ISRAEL HISTORY MAPS ATLAS

3000 YEARS OF GEOGRAPHIC CHRONOLOGY OF JEWISH SOVEREIGNTY IN ISRAEL

By Ilan Reiner and Amir Reiner

SPECIAL ISRAEL **70** INDEPENDENCE DAY EDITION

Created and Produced by Amir Reiner
Research and Graphics by Ilan Reiner

Cover design and Page layout by Ilan Reiner
Editor: Aviva Lee, Aviva@AvivaLee.net 646.353.0267
Linguistic Editor: Iris Israeli, iris.edit1@gmail.com

ISBN-13: 978-0-692459-32-4
ISBN-10: 0-692459-32-4

Revision 7.1 (November 2019, Chesvan 5779)

Earth Photo on main cover by NASA. See "About the Project" for additional photo credits.

Table of Contents

Forward

Israel History Maps: A Geographical Chronology of Jewish Sovereignty in Israel, is a unique project intended in providing the users with a knowledge base and visual introduction to the history of the Jewish people in Israel in relation to the history of other nations in the same area. It portrays the history of Jewish rule in the land of Israel from a historical and geographic point of view. Watch how 3,000 years of history unfolds in a consistent series of over 50 maps! Simple and easy to understand, the maps are all in a uniform scale and divided into several periods, accompanied with an overall timeline.

This project can be a great visual aid to students, teachers and community leaders as it shows the changes in the borders in Israel over the past 3,500 years. This endeavor traces the historical connection between the Jewish people and the land of Israel and identifies the eras in which they had any level of sovereignty. This is accomplished by using easy-to-understand graphics that do not overwhelm the viewer with extensive information. It can be used as a teaching aid in Bible studies, history and geography classes as well as Jewish studies classes.

The project describes the various divisions of the land, and the changes in political and administrative borders throughout history. It consists of over 50 maps, beginning with the Hebrew settlement after the exodus from Egypt up to present day. For organization purposes, we have decided to subdivide this continuity into three main eras of Israelite or Jewish sovereignty in Israel, with eras of exile between them.

The First Era would begin with the conquest of Canaan by Joshua through the days of judges, the Kingdoms of David and his son Solomon, and will end with the destruction of the First Temple and the exile of the Jews by the Babylonians. The first exile was relatively a short one, lasting only several decades.

The Second Era coincides with the period of the Second Temple, a period that spans over about four centuries. It begins from the return of the Jews to Israel after the Babylonian Exile, through the Hasmonean and Herod's kingdoms and ends with the Great Jewish Revolt and destruction of the Second Temple by the Romans.

The period of the second exile begins with Roman rule over Israel. But shortly after, another uprising, the Bar Kochva revolt, establishes Jewish independence for a short period of a few years. Although Jewish independence was established, it was for a very short time and cannot be considered an era. After the revolt was put down, Jews found themselves in exile for nearly two millennia, as various empires conquer and subsequently lost their rule over Israel.

The Third Era begins with the establishment of the State of Israel in the last century. It continues through the various conflicts that the State of Israel endured and the peace accords she signed with her neighbors.

The uniqueness of the maps of Israel in this project are:

- A series of over 50 maps of Israel, in chronological order, divided into historical eras
- All of the maps are in a uniform scale, allowing for better understanding border changes and modifications
- The maps are very clear and easy to understand
- A Dynamic timeline (with Hebrew years) puts every specific map in historical context
- Maps of foreign rule bring the Jewish rule in context to foreign rule

Using this project, viewers and students are able to better understand how various time periods relate to each others, the extent of Jewish sovereignty in various time periods and the depth of the connection between the Jewish people and the land of Israel.

A great effort was put into the careful preparation of this project. The maps were created specifically for this project, by a graphic designer, who is knowledgeable with the history and geography of Israel and the Jewish people. Each map was prepared after extensive research of the period and with great attention to details.

Israel History Maps became a reality in its current format with the patience and support of both our spouses, Neda and Maya, to whom we owe many thanks for advising and encouraging us along the way. Many thanks also go to all those who purchased our initial version of the maps, provided valuable feedback and gave us great reviews. We would also like to thank Aviva Lee (Aviva@AvivaLee.net) for her methodological and comprehensive editing, as well as Iris Israeli (iris.edit1@gmail.com), Linguistic Editor who is a specialist in Jewish and Hebrew linguistic editing, for the final polish and professional touch.

In today's reality, we hope that this project shall serve as another tool for enhancing the connection between Jews and Israel.

We encourage you to share your thoughts and check out new information regarding Israel History Maps on our website:
www.IsraelHistoryMaps.com

Ilan Reiner and Amir Reiner
IsraelHistoryMaps@gmail.com
Los Angeles, CA and Haifa, Israel
January 2014, Shevat 5774

About the Authors

Ilan Reiner is a history and geography researcher, especially in regards to Jewish history during the Second Temple period, as well as a Bible scholar. After full military service as a programmer and system administrator and graduating from Israel's Technion Architecture school, he's been working as an architectural designer and project manager at various architecture firms. With a detail-oriented approach, he prefers clean contemporary designs that appeal to a wider group of people. He loves the Bible and has twice won first place in Israel's Youth National Bible Contest (Hidon Tanach). His vast knowledge in Jewish history and the Bible, along with his design skills, helped him with the extensive research in preparing the Israel History Maps set. Ilan lives in Los Angeles with his wife and son, and is very active in his community.

Amir Reiner is very much involved with start-ups and technological innovations, while always on the lookout for new and exciting history books. He completed full military service in the Israeli Air Force. A graduate of Israel's Technion School of Industrial Engineering and Management and with an MBA from Haifa University, he works in the field of information system analysis. After participating in the prestigious "Online Ambassadors" program, he enjoys defending Israel on various web sites. His love for Israel and her history as well as his fascination with creating new media to deliver messages, sparked the idea to create the Israel History Maps project. Amir lives in Haifa, Israel with his wife and is active with various organizations that support Israel.

About the Project

While developing this project we had to face many challenges and make tough decisions in order to stick to our original intent: Our main goal is that the maps will show a geo-political overview of the region to demonstrate long term shifts of influence and powers in the land of Israel.

When it came to making decisions about which maps to include or design and decide upon the layout options, we always opted to stay in line with our "Mission Statement" (as described at the beginning of the Forward). To the extent that it was possible, we picked everything that is easy to read and understand with respect to the geography and the history of Israel.

Content

The first choice we made was regarding the map itself. We decided that all maps would be in one uniform scale. This would make it easy to compare different periods. Hence, in some cases, we were unable to show the full extent of rule, such as in the period of David and Solomon. We preferred to omit some areas that are less relevant, and to keep the map at a scale that is easy to read without overburdening the reader with excessive information. There can always be more information added to each map: river names, more cities, significant historic locations, etc.. We showed the main rivers and lakes, without labeling them since we didn't believe the labels contributed to our "Mission Statement". As for cities, we preferred to include cities that were habitable at most of the time periods.

Accuracy

Despite our best efforts to make the maps and the historical overview as accurate as possible, there might be some information or content that is controversial. This is especially true in regards to all maps before the common era. When it comes to events during the time of the Bible, we used the Bible as a source as well as common historic and archaeological studies. That being said, the Bible is not a science book and not everything there can be taken at face value with regards to historical or geographical information. Also archeology isn't an exact science, and often new discoveries contradict common theories. Therefore, in most cases we decided to portray the most common theory that is not contradicted by the plain understanding of the Bible.

Dates

The exact year in which specific events took place until modern times are often controversial. This is more so when discussing the change in sovereignty as it tends to be more of a process. We used the acceptable historical dates when noting events. However, there is a discrepancy of about 164 years between the accepted historical date of the destruction of the First Temple in 586 BCE and the Seder Olam Rabba which sets it to 422 BCE. This would affect all events up until the 2nd century BCE. On the timeline there are the common years and beside them, in square brackets, the Hebrew years since creation.

Format (layout)

The general layout of the map page is having the map on the right side. On the lower right side of the map there's a legend, north symbol and a scale bar. To its left there's the timeline. On the left side of the page there is the historical overview and below it a reference image This format is consistent and allows the reader to either focus only on the maps or expand to additional contents.

Map Format and Graphics

To keep the maps simple, legible and graphically pleasing (fewest color codes), we used the following convention: Areas that were under some level of Hebrew or Jewish rule are shaded in green with green borders. Areas that were under foreign rule, are bordered with a gray line. The area of Judea or Israel, when under foreign rule, is shaded gray with a gray line.
As for labels, a regular type font is used to label kingdoms, countries or districts; an italic type is used to label nations or tribes that inhabited the area.
The timeline itself is color divided into the various periods of rule. Each period is accompanied with the year it began and ended. Both common and Hebrew year since creation (in square brackets) are indicated.

Brief Historical Overview

Each map is accompanied with a brief historical overview that describes the main events or turning points of the period discussed, mainly from a geopolitical standpoint (that would affect the borders). There might be significant events omitted from the overview, since we were not able to include everything. Also in this case, some facts are disputable and we followed the same rationale of accuracy as in the maps, while always opting for brevity. Numerous books have been written on almost every period and can be referred to for further in-depth understanding of any specific period.

Images

To each map (as well and the era beginning and ending pages) we added an image. It was our intention to give a visual association to the occurrences described in the map and the historical overview of that period. In cases where the image is an artwork, we opted for an image that would reflect the description of the period, rather than reflecting historical or archaeological accuracy. In no way should any artwork presented here be taken as an accurate accounting of what happened. As a general rule, the use of any imagery, artwork or photos in this project do not suggest that the author, artists, photographer, licensor or the website hosting the content, endorse us, or the project or the use of the image in this project.

In regards to copyright, we made every effort to respect their copyright status. Most images are in the public domain in the United States (and many other countries) and were obtained online. Some images were released to the public domain, accompanied with the statement: "I, the copyright holder of this work, release this work into the public domain. This applies worldwide." Other images are considered public domain because their copyright has expired, and were accompanied with the statement: "This image is in the public domain [in the United States] because its copyright has expired. This applies to Australia, the European Union and those countries with a copyright term of life of the author plus 70 years." To these images, the proper associated United States Public Domain tag would be {{US-PD}} or {{US-1923}} if it were published before 1923 outside the US. In all cases of artwork, we accompanied the description of the image with the name of the artist.

Some of the photos were licensed under the Creative Commons Attribution 2.5 Generic license. This allows us to share and remix the work, in the condition that we attribute the work in the manner specified by the author or licensor (but not in any way that suggests that they endorse us or our use of the work). In those cases we included the name of the photographer. Other photos are in public domain in the United States because it is a work prepared by an officer or employee of the United States Government as part of that person's official duties under the terms of Title 17, Chapter 1, Section 105 of the US Code. Some of the other photos (about a dozen) are not accompanied with any attribution since we hold exclusive copyrights to those works. As for any satellite views, those were taken by NASA and as such regarded as Public Domain.

Please contact us if you have any questions or comments regarding the copyright status of a specific image, or if you feel we have unintentionally violated any of the copyrights.

Introduction

The origins of the Israelites, and later on - the Jewish people, can be traced back to over three thousand years ago. The Bible tells us of a tribe who migrated to Egypt during famine years, growing to become a big nation, always yearning to return to the land promised to their ancestors by their God. After their exodus from Egypt (in the 12th century BCE), they traveled through the desert to the promised land - Israel. The land that they were promised was one of milk and honey, but also at that point occupied. A divine promise to inherit the land is something to believe in, but when coming to claim that land, the Israelites needed to use force, strategy and have faith in God.

Although several small kingdoms were conquered by the Israelites before crossing the Jordan River into the promised land, the actual beginning of the First Era of Israelite Rule in Israel can be defined with the conquests of Joshua. It continues through the period of settlement (judges), and the establishment of a monarchy by King Saul who was appointed by God. Ultimately it was King David and his son, King Solomon, who truly united all the Israelite tribes, building the First Temple in the new capital - Jerusalem, and establishing one of the biggest and wealthiest kingdoms of that period.

That kingdom didn't last long and soon after King Solomon's death, it was split by a civil war between two groups of tribes into the kingdoms of Judah and Israel. The two sister kingdoms coexisted for several centuries, sometimes as partners and sometimes as warring rivals. For the most part, the northern Kingdom of Israel was stronger, bigger (in populace and area) and wealthier than the Kingdom of Judah. After several centuries, the northern Kingdom of Israel was conquered and destroyed by the Assyrian Kingdom in the 7th century BCE, and the southern Kingdom of Judah was all that remained of the once great kingdom of David and Solomon. The populace of the Kingdom of Israel was exiled, dispersed throughout the Assyrian Kingdom and lost forever. Furthermore, the days of the Kingdom of Judah were not long, and soon it faced the strongest kingdom to ever exist until that time - the (Neo) Babylonian empire. The First Era ends with the destruction of the First Temple, the burning of Jerusalem and the exile of the Jews by the Babylonians (a period that lasted several decades).

All this is told to us by the Hebrew Bible. Although it is not a history or a fact-finding book, there are numerous descriptions of the conquests and settlements in the land of Israel (mostly for the purpose of demonstrating God's fulfillment of the promise). Conclusive and irrefutable archaeological evidence are yet to be found, but every now and then a new discovery supports the biblical story to some degree or another. However, archeology is uncovering more and more evidence of Jewish influence, rule and development in Israel during the Second Era of Jewish sovereignty in Israel.

The Second Era of Jewish rule in Israel begins at the establishment of a Jewish autonomy within the Persian Empire by the Jews who returned to Israel after the Babylonian Exile. They had rebuilt the city of Jerusalem and built the Second Temple at its center. Later, after Alexander the Great's conquest, the Jewish autonomy was under Hellenistic rule. When tension between the Jews and the Seleucid Kingdom descended into armed conflict, the Jews gained full independence with the Hasmonean revolt, and re-established the Jewish kingdom. Later this kingdom came under partial Roman rule and influence, as the Hasmonean kings sought alliance with the rising Roman Empire.

Shortly after, the Romans appointed Herod as the king of Judea, backed up with Roman troops. He destroyed the Hasmonean dynasty, established Judea as a kingdom (no longer a Roman province, but still with allegiance to Rome), and then set the path to making Judea a great kingdom. He expanded the boundaries of the Jewish kingdom, built numerous cities, buildings and infrastructures, and practically rebuilt the Temple in Jerusalem. The Jewish kingdom enjoyed many days of economic growth and prosperity, despite some civil unrest and disapproval of King Herod. After his death, his descendants were unable to maintain the kingdom, and it fell under direct Roman rule. As tension grew between the Jewish population and the Roman government, a violent conflict was inevitable. The Jews revolted against the Romans, in what also became an internal Jewish civil war. After four years, Roman legions stormed Jerusalem, destroyed the Temple, burned down the city and exiled many of the Jews to be sold as slaves around the Roman world. This concluded the Second Era of Jewish Sovereignty.

Although the Jewish kingdom no longer existed, many of the Jews lived in northern Israel under Roman rule in the Galilee region and other provinces. Less than 70 years after the Great Revolt, there was another uprising in Israel. The Bar Kochva revolt established Jewish independence for a brief time, until it was put down brutally by a huge part of the Roman army. The Jewish population in Israel suffered an enormous loss and Jews were no longer able to rule Israel for nearly two millennia, as various empires conquered and subsequently lost their rule over Israel.

The Third Era begins with the establishment of the State of Israel in 1948. It continues through the various conflicts that the State of Israel endured and the peace accords that Israel signed with her neighbors, until the present day. In this era it is demonstrated how the borders of the new country, created under mandate of the United Nations, shifted significantly in less than seven decades. The borders of the newly established state were theoretical as Israel was born into war, since immediately after declaring independence, all surrounding Arab countries attacked Israel. The newborn country fought for her survival and right to exist during the War of Independence. The cease-fire borders were significantly different. Israel expanded her borders significantly after the Six Day War (1967), and returned most of that new territory after signing the peace treaty with Egypt and later on with Jordan. Several other territories were given to the Palestinian Authority as part of various agreements.

The following easy-to-understand maps and chronological timeline will demonstrate the modifications of the governance, influence and jurisdiction in the Land of Israel over the past three millennia, from Biblical times to the modern period.

The Land
Satellite map

This satellite image (on the right) depicts Israel according to the size used in the forthcoming maps. This image was taken by NASA in the early 2000's shows the habitable areas in the early 21st century. These true-color images were acquired by the Moderate Resolution Imaging Spectroradiometer (MODIS) aboard the Aqua and Terra satellites.

Credit: Jeff Schmaltz, MODIS Rapid Response Team, NASA/GSFC

Metadata
Data Date: January 6, 2003
Visualization Date: January 7, 2003
Sensor(s): Terra - MODIS

Below is an image of Israel and the Nile delta at night. This image by NASA was acquired on November 28, 2010 ISS crew on the International Space Station.

From the Earth Observatory web site:
"One of the fascinating aspects of viewing Earth at night is how well the lights show the distribution of people. In this view, besides the Nile delta, another brightly lit region is visible along the eastern coastline of the Mediterranean—the Tel-Aviv metropolitan area in Israel (image right). To the east of Tel-Aviv lies Amman, Jordan. The two major water bodies that define the western and eastern coastlines of the Sinai Peninsula—the Gulf of Suez and the Gulf of Aqaba—are outlined by lights along their coastlines (image lower right).

© MAP COURTESY OF NASA

The Land

Topographic map

Despite its small size, Israel is home to a variety of geographic features, from the Negev desert in the south to the inland fertile Jezreel Valley, mountain ranges of the Galilee, Carmel and toward the Golan in the north. The Israeli Coastal Plain on the shores of the Mediterranean is home to the majority of the nation's population. East of the central highlands lies the Jordan Rift Valley, which forms a small part of the 6,500-kilometer (4,039 mi) Great Rift Valley.

The Jordan River runs along the Jordan Rift Valley, from Mount Hermon through the Hulah Valley and the Sea of Galilee to the Dead Sea, the lowest point on the surface of the Earth. Further south is the Arabah, ending with the Gulf of Eilat, part of the Red Sea. Unique to Israel and the Sinai Peninsula are makhteshim, or erosion cirques. The largest makhtesh in the world is Ramon Crater in the Negev, which measures 40 by 8 kilometers (25 by 5 mi). A report on the environmental status of the Mediterranean basin states that Israel has the largest number of plant species per square meter of all the countries in the basin.

Temperatures in Israel vary widely, especially during the winter. The more mountainous regions can be windy, cold, and sometimes snowy; Jerusalem usually receives at least one snowfall each year. Meanwhile, coastal cities, such as Tel Aviv and Haifa, have a typical Mediterranean climate with cool, rainy winters and long, hot summers. The area of Beersheba and the Northern Negev has a semi-arid climate with hot summers, cool winters and fewer rainy days than the Mediterranean climate. The Southern Negev and the Arava areas have desert climate with very hot and dry summers, and mild winters with few days of rain. The highest temperature in the continent of Asia (53.7 °C or 128.7 °F) was recorded in 1942 at Tirat Zvi kibbutz in the northern Jordan river valley.

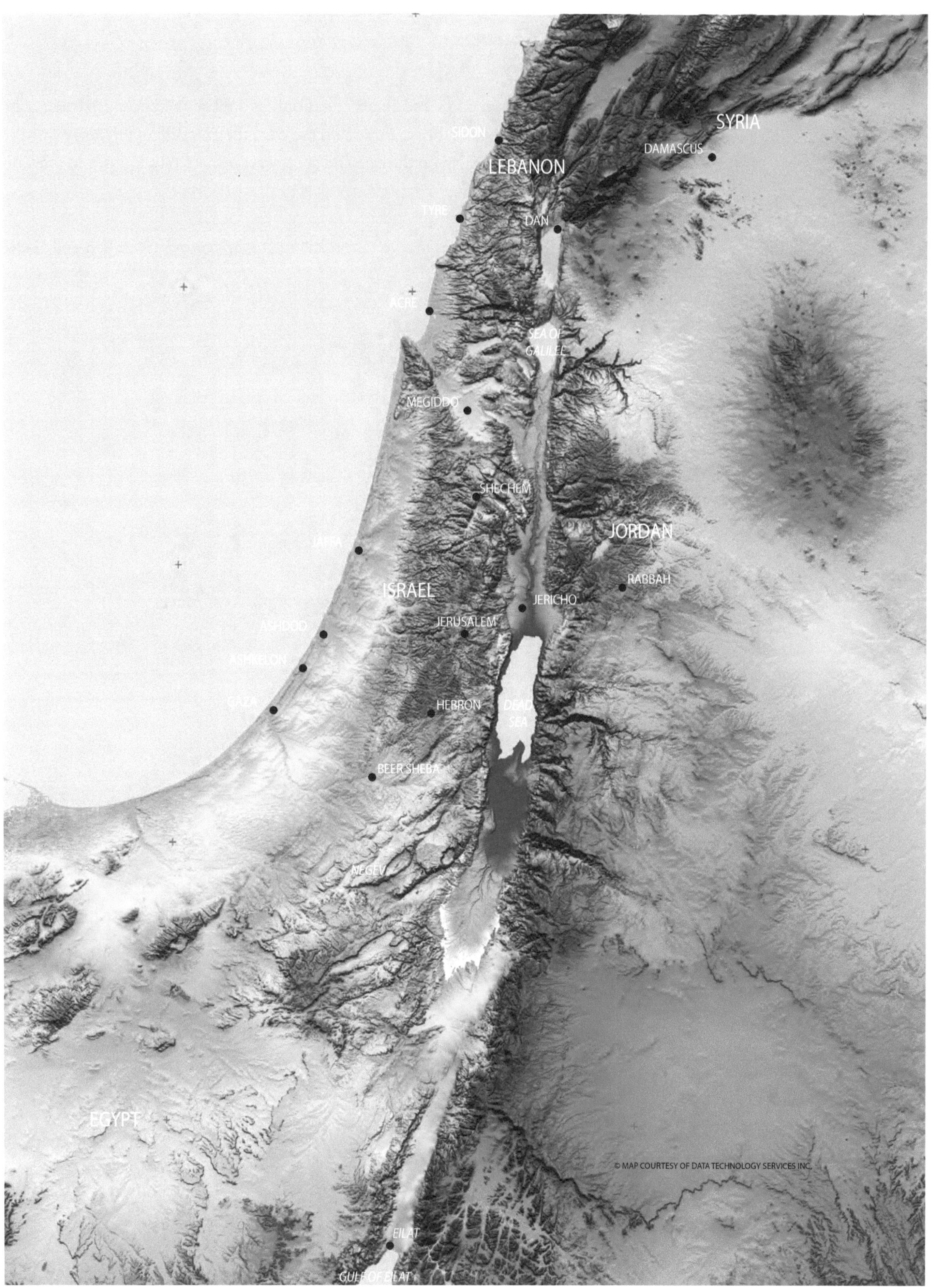
SYRIA
SIDON
DAMASCUS
LEBANON
TYRE
DAN
ACRE
SEA OF
GALILEE
MEGIDDO
SHECHEM
JORDAN
JAFFA
RABBAH
ISRAEL
JERICHO
ASHDOD
JERUSALEM
ASHKELON
GAZA
HEBRON
DEAD
SEA
BEER SHEBA
NEGEV
EGYPT
© MAP COURTESY OF DATA TECHNOLOGY SERVICES INC.
EILAT
GULF OF EILAT

The Land
Google map

In the Google map of Israel (in the page across) the main cities and roads stand out, as well as the current borders. She shares land borders with Lebanon in the north, Syria in the northeast, Jordan on the east, the Palestinian territories (or the Palestinian Authority) comprising the West Bank and Gaza Strip on the east and southwest respectively, Egypt and the Gulf of Aqaba in the Red Sea to the south.

Israel has three main metropolitan areas - Tel Aviv (Gush Dan, as shown in the enlarged map below); Jerusalem and Haifa. Second level metropolitan areas are Be'er Sheba and Nazareth.

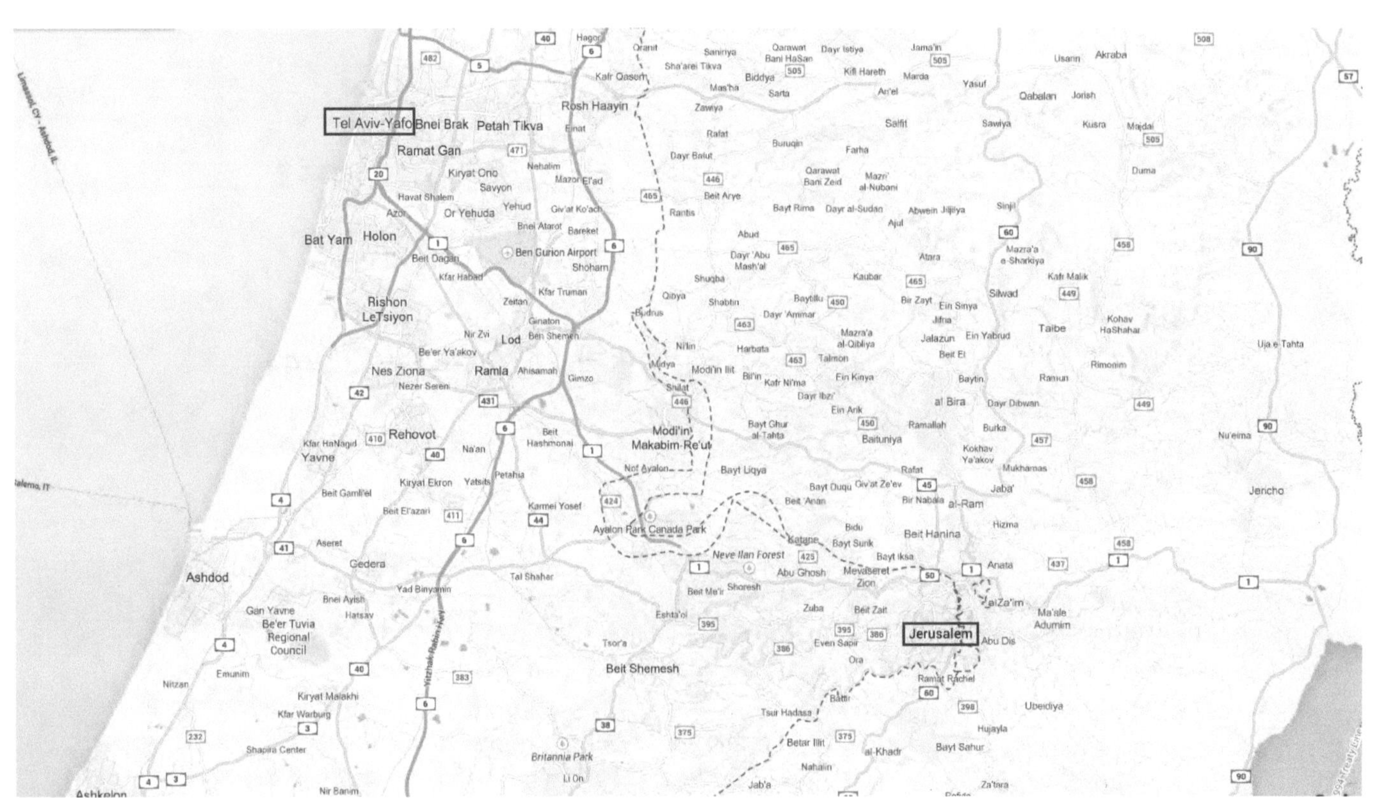

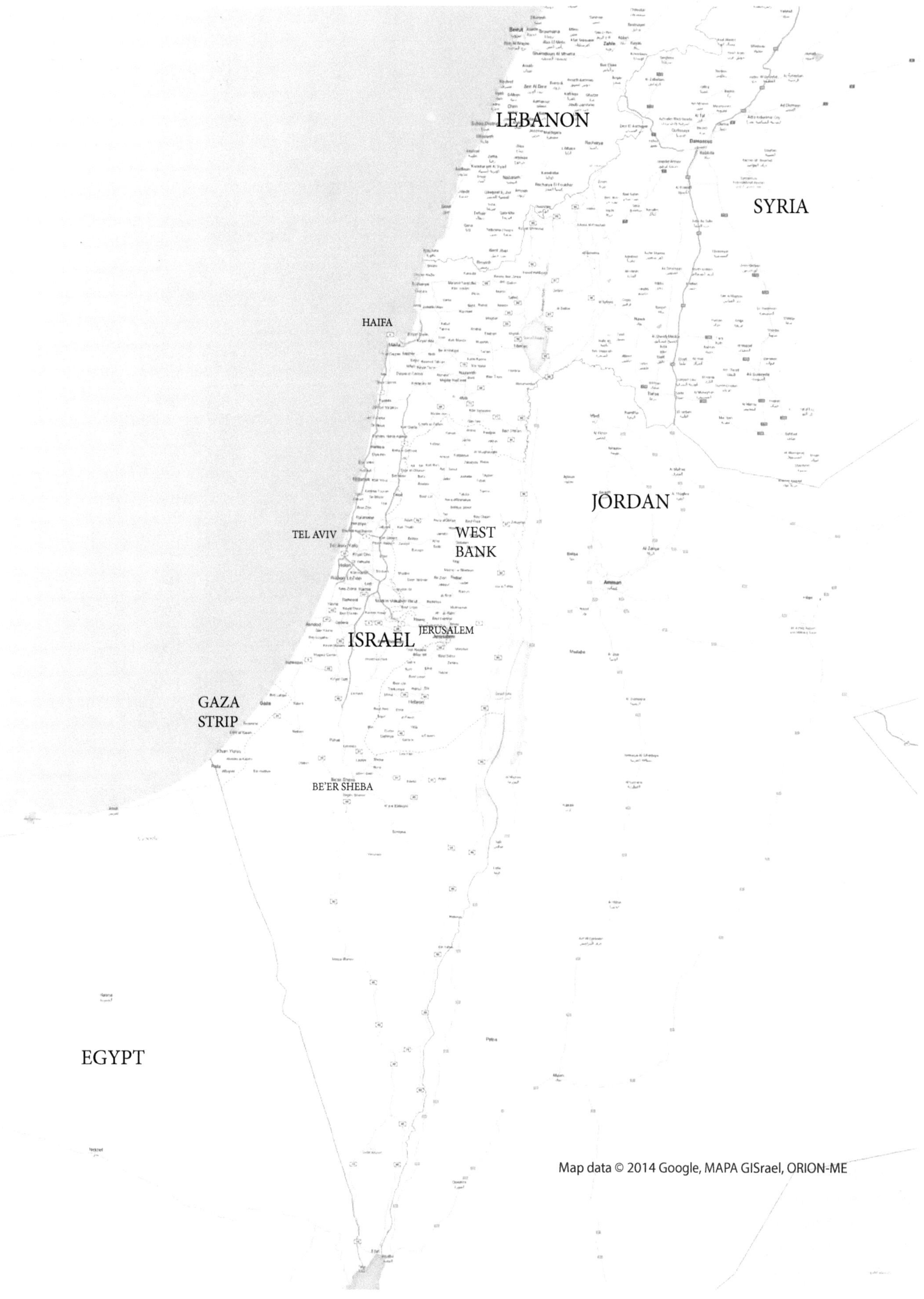
LEBANON
SYRIA
HAIFA
JORDAN
TEL AVIV
WEST
BANK
ISRAEL
JERUSALEM
GAZA
STRIP
BE'ER SHEBA
EGYPT
Map data © 2014 Google, MAPA GISrael, ORION-ME

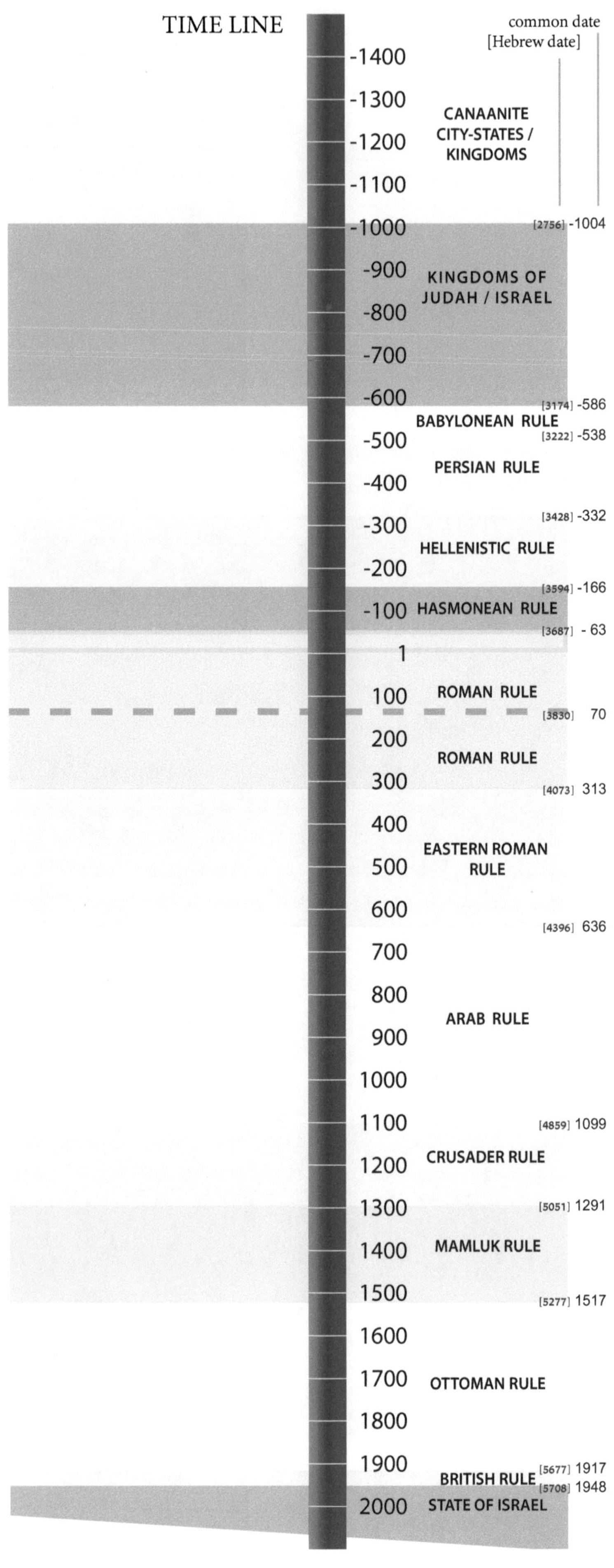
TIME LINE
common date
[Hebrew date]
-1400
-1300
-1200
-1100
CANAANITE CITY-STATES / KINGDOMS
[2756] -1004
-1000
-900
-800
-700
-600
KINGDOMS OF JUDAH / ISRAEL
[3174] -586
BABYLONEAN RULE
[3222] -538
-500
-400
PERSIAN RULE
[3428] -332
-300
-200
HELLENISTIC RULE
[3594] -166
-100
HASMONEAN RULE
[3687] - 63
1
100
ROMAN RULE
[3830] 70
200
300
ROMAN RULE
[4073] 313
400
500
600
EASTERN ROMAN RULE
[4396] 636
700
800
900
1000
ARAB RULE
[4859] 1099
1100
1200
CRUSADER RULE
[5051] 1291
1300
1400
MAMLUK RULE
[5277] 1517
1500
1600
1700
1800
1900
OTTOMAN RULE
[5677] 1917
BRITISH RULE
[5708] 1948
2000
STATE OF ISRAEL

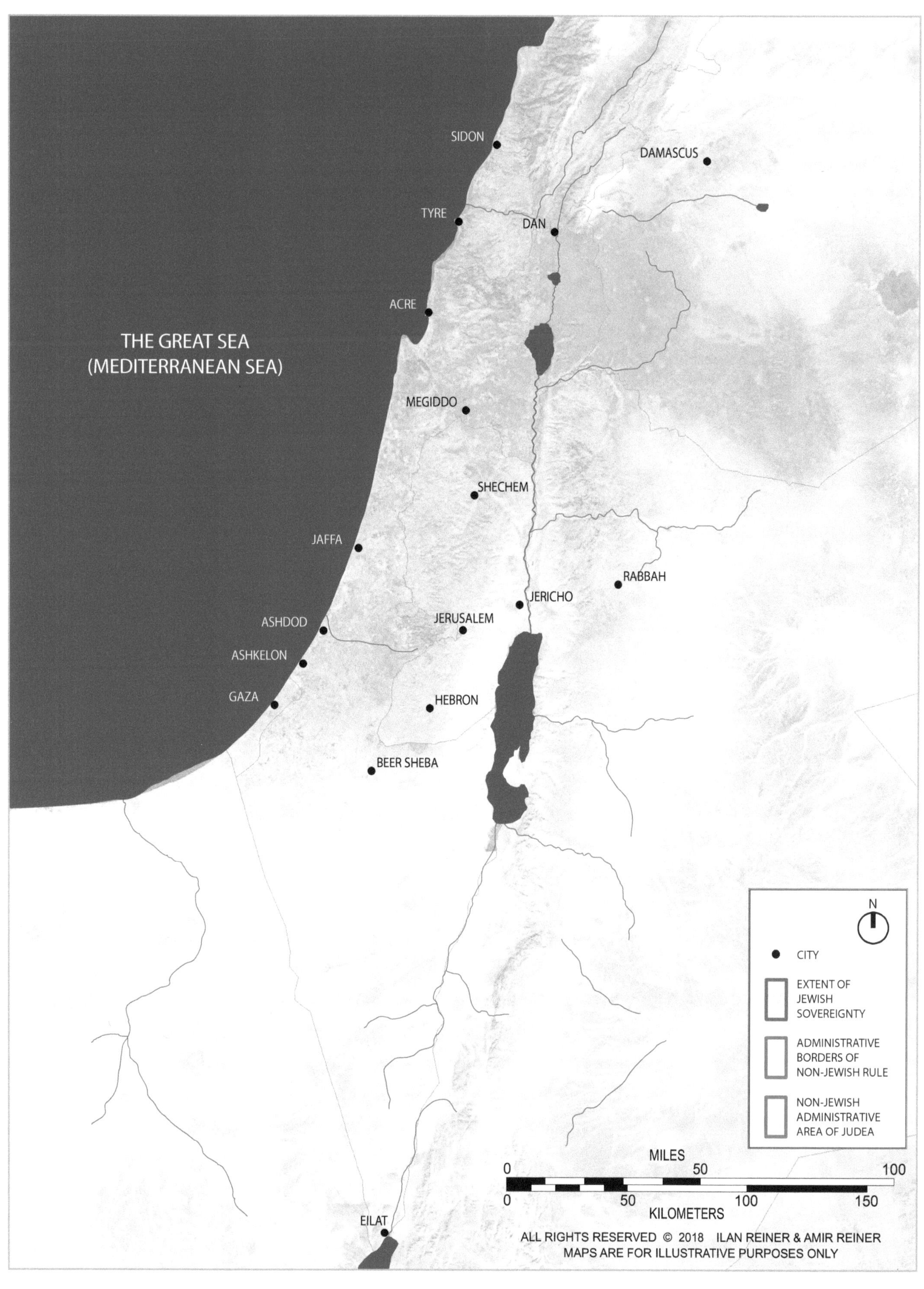
THE GREAT SEA
(MEDITERRANEAN SEA)
SIDON
DAMASCUS
TYRE
DAN
ACRE
MEGIDDO
SHECHEM
JAFFA
RABBAH
JERICHO
ASHDOD
JERUSALEM
ASHKELON
GAZA
HEBRON
BEER SHEBA
EILAT
N
CITY
EXTENT OF
JEWISH
SOVEREIGNTY
ADMINISTRATIVE
BORDERS OF
NON-JEWISH RULE
NON-JEWISH
ADMINISTRATIVE
AREA OF JUDEA
MILES
0
50
100
0
50
100
150
KILOMETERS
ALL RIGHTS RESERVED © 2018 ILAN REINER & AMIR REINER
MAPS ARE FOR ILLUSTRATIVE PURPOSES ONLY

Canaanite Cities and Kingdoms
Late Bronze Age and Iron Age I
12th & 13th century BCE

Cities and kingdoms existed in the land of Canaan for many centuries before the Hebrew people arrived. Some of them, such as Shechem, Moab, Jericho and Edom, are mentioned in the Bible (Genesis 33; Deuteronomy 2 & 3; Joshua 2; etc.) as well as in Egyptian letters. This area was under Egyptian influence or direct rule at various times. It was a strategic location connecting Egypt with Mesopotamia and Asia Minor. The various kingdoms and cities consisted of different nations that were often at war with each other.

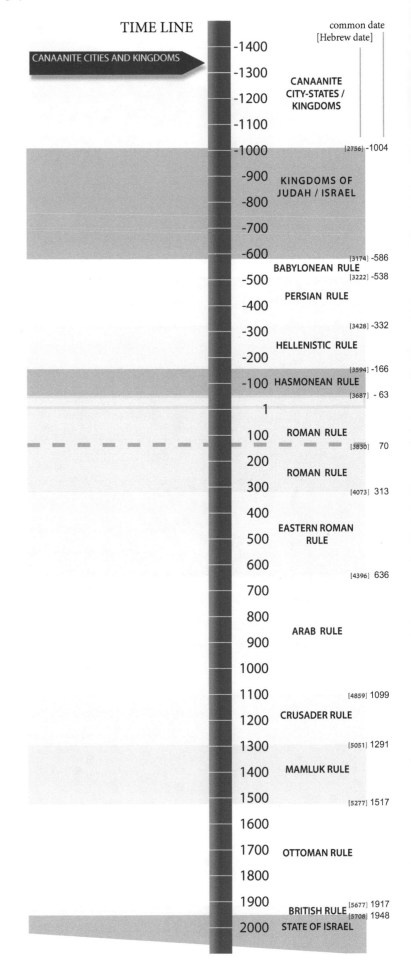

The name Canaan written in hieroglyphs
Using free hieroglyphic fonts

TIME LINE

common date
[Hebrew date]

CANAANITE CITIES AND KINGDOMS

-1400
-1300
-1200
-1100
-1000
-900
-800
-700
-600
-500
-400
-300
-200
-100
1
100
200
300
400
500
600
700
800
900
1000
1100
1200
1300
1400
1500
1600
1700
1800
1900
2000

CANAANITE CITY-STATES / KINGDOMS
[2756] -1004
KINGDOMS OF JUDAH / ISRAEL
[3174] -586
BABYLONEAN RULE
[3222] -538
PERSIAN RULE
[3428] -332
HELLENISTIC RULE
[3594] -166
HASMONEAN RULE
[3687] - 63
ROMAN RULE
[3830] 70
ROMAN RULE
[4073] 313
EASTERN ROMAN RULE
[4396] 636
ARAB RULE
[4859] 1099
CRUSADER RULE
[5051] 1291
MAMLUK RULE
[5277] 1517
OTTOMAN RULE
[5677] 1917
BRITISH RULE
[5708] 1948
STATE OF ISRAEL

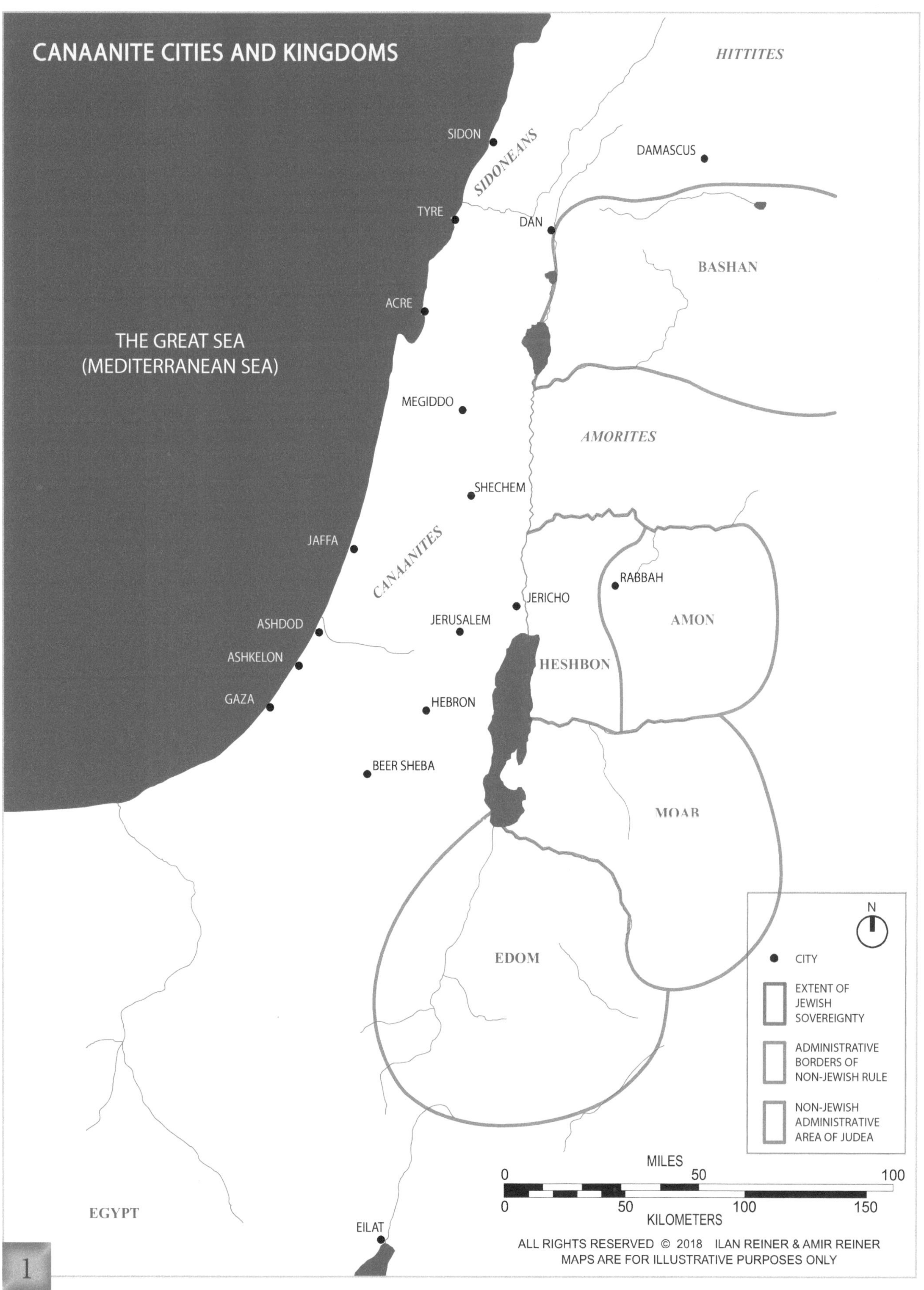
CANAANITE CITIES AND KINGDOMS
HITTITES
SIDON
SIDONEANS
DAMASCUS
TYRE
DAN
BASHAN
ACRE
THE GREAT SEA
(MEDITERRANEAN SEA)
MEGIDDO
AMORITES
SHECHEM
JAFFA
CANAANITES
RABBAH
JERICHO
AMON
JERUSALEM
ASHDOD
HESHBON
ASHKELON
GAZA
HEBRON
BEER SHEBA
MOAB
EDOM
N
CITY
EXTENT OF
JEWISH
SOVEREIGNTY
ADMINISTRATIVE
BORDERS OF
NON-JEWISH RULE
NON-JEWISH
ADMINISTRATIVE
AREA OF JUDEA
MILES
0
50
100
0
50
100
150
KILOMETERS
EGYPT
EILAT
1

Era of Settlement
Conquest and Settlement
about 1230 BCE

As the Hebrew tribes were on their journey to Canaan (where they intended on settling), several Amorite kingdoms waged war on them (Numbers 21). As a result, the first settlement of the Hebrew people was on the east bank of the Jordan River. This area was scarcely populated and was mainly used as grazing area for cattle. According to the Bible (Numbers 32), this area was given to two and a half tribes and the rest of the tribes settled to the west of the Jordan River.

Mosaic of the 12 Tribes of Israel
From Givat Mordechai synagogue wall in Jerusalem

TIME LINE

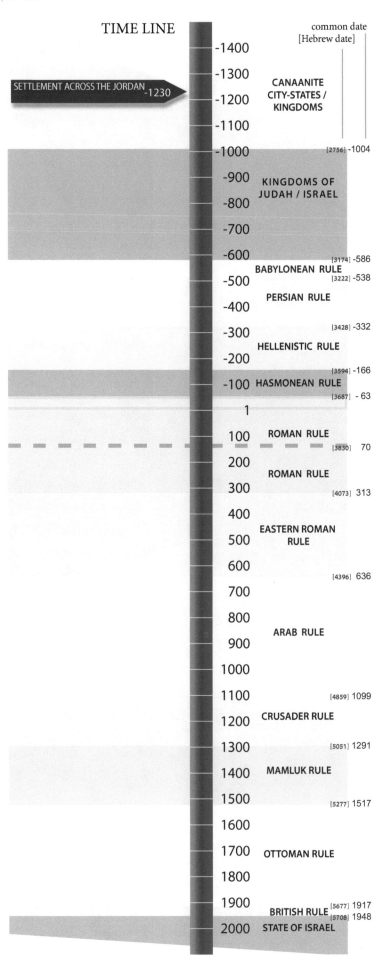

common date
[Hebrew date]

SETTLEMENT ACROSS THE JORDAN -1230

-1400
-1300
-1200 CANAANITE CITY-STATES / KINGDOMS
-1100
-1000 [2756] -1004
-900 KINGDOMS OF JUDAH / ISRAEL
-800
-700
-600 [3174] -586
BABYLONEAN RULE [3222] -538
-500
PERSIAN RULE
-400
-300 [3428] -332
HELLENISTIC RULE
-200
[3594] -166
-100 HASMONEAN RULE
[3687] - 63
1
100 ROMAN RULE
[3830] 70
200 ROMAN RULE
300 [4073] 313
400
500 EASTERN ROMAN RULE
600
[4396] 636
700
800
900 ARAB RULE
1000
1100 [4859] 1099
1200 CRUSADER RULE
1300 [5051] 1291
1400 MAMLUK RULE
1500 [5277] 1517
1600
1700 OTTOMAN RULE
1800
1900 [5677] 1917
BRITISH RULE [5708] 1948
2000 STATE OF ISRAEL

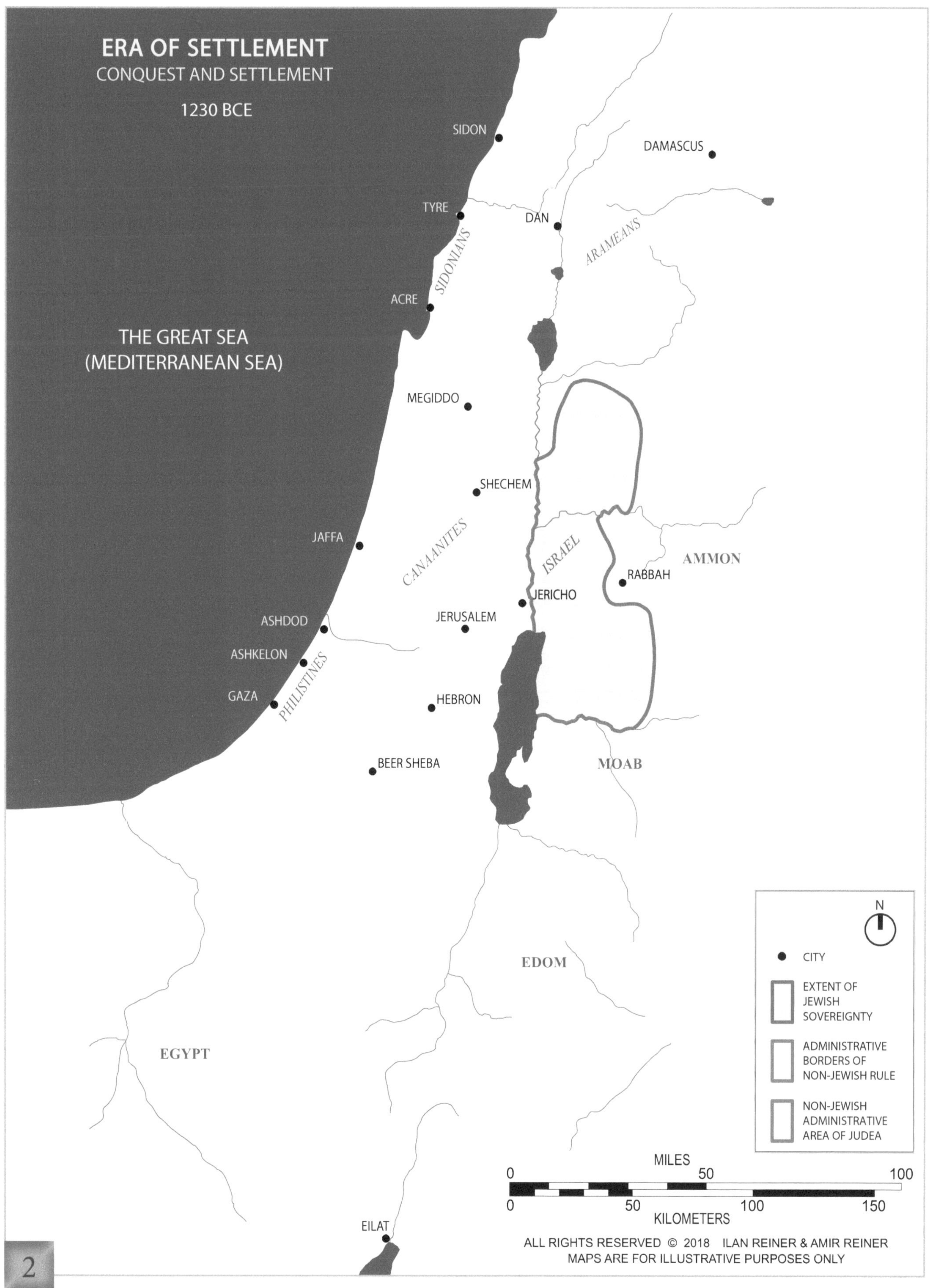
ERA OF SETTLEMENT
CONQUEST AND SETTLEMENT
1230 BCE
SIDON
DAMASCUS
TYRE
DAN
SIDONIANS
ARAMEANS
ACRE
THE GREAT SEA
(MEDITERRANEAN SEA)
MEGIDDO
SHECHEM
JAFFA
CANAANITES
ISRAEL
AMMON
RABBAH
JERICHO
ASHDOD
JERUSALEM
ASHKELON
PHILISTINES
GAZA
HEBRON
BEER SHEBA
MOAB
EDOM
EGYPT
EILAT
N
CITY
EXTENT OF JEWISH SOVEREIGNTY
ADMINISTRATIVE BORDERS OF NON-JEWISH RULE
NON-JEWISH ADMINISTRATIVE AREA OF JUDEA
MILES
0
50
100
0
50
100
150
KILOMETERS
ALL RIGHTS RESERVED © 2018 ILAN REINER & AMIR REINER
MAPS ARE FOR ILLUSTRATIVE PURPOSES ONLY
2

Beginning of the First Era of Hebrew Rule in the Land of Israel

about 1240 BCE to 586 BCE

Although several small kingdoms were conquered by the Israelites before crossing the Jordan River into the promised land, the actual beginning of the First Era of Israelite Rule in Israel can be defined with the conquests of Joshua. It continues through the period of settlement (Judges), and the establishment of a monarchy by King Saul who was appointed by God. Ultimately it was King David and his son, King Solomon, who truly united all the Israelite tribes, building the First Temple in the new capital - Jerusalem, and establishing one of the biggest and wealthiest kingdoms of that period.

That kingdom didn't last long and soon after King Solomon's death, it was split by a civil war between two groups of tribes into the kingdoms of Judah and Israel. The two sister kingdoms coexisted for several centuries, sometimes as partners and sometimes as warring rivals. For the most part, the northern Kingdom of Israel was stronger, bigger (in populace and area) and wealthier than the Kingdom of Judah. After several centuries, the northern Kingdom of Israel was conquered and destroyed by the Assyrian Kingdom in the 7th century BCE, and the southern Kingdom of Judah was all that remained of the once great kingdom of David and Solomon. The populace of the Kingdom of Israel was exiled, dispersed throughout the Assyrian Kingdom and lost forever. Furthermore, the days of the Kingdom of Judah were not long, and soon it faced the strongest kingdom to ever exist until that time - the (Neo) Babylonian empire. The First Era ends with the destruction of the First Temple, the burning of Jerusalem and the exile of the Jews by the Babylonians for a period of several decades.

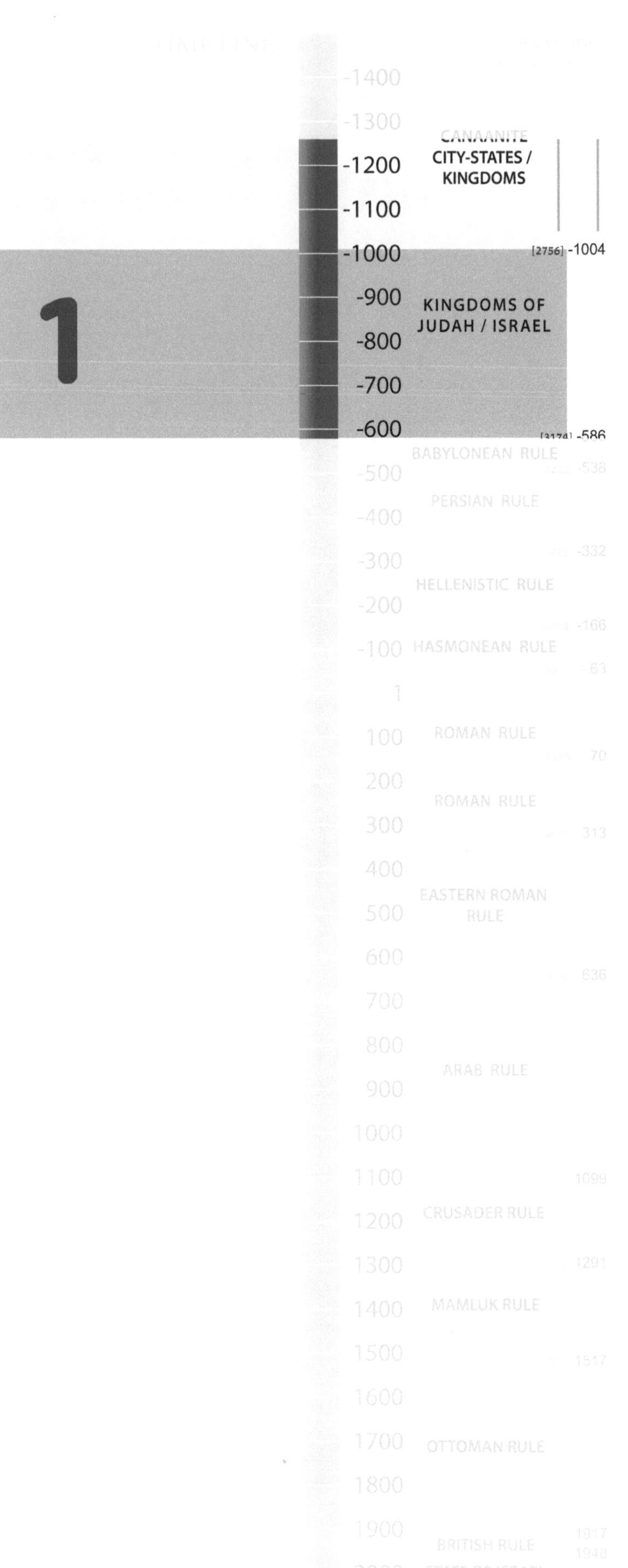

BEGINNING OF THE FIRST ERA OF HEBREW RULE IN THE LAND OF ISRAEL

CONQUEST OF CANAAN BY JOSHUA

-1230 TO -586

The Battle of Jericho
Woodcut by Julius Schnorr von Carolsfeld

Joshua's Conquests
End of Conquest and Settlement
about 1230 BCE to 1200 BCE

Joshua led the Israelite people in the first wave of conquest and settlement in Canaan. The strategy was to penetrate the land by way of Jericho, then establish a stronghold over the central mountain region, thus splitting the northern cities from the southern cities. After many years, thirty one cities were conquered (as listed in the Bible - Joshua 12), and the Israelite tribes gained a stronghold in the land. They settled mainly in the mountainous region, leaving the coastal regions unconquered.

The Children of Israel Crossing the Jordan
by Gustave Dore

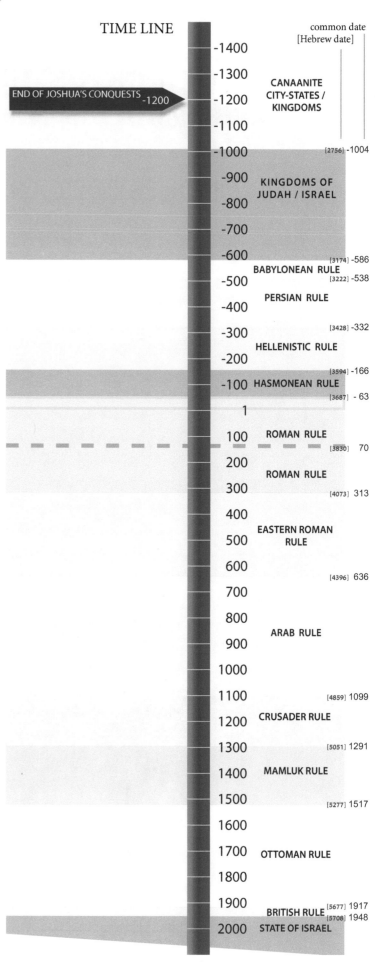

TIME LINE

END OF JOSHUA'S CONQUESTS -1200

common date [Hebrew date]

Period	common date [Hebrew date]
CANAANITE CITY-STATES / KINGDOMS	
KINGDOMS OF JUDAH / ISRAEL	[2756] -1004
BABYLONEAN RULE	[3174] -586
PERSIAN RULE	[3222] -538
HELLENISTIC RULE	[3428] -332
HASMONEAN RULE	[3594] -166
ROMAN RULE	[3687] - 63
ROMAN RULE	[3830] 70
EASTERN ROMAN RULE	[4073] 313
ARAB RULE	[4396] 636
CRUSADER RULE	[4859] 1099
MAMLUK RULE	[5051] 1291
OTTOMAN RULE	[5277] 1517
BRITISH RULE	[5677] 1917
STATE OF ISRAEL	[5708] 1948

-1400, -1300, -1200, -1100, -1000, -900, -800, -700, -600, -500, -400, -300, -200, -100, 1, 100, 200, 300, 400, 500, 600, 700, 800, 900, 1000, 1100, 1200, 1300, 1400, 1500, 1600, 1700, 1800, 1900, 2000

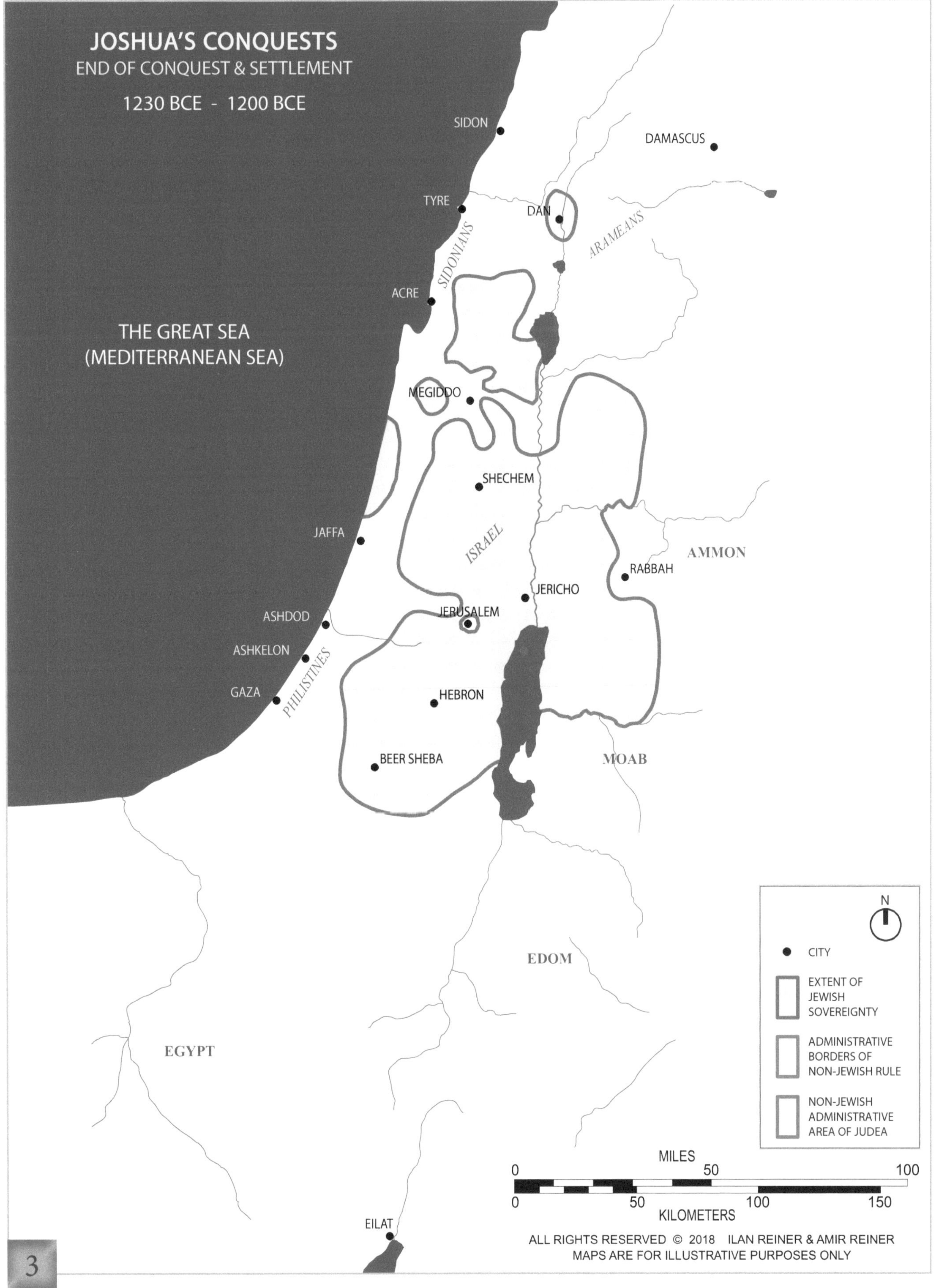

JOSHUA'S CONQUESTS
END OF CONQUEST & SETTLEMENT
1230 BCE - 1200 BCE
SIDON
DAMASCUS
TYRE
DAN
SIDONIANS
ARAMEANS
ACRE
THE GREAT SEA
(MEDITERRANEAN SEA)
MEGIDDO
SHECHEM
JAFFA
ISRAEL
AMMON
RABBAH
JERICHO
ASHDOD
JERUSALEM
ASHKELON
PHILISTINES
GAZA
HEBRON
BEER SHEBA
MOAB
N
CITY
EXTENT OF JEWISH SOVEREIGNTY
ADMINISTRATIVE BORDERS OF NON-JEWISH RULE
NON-JEWISH ADMINISTRATIVE AREA OF JUDEA
EDOM
EGYPT
MILES
0
50
100
0
50
100
150
KILOMETERS
EILAT
ALL RIGHTS RESERVED © 2018 ILAN REINER & AMIR REINER
MAPS ARE FOR ILLUSTRATIVE PURPOSES ONLY
3

Tribal Allotments of Israel
Time of the Judges
about 1200 BCE to 1050 BCE

Settlement of the Hebrew tribes was a long and complex process, spanning over many generations. Borders shifted often as various tribes gained or lost strength. In the book of Joshua (Chapter 18) it is described that surveyors from each tribe were sent to investigate the land. The land was then allotted to the tribes according to their size. The boundaries between the tribes are mentioned in the book of Joshua (Chapters 15-19). But, this most likely reflects the boundaries also during the majority of the period of Judges. Note that the tribe of Dan eventually migrated north from their original coastal region.

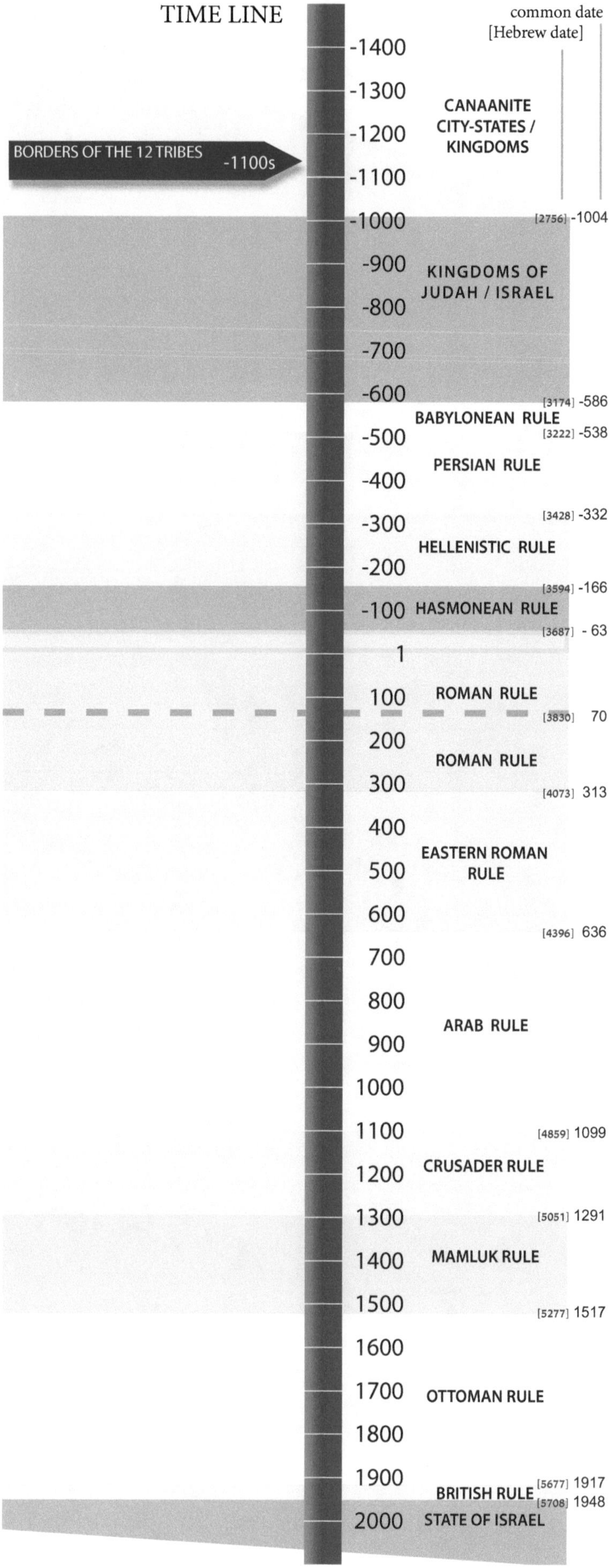

Border Stone from Ancient Mesopotamia
appears in History of ... Babylonia and Assyria (1906)

TIME LINE

common date
[Hebrew date]

BORDERS OF THE 12 TRIBES -1100s

Time line	Period	common date [Hebrew date]
-1400		
-1300	CANAANITE CITY-STATES / KINGDOMS	
-1200		
-1100		
-1000		[2756] -1004
-900	KINGDOMS OF JUDAH / ISRAEL	
-800		
-700		
-600		[3174] -586
-500	BABYLONEAN RULE	[3222] -538
-400	PERSIAN RULE	
-300		[3428] -332
-200	HELLENISTIC RULE	
-100	HASMONEAN RULE	[3594] -166
1		[3687] - 63
100	ROMAN RULE	[3830] 70
200	ROMAN RULE	
300		[4073] 313
400		
500	EASTERN ROMAN RULE	
600		[4396] 636
700		
800		
900	ARAB RULE	
1000		
1100		[4859] 1099
1200	CRUSADER RULE	
1300		[5051] 1291
1400	MAMLUK RULE	
1500		[5277] 1517
1600		
1700	OTTOMAN RULE	
1800		
1900	BRITISH RULE	[5677] 1917
2000	STATE OF ISRAEL	[5708] 1948

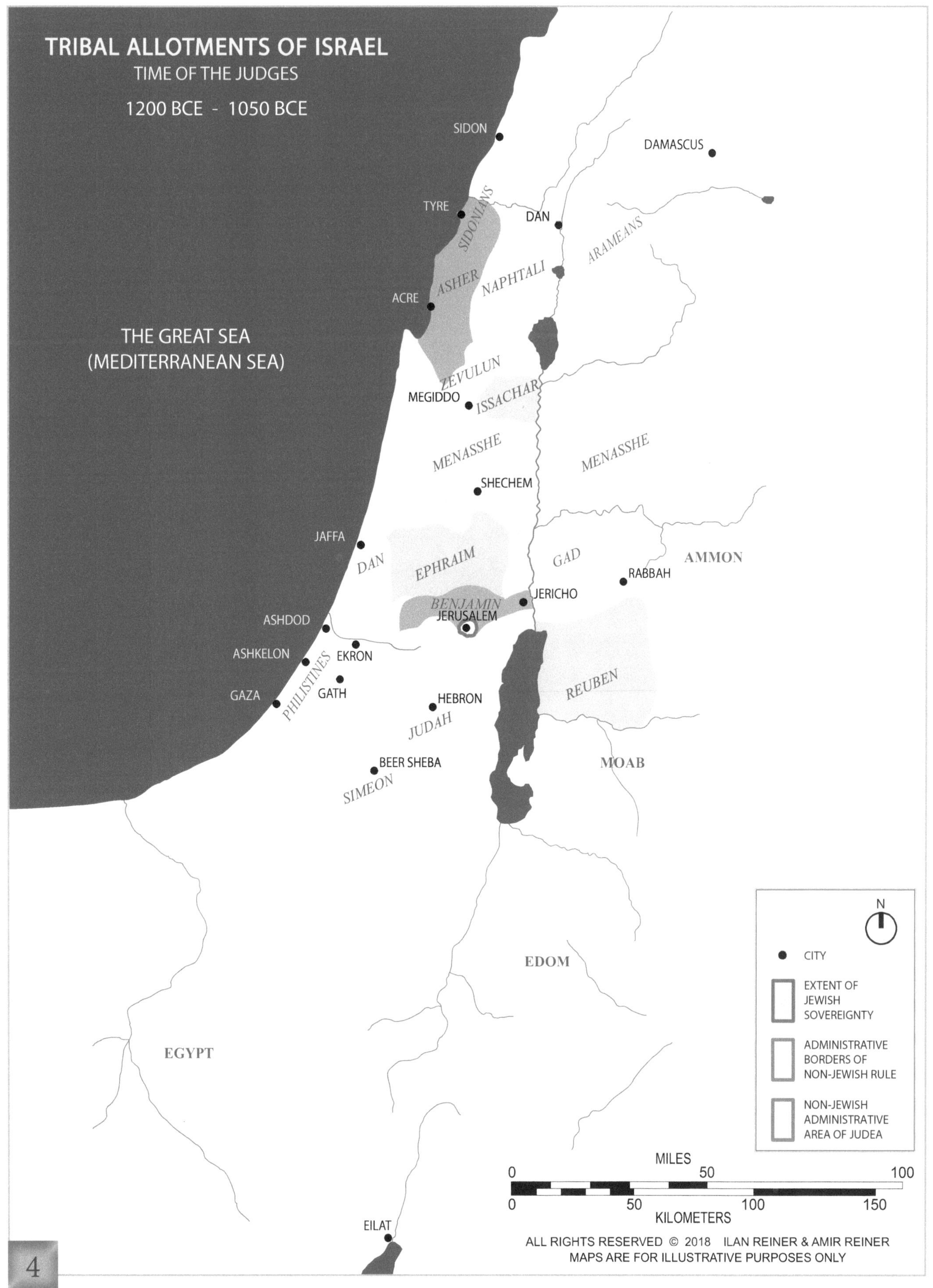

TRIBAL ALLOTMENTS OF ISRAEL
TIME OF THE JUDGES
1200 BCE - 1050 BCE
SIDON
DAMASCUS
TYRE
SIDONIANS
DAN
ARAMEANS
NAPHTALI
ASHER
ACRE
THE GREAT SEA
(MEDITERRANEAN SEA)
ZEVULUN
MEGIDDO
ISSACHAR
MENASSHE
MENASSHE
SHECHEM
JAFFA
DAN
EPHRAIM
GAD
AMMON
RABBAH
JERICHO
BENJAMIN
JERUSALEM
ASHDOD
ASHKELON
EKRON
PHILISTINES
GATH
GAZA
HEBRON
REUBEN
JUDAH
BEER SHEBA
MOAB
SIMEON
EDOM
EGYPT
EILAT
N
CITY
EXTENT OF JEWISH SOVEREIGNTY
ADMINISTRATIVE BORDERS OF NON-JEWISH RULE
NON-JEWISH ADMINISTRATIVE AREA OF JUDEA
MILES
0 50 100
0 50 100 150
KILOMETERS
ALL RIGHTS RESERVED © 2018 ILAN REINER & AMIR REINER
MAPS ARE FOR ILLUSTRATIVE PURPOSES ONLY
4

King Saul
From Tribal Leadership to Kingdom
about 1014 BCE to 1011 BCE

After a period of tribal leaders (Judges) who formed temporary tribal alliances to defend against hostile nations, the people decided to anoint a king. The tribes of Israel were united under a monarchy for the first time. King Saul was the first official king, anointed by the prophet Samuel as commanded by God (1 Samuel 8-9). Saul formed a standing army that was used to secure the kingdom and to unify the various territories that were already settled (1 Samuel 14). The Philistines were the main enemy, with five major cities along the southern coastal region of Canaan. Ultimately, King Saul died, and the Israeli army defeated, in battle against the Philistines.

Death of King Saul
by Elie Marcuse, 1848 {{PD-US}}

TIME LINE

KINGDOM OF ISRAEL - SAUL -1011

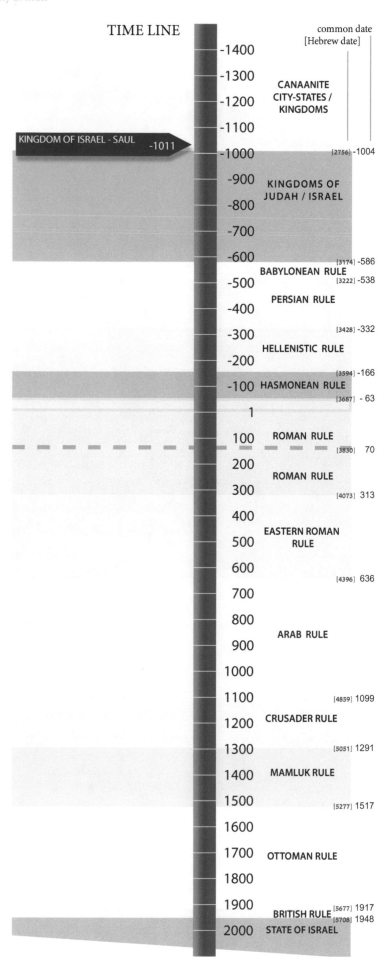

Scale	Period	common date [Hebrew date]
-1400		
-1300	CANAANITE CITY-STATES / KINGDOMS	
-1200		
-1100		
-1000		[2756] -1004
-900	KINGDOMS OF JUDAH / ISRAEL	
-800		
-700		
-600		[3174] -586
	BABYLONEAN RULE	[3222] -538
-500		
-400	PERSIAN RULE	
-300		[3428] -332
-200	HELLENISTIC RULE	
		[3594] -166
-100	HASMONEAN RULE	[3687] - 63
1		
100	ROMAN RULE	[3830] 70
200	ROMAN RULE	
300		[4073] 313
400		
500	EASTERN ROMAN RULE	
600		[4396] 636
700		
800	ARAB RULE	
900		
1000		
1100		[4859] 1099
1200	CRUSADER RULE	
1300		[5051] 1291
1400	MAMLUK RULE	
1500		[5277] 1517
1600		
1700	OTTOMAN RULE	
1800		
1900	BRITISH RULE	[5677] 1917
		[5708] 1948
2000	STATE OF ISRAEL	

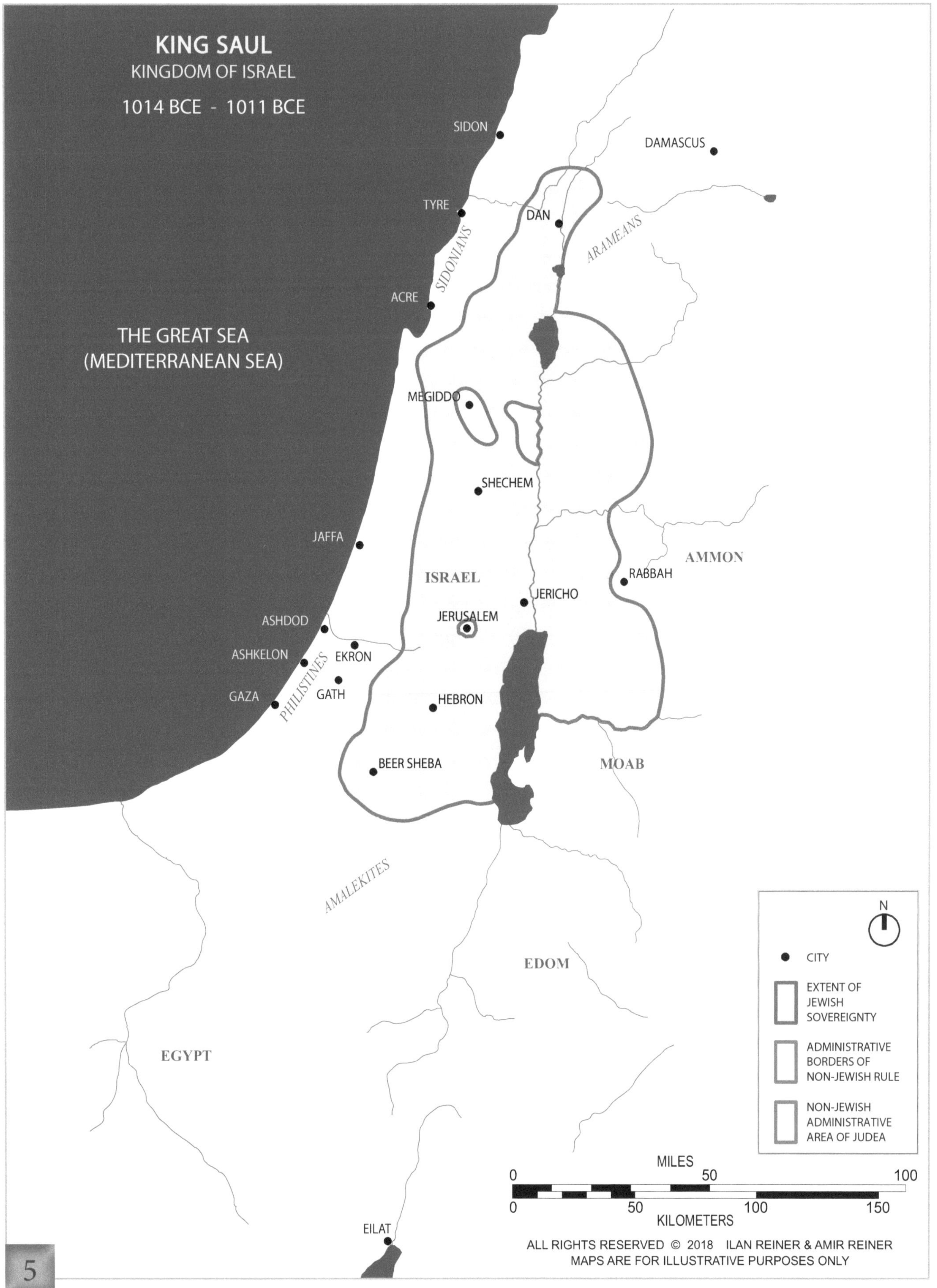

KING SAUL
KINGDOM OF ISRAEL
1014 BCE - 1011 BCE
SIDON
DAMASCUS
TYRE
DAN
SIDONIANS
ARAMEANS
ACRE
THE GREAT SEA
(MEDITERRANEAN SEA)
MEGIDDO
SHECHEM
JAFFA
ISRAEL
AMMON
RABBAH
JERICHO
JERUSALEM
ASHDOD
ASHKELON
EKRON
GAZA
PHILISTINES
GATH
HEBRON
BEER SHEBA
MOAB
AMALEKITES
EDOM
EGYPT
EILAT
N
CITY
EXTENT OF JEWISH SOVEREIGNTY
ADMINISTRATIVE BORDERS OF NON-JEWISH RULE
NON-JEWISH ADMINISTRATIVE AREA OF JUDEA
MILES
0 50 100
0 50 100 150
KILOMETERS
ALL RIGHTS RESERVED © 2018 ILAN REINER & AMIR REINER
MAPS ARE FOR ILLUSTRATIVE PURPOSES ONLY
5

King David and King Solomon
United Kingdom of Israel and Judah
about 1004 BCE to 931 BCE

Under the rule of King David and King Solomon, perhaps the greatest kings in the history of the Jewish people, Israel experienced the greatest expansion ever - along with economic prosperity. Cities from northern Syria of today to the Red Sea were under direct control or influence of the young Hebrew kingdom (2 Samuel 24). Jerusalem became the new capital and the primary religious center with the building of the Temple. It was a time of abundance and peace, with many public works, such as the building of the First Temple in Jerusalem and the grand palace (1 Kings 5). Towards the end of Solomon's rule there were various revolts that threatened the stability of the kingdom. These were mainly due to the high taxation that was imposed on the people.

Remains of King David's Palace in Jerusalem or Kings of the House of David (according to Eilat Mazer)

TIME LINE

ISRAEL - DAVID & SOLOMON -931

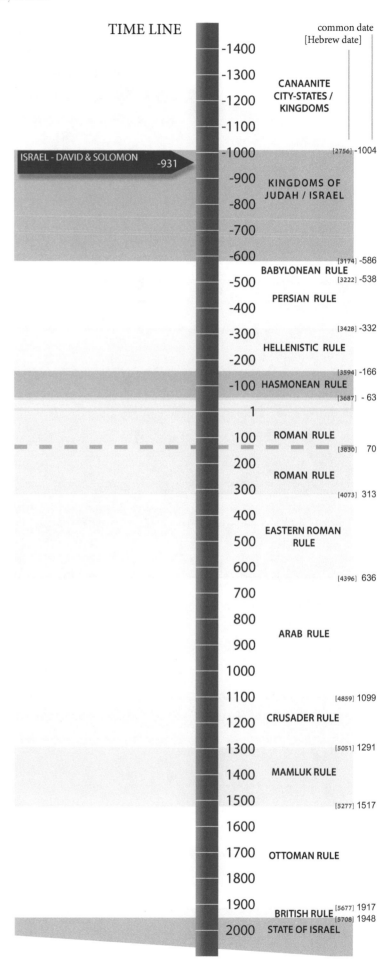

common date [Hebrew date]

-1400
-1300
-1200
-1100
-1000
-900
-800
-700
-600
-500
-400
-300
-200
-100
1
100
200
300
400
500
600
700
800
900
1000
1100
1200
1300
1400
1500
1600
1700
1800
1900
2000

CANAANITE CITY-STATES / KINGDOMS
[2756] -1004
KINGDOMS OF JUDAH / ISRAEL
[3174] -586
BABYLONEAN RULE
[3222] -538
PERSIAN RULE
[3428] -332
HELLENISTIC RULE
[3594] -166
HASMONEAN RULE
[3687] - 63
ROMAN RULE
[3830] 70
ROMAN RULE
[4073] 313
EASTERN ROMAN RULE
[4396] 636
ARAB RULE
[4859] 1099
CRUSADER RULE
[5051] 1291
MAMLUK RULE
[5277] 1517
OTTOMAN RULE
[5677] 1917
BRITISH RULE
[5708] 1948
STATE OF ISRAEL

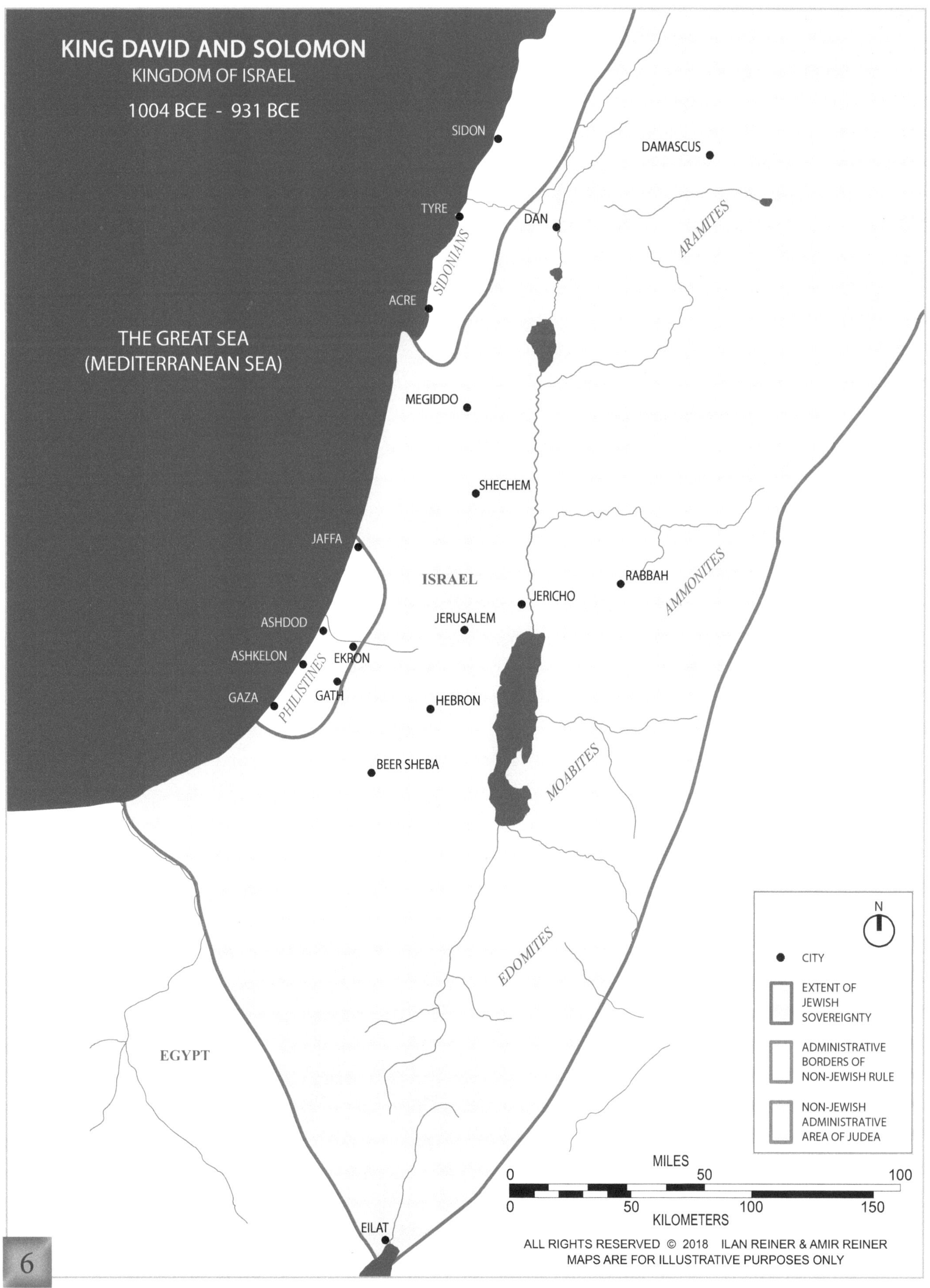

KING DAVID AND SOLOMON
KINGDOM OF ISRAEL
1004 BCE - 931 BCE
SIDON
DAMASCUS
TYRE
DAN
SIDONIANS
ARAMITES
ACRE
THE GREAT SEA
(MEDITERRANEAN SEA)
MEGIDDO
SHECHEM
JAFFA
ISRAEL
RABBAH
AMMONITES
JERICHO
ASHDOD
JERUSALEM
ASHKELON
EKRON
PHILISTINES
GAZA
GATH
HEBRON
BEER SHEBA
MOABITES
EDOMITES
EGYPT
EILAT
N
CITY
EXTENT OF JEWISH SOVEREIGNTY
ADMINISTRATIVE BORDERS OF NON-JEWISH RULE
NON-JEWISH ADMINISTRATIVE AREA OF JUDEA
MILES
0
50
100
0
50
100
150
KILOMETERS
ALL RIGHTS RESERVED © 2018 ILAN REINER & AMIR REINER
MAPS ARE FOR ILLUSTRATIVE PURPOSES ONLY
6

Divided Kingdom
Kingdom of Israel and Kingdom of Judah
about 931 BCE to 875 BCE

Shortly after King Solomon's death, the northern tribes rebelled and split off to establish the Kingdom of Israel in northern Israel (1 Kings 12). The Kingdom of Judah consisted mainly of the tribes of Judah, Simon and Levites, while the other ten Hebrew tribes formed the Kingdom of Israel. Immediately after, Egyptian Pharaoh Sheshonk I invaded both kingdoms, and plundered the Temple in Jerusalem. Over the next century, despite sharing a common heritage, culture and religion, the two sister kingdoms exhibited religious rivalry and were at war with one another for the most part. Hence, the border between the Kingdoms often shifted. Their divisiveness led to overall military and political weakness, which encouraged many foreign cities and smaller kingdoms that were once under their control, to gain independence and wage war against the Hebrew kingdoms.

TIME LINE

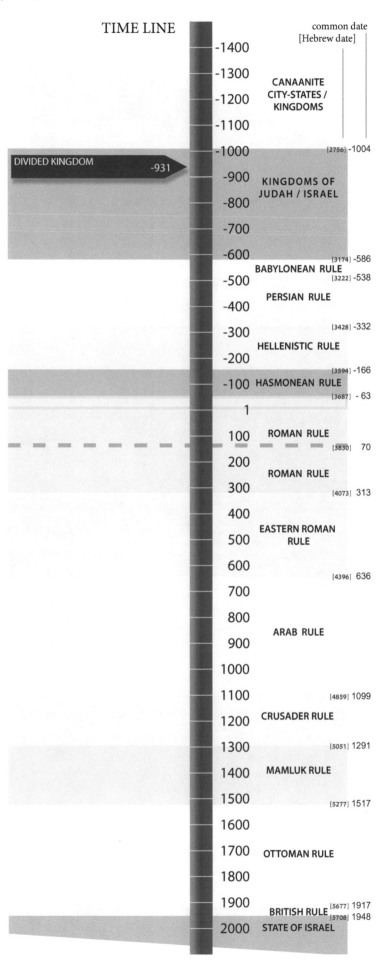

common date [Hebrew date]

-1400
-1300
-1200
-1100
CANAANITE CITY-STATES / KINGDOMS
[2756] -1004
-1000
DIVIDED KINGDOM -931
-900
-800
-700
-600
KINGDOMS OF JUDAH / ISRAEL
[3174] -586
BABYLONEAN RULE
[3222] -538
-500
-400
PERSIAN RULE
[3428] -332
-300
-200
HELLENISTIC RULE
[3594] -166
-100
HASMONEAN RULE
[3687] - 63
1
100
ROMAN RULE
[3830] 70
200
300
ROMAN RULE
[4073] 313
400
500
EASTERN ROMAN RULE
600
[4396] 636
700
800
900
1000
ARAB RULE
1100
[4859] 1099
1200
CRUSADER RULE
1300
[5051] 1291
1400
MAMLUK RULE
1500
[5277] 1517
1600
1700
1800
1900
OTTOMAN RULE
[5677] 1917
BRITISH RULE
[5708] 1948
2000
STATE OF ISRAEL

King Rehoboam, son of King Solomon
Fragment of a wall painting in Basel Town Hall

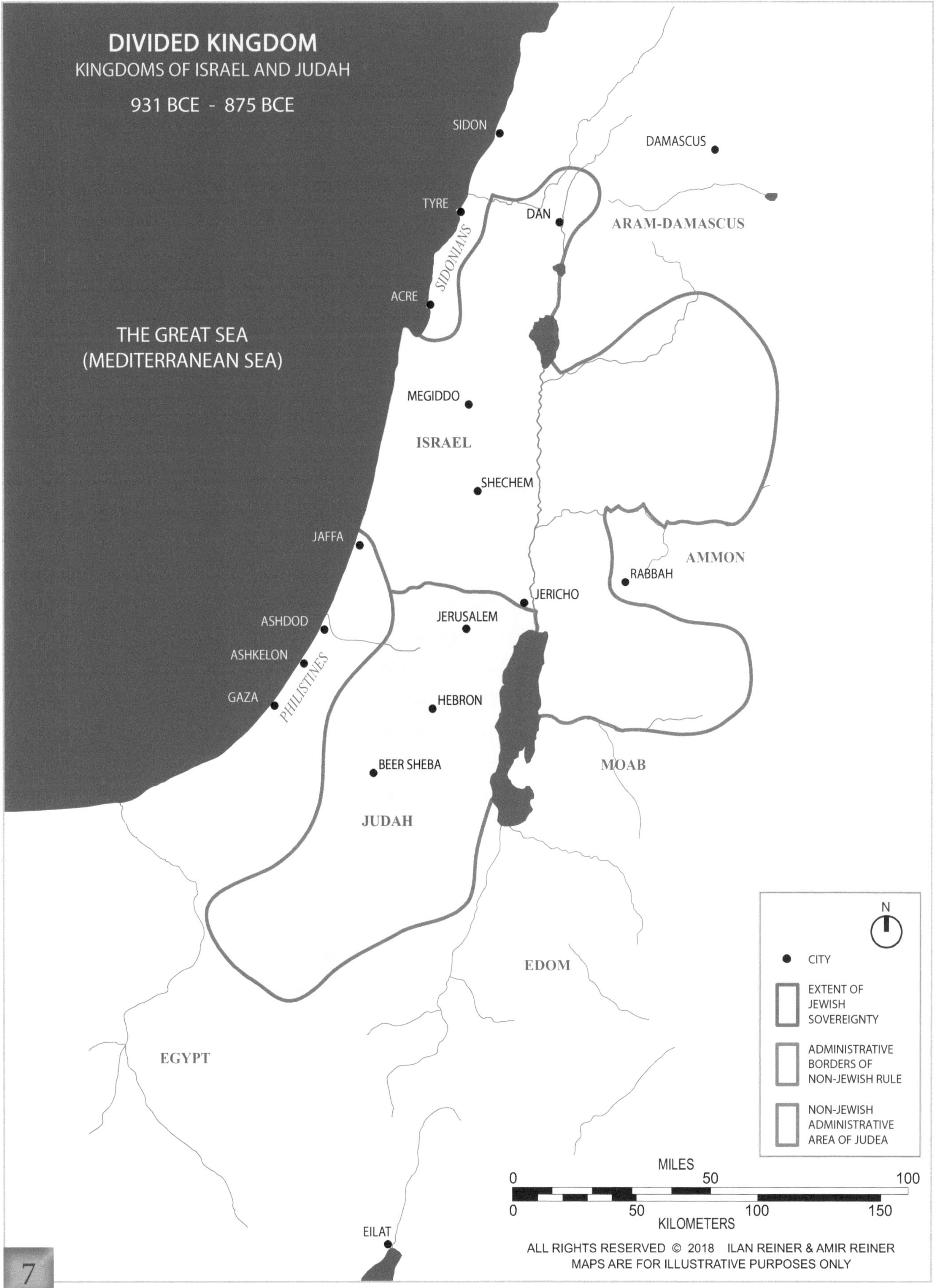

DIVIDED KINGDOM
KINGDOMS OF ISRAEL AND JUDAH
931 BCE - 875 BCE
SIDON
DAMASCUS
TYRE
DAN
ARAM-DAMASCUS
SIDONIANS
ACRE
THE GREAT SEA
(MEDITERRANEAN SEA)
MEGIDDO
ISRAEL
SHECHEM
JAFFA
AMMON
RABBAH
JERICHO
ASHDOD
JERUSALEM
ASHKELON
PHILISTINES
GAZA
HEBRON
BEER SHEBA
MOAB
JUDAH
N
CITY
EXTENT OF JEWISH SOVEREIGNTY
ADMINISTRATIVE BORDERS OF NON-JEWISH RULE
NON-JEWISH ADMINISTRATIVE AREA OF JUDEA
EDOM
EGYPT
MILES
0
50
100
0
50
100
150
KILOMETERS
EILAT
ALL RIGHTS RESERVED © 2018 ILAN REINER & AMIR REINER
MAPS ARE FOR ILLUSTRATIVE PURPOSES ONLY
7

King Ahab and King Jehoshaphat
The Hebrew Kingdoms Recovering
about 875 BCE to 850 BCE

This era was a time of growth for both kingdoms, as they prospered through peace and a strong alliance between them. They took advantage of the decline of regional powers in order to expand their borders and influence (1 Kings 20). On one occasion, Jehoshaphat - King of Judah - joined Ahab, King of Israel, in an offensive war against Aram Damascus in the north (1 Kings 22). Prosperity and military triumphs were overshadowed by great social injustice and decline in spirituality (1 Kings 21).

TIME LINE

AHAB AND JEHOSHAPHAT -860

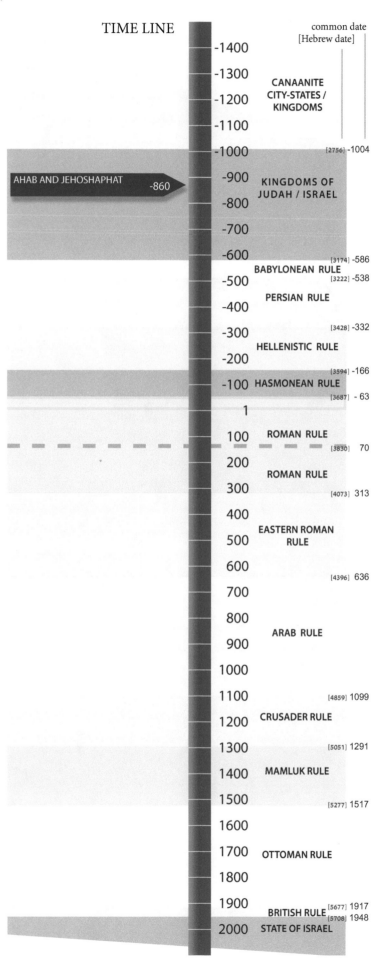

common date [Hebrew date]

Scale	Period	Date
-1400		
-1300	CANAANITE CITY-STATES / KINGDOMS	
-1200		
-1100		
-1000		[2756] -1004
-900	KINGDOMS OF JUDAH / ISRAEL	
-800		
-700		
-600		[3174] -586
	BABYLONEAN RULE	[3222] -538
-500		
-400	PERSIAN RULE	
-300		[3428] -332
-200	HELLENISTIC RULE	
-100		[3594] -166
	HASMONEAN RULE	[3687] - 63
1		
100	ROMAN RULE	[3830] 70
200	ROMAN RULE	
300		[4073] 313
400		
500	EASTERN ROMAN RULE	
600		[4396] 636
700		
800		
900	ARAB RULE	
1000		
1100		[4859] 1099
1200	CRUSADER RULE	
1300		[5051] 1291
1400	MAMLUK RULE	
1500		[5277] 1517
1600		
1700	OTTOMAN RULE	
1800		
1900	BRITISH RULE	[5677] 1917
2000	STATE OF ISRAEL	[5708] 1948

Death of King Ahab in battle against Aram
By: Gustave Dore

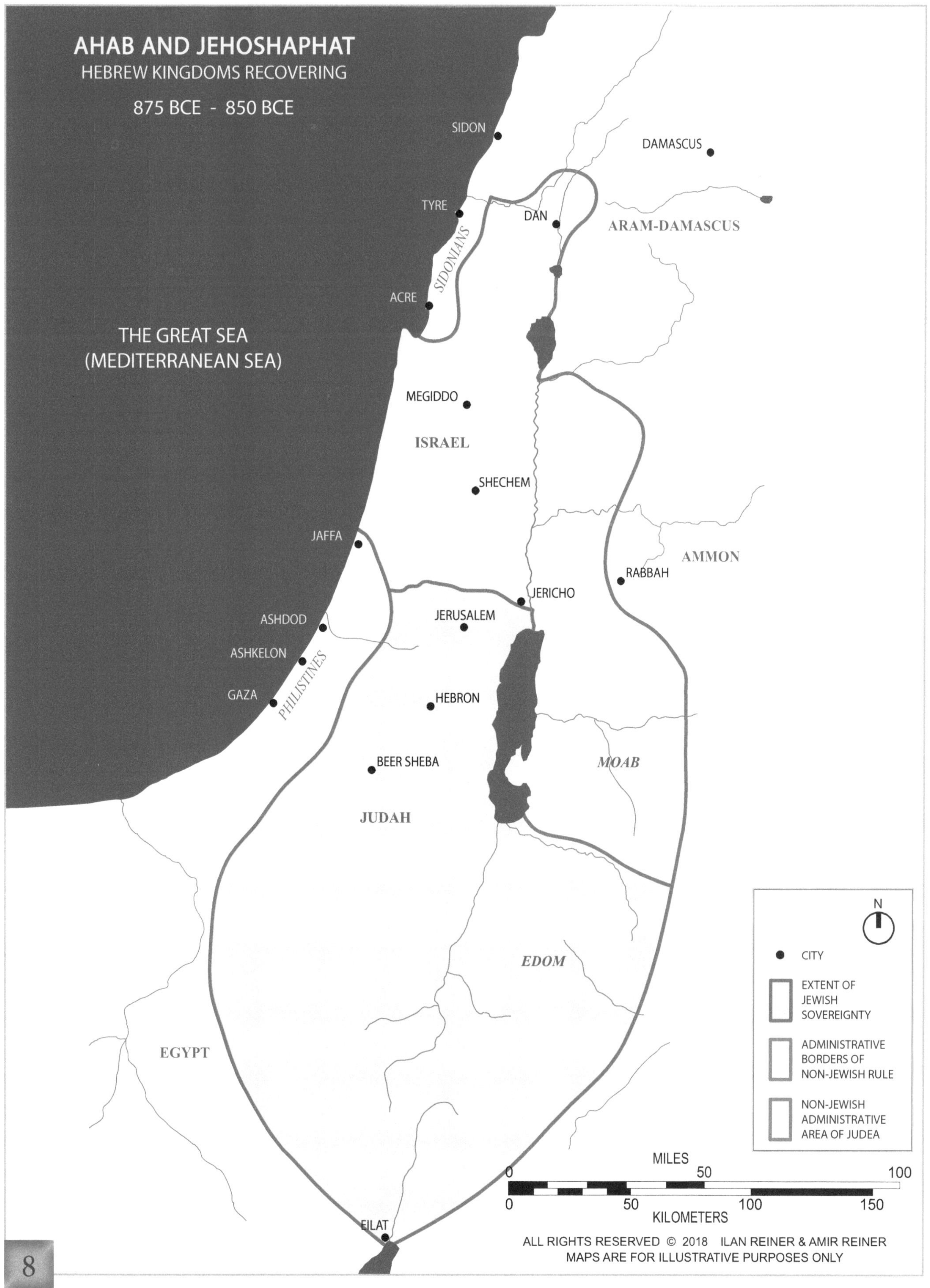
AHAB AND JEHOSHAPHAT
HEBREW KINGDOMS RECOVERING
875 BCE - 850 BCE
SIDON
DAMASCUS
TYRE
DAN
ARAM-DAMASCUS
SIDONIANS
ACRE
THE GREAT SEA
(MEDITERRANEAN SEA)
MEGIDDO
ISRAEL
SHECHEM
JAFFA
AMMON
RABBAH
JERICHO
JERUSALEM
ASHDOD
ASHKELON
PHILISTINES
GAZA
HEBRON
BEER SHEBA
MOAB
JUDAH
EDOM
EGYPT
EILAT
N
CITY
EXTENT OF JEWISH SOVEREIGNTY
ADMINISTRATIVE BORDERS OF NON-JEWISH RULE
NON-JEWISH ADMINISTRATIVE AREA OF JUDEA
MILES
0 50 100
0 50 100 150
KILOMETERS
ALL RIGHTS RESERVED © 2018 ILAN REINER & AMIR REINER
MAPS ARE FOR ILLUSTRATIVE PURPOSES ONLY
8

Rise of Aram Damascus
King Jehu and King Joash
about 840 BCE to 800 BCE

A shift in regional powers allowed the kingdom of Aram Damascus to gain control over neighboring Aramaic Kingdoms and unite them into one strong army. This allowed Aram Damascus to expand her borders southward, and to conquer large areas that were once under influence or rule of the Kingdom of Israel. At this point, both kingdoms, Judah and Israel, were weak from internal wars and political conflicts. Philistines, Moabites, Edomites and others took advantage and regained their independence after long years of being under Hebrew rule.

Aramaen funeral stele (found in Syria)
On display at the Louvre Museum

TIME LINE

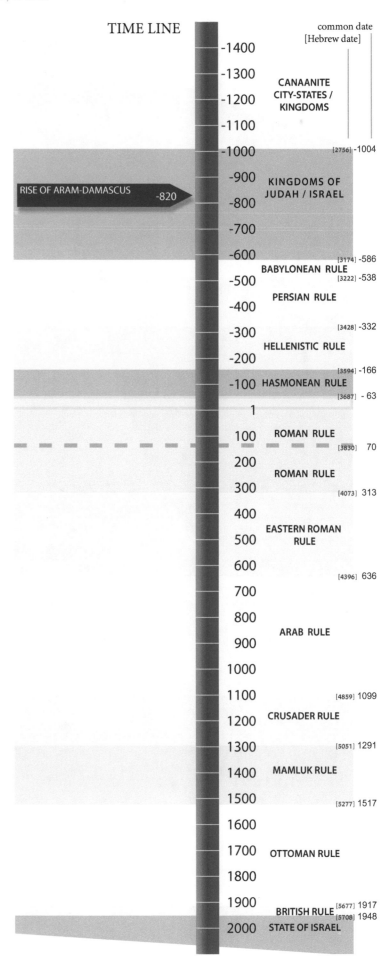

common date
[Hebrew date]

-1400 -1300 -1200 -1100 -1000 -900 -800 -700 -600 -500 -400 -300 -200 -100 1 100 200 300 400 500 600 700 800 900 1000 1100 1200 1300 1400 1500 1600 1700 1800 1900 2000

RISE OF ARAM-DAMASCUS -820

CANAANITE CITY-STATES / KINGDOMS
[2756] -1004
KINGDOMS OF JUDAH / ISRAEL
[3174] -586
BABYLONEAN RULE
[3222] -538
PERSIAN RULE
[3428] -332
HELLENISTIC RULE
[3594] -166
HASMONEAN RULE
[3687] - 63
ROMAN RULE
[3830] 70
ROMAN RULE
[4073] 313
EASTERN ROMAN RULE
[4396] 636
ARAB RULE
[4859] 1099
CRUSADER RULE
[5051] 1291
MAMLUK RULE
[5277] 1517
OTTOMAN RULE
[5677] 1917
BRITISH RULE
[5708] 1948
STATE OF ISRAEL

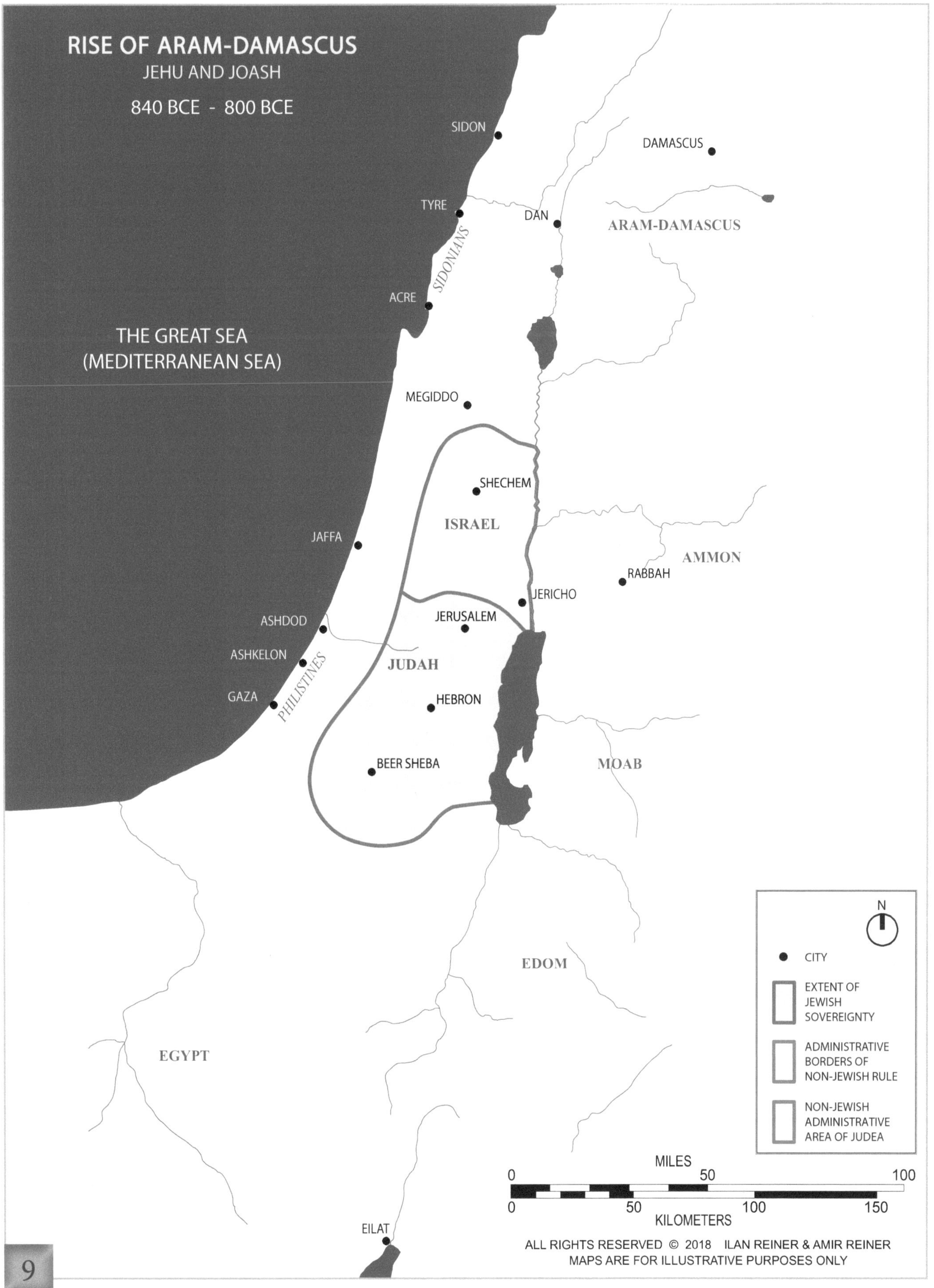

RISE OF ARAM-DAMASCUS
JEHU AND JOASH
840 BCE - 800 BCE
SIDON
DAMASCUS
TYRE
DAN
ARAM-DAMASCUS
SIDONIANS
ACRE
THE GREAT SEA
(MEDITERRANEAN SEA)
MEGIDDO
SHECHEM
ISRAEL
JAFFA
AMMON
RABBAH
JERICHO
JERUSALEM
ASHDOD
ASHKELON
JUDAH
PHILISTINES
GAZA
HEBRON
BEER SHEBA
MOAB
N
CITY
EXTENT OF JEWISH SOVEREIGNTY
ADMINISTRATIVE BORDERS OF NON-JEWISH RULE
NON-JEWISH ADMINISTRATIVE AREA OF JUDEA
EDOM
EGYPT
MILES
0
50
100
0
50
100
150
KILOMETERS
EILAT
ALL RIGHTS RESERVED © 2018 ILAN REINER & AMIR REINER
MAPS ARE FOR ILLUSTRATIVE PURPOSES ONLY
9

King Uzziah and King Jeroboam II
Kingdom of Judah and Kingdom of Israel
about 769 BCE to 748 BCE

This was a time when both kingdoms were at peace and thus flourished. The Assyrian Empire was experiencing internal difficulties, yet still engaged in military campaigns that exhausted Aram Damascus's military strength. This allowed for the joined forces of Israel and Judah to expand their borders and influence, second only to the times of David and Solomon (2 Kings 14). New Israeli towns grew east of the Jordan, and commerce provided for economic growth. In Judah, King Uzziah defeated the Philistines and expanded the border south, building the city of Eilat, opening up the port to increased commerce (2 Chronicles 26). Both kingdoms fortified many cities and strengthened their military.

King Uzziah
By: Rembrandt

TIME LINE

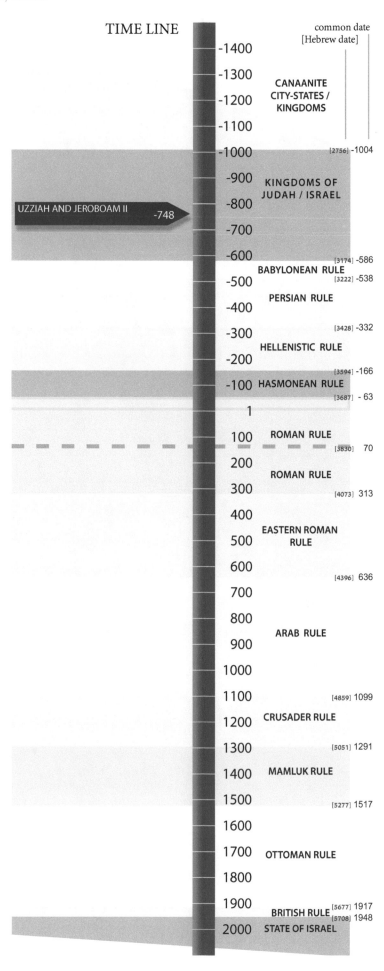

common date
[Hebrew date]

-1400
-1300
CANAANITE CITY-STATES / KINGDOMS
-1200
-1100
-1000 [2756] -1004
-900
KINGDOMS OF JUDAH / ISRAEL
-800
UZZIAH AND JEROBOAM II -748
-700
-600 [3174] -586
BABYLONEAN RULE
-500 [3222] -538
PERSIAN RULE
-400
-300 [3428] -332
HELLENISTIC RULE
-200 [3594] -166
-100 HASMONEAN RULE
[3687] - 63
1
100 ROMAN RULE
[3830] 70
200
ROMAN RULE
300 [4073] 313
400
EASTERN ROMAN RULE
500
600 [4396] 636
700
800
ARAB RULE
900
1000
1100 [4859] 1099
CRUSADER RULE
1200
1300 [5051] 1291
MAMLUK RULE
1400
1500 [5277] 1517
1600
1700 OTTOMAN RULE
1800
1900 [5677] 1917
BRITISH RULE [5708] 1948
2000 STATE OF ISRAEL

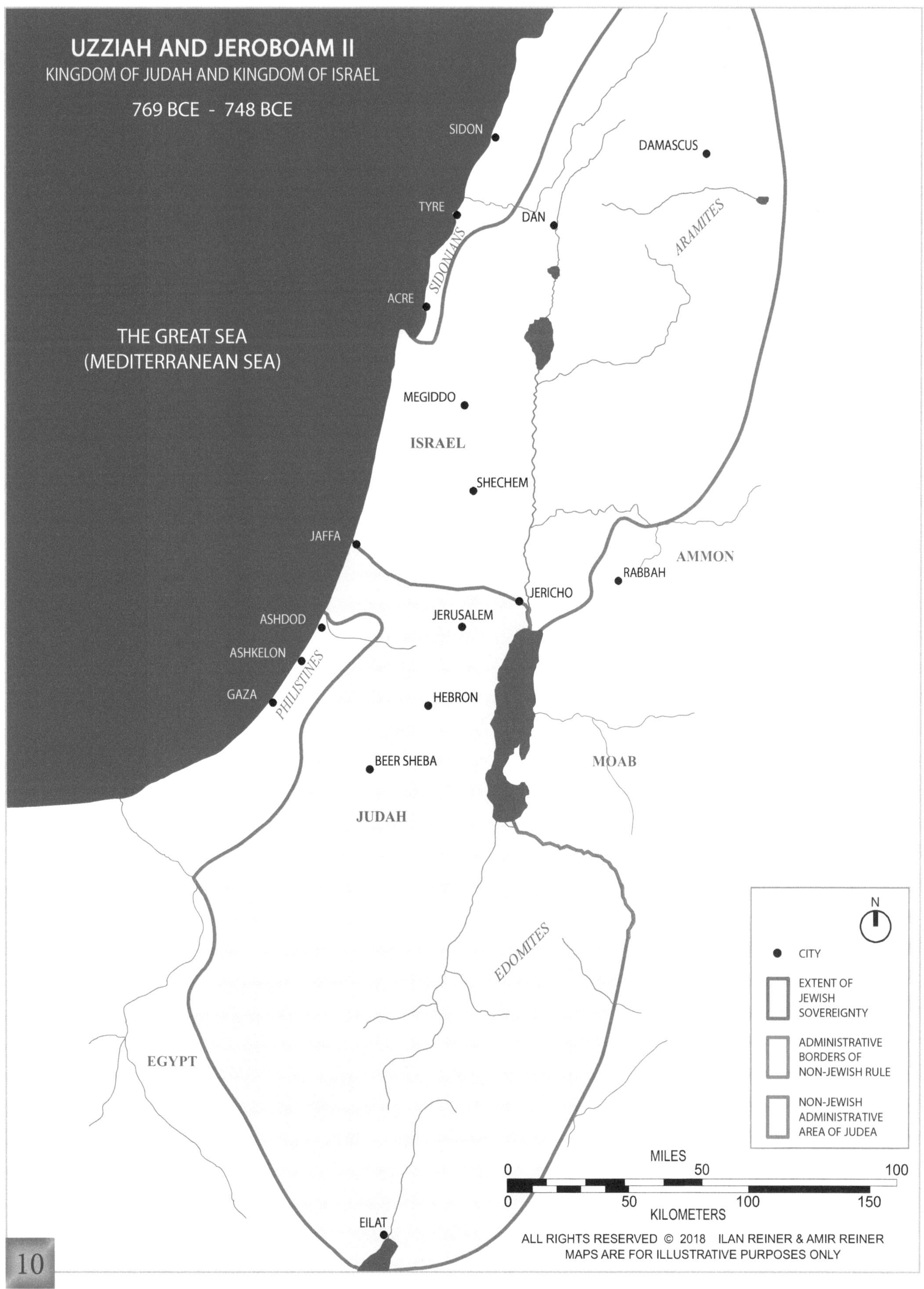
UZZIAH AND JEROBOAM II
KINGDOM OF JUDAH AND KINGDOM OF ISRAEL
769 BCE - 748 BCE
SIDON
DAMASCUS
TYRE
DAN
SIDONIANS
ARAMITES
ACRE
THE GREAT SEA (MEDITERRANEAN SEA)
MEGIDDO
ISRAEL
SHECHEM
JAFFA
AMMON
RABBAH
JERICHO
JERUSALEM
ASHDOD
ASHKELON
PHILISTINES
GAZA
HEBRON
BEER SHEBA
MOAB
JUDAH
EDOMITES
EGYPT
EILAT
N
CITY
EXTENT OF JEWISH SOVEREIGNTY
ADMINISTRATIVE BORDERS OF NON-JEWISH RULE
NON-JEWISH ADMINISTRATIVE AREA OF JUDEA
MILES
0
50
100
0
50
100
150
KILOMETERS
10

Fall of the Kingdom of Israel
King Hezekiah of Judah
about 722 BCE to 680 BCE

As the Assyrian Empire expanded their influence across the Middle East, the Kingdom of Israel refused to become a vassal kingdom and rebelled. The Assyrian army quickly marched in, destroying many cities, including the capital Samaria, and exiling the people. The fall of the northern sister kingdom came as a shock to the Hebrews in both kingdoms. Despite the rivalry, the Kingdom of Israel was still part of a single nation. The Assyrian Empire also conquered and destroyed many cities in Judah and laid siege on Jerusalem. This was a time of great decline to the Jewish kingdom. The Bible tells us of significant religious reforms that King Hezekiah performed and also several construction projects, such as the Shiloah (Siloam) water underground aqueduct, bringing water to the city of Jerusalem (2 Kings 18-20). His son, Menasshe, ruled for many decades, managing to avoid interfering with international affairs.

Assyrian archers (from Palace of Nineveh)
On display at the British Museum

TIME LINE

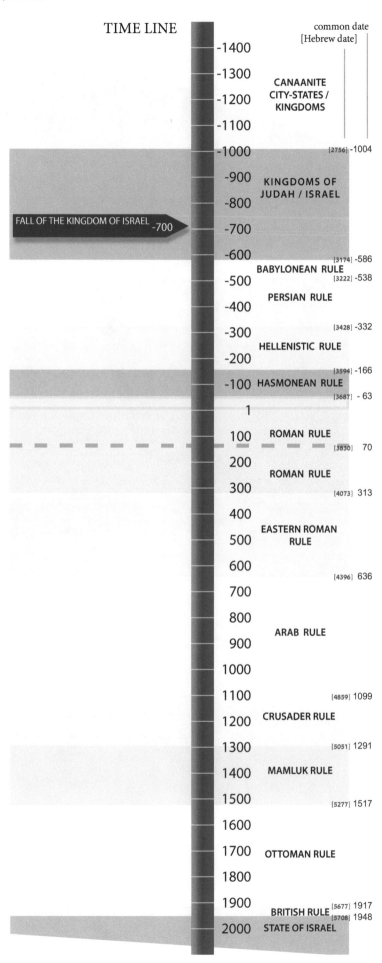

common date
[Hebrew date]

Scale	Period	Boundary
-1400		
-1300	CANAANITE CITY-STATES / KINGDOMS	
-1200		
-1100		
-1000		[2756] -1004
-900	KINGDOMS OF JUDAH / ISRAEL	
-800		
-700	FALL OF THE KINGDOM OF ISRAEL -700	
-600		[3174] -586
-500	BABYLONEAN RULE	[3222] -538
-400	PERSIAN RULE	
-300		[3428] -332
-200	HELLENISTIC RULE	
-100	HASMONEAN RULE	[3594] -166
1		[3687] - 63
100	ROMAN RULE	[3830] 70
200	ROMAN RULE	
300		[4073] 313
400		
500	EASTERN ROMAN RULE	
600		[4396] 636
700		
800		
900	ARAB RULE	
1000		
1100		[4859] 1099
1200	CRUSADER RULE	
1300		[5051] 1291
1400	MAMLUK RULE	
1500		[5277] 1517
1600		
1700	OTTOMAN RULE	
1800		
1900	BRITISH RULE	[5677] 1917
2000	STATE OF ISRAEL	[5708] 1948

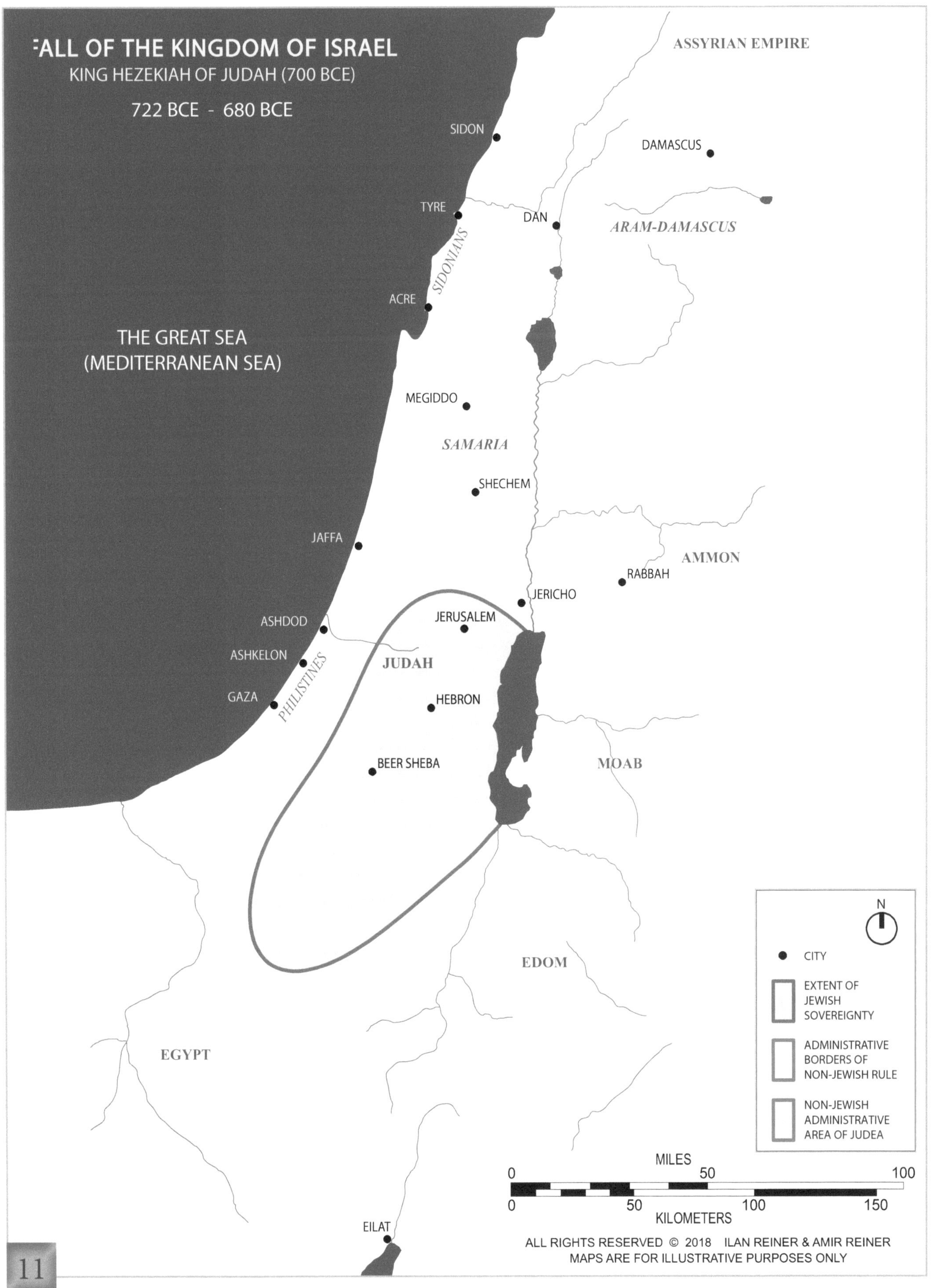

FALL OF THE KINGDOM OF ISRAEL
KING HEZEKIAH OF JUDAH (700 BCE)
722 BCE - 680 BCE
ASSYRIAN EMPIRE
SIDON
DAMASCUS
TYRE
DAN
ARAM-DAMASCUS
SIDONIANS
ACRE
THE GREAT SEA
(MEDITERRANEAN SEA)
MEGIDDO
SAMARIA
SHECHEM
JAFFA
AMMON
RABBAH
JERICHO
JERUSALEM
ASHDOD
ASHKELON
JUDAH
GAZA
PHILISTINES
HEBRON
BEER SHEBA
MOAB
EDOM
EGYPT
EILAT
N
CITY
EXTENT OF JEWISH SOVEREIGNTY
ADMINISTRATIVE BORDERS OF NON-JEWISH RULE
NON-JEWISH ADMINISTRATIVE AREA OF JUDEA
MILES
0
50
100
0
50
100
150
KILOMETERS
11

King Josiah
Kingdom of Judah
about 649 BCE to 609 BCE

The downfall of the Assyrian Empire allowed the Kingdom of Judah to regain her strength and influence in the region. King Josiah was able to expand the borders significantly and he also initiated extreme religious reforms (2 Kings 23). He was killed in battle at Megiddo while trying to meddle in a conflict between Egypt and Babylon. The battle ended in a draw. But, the Egyptians retaliated by placing Judah under their political influence and appointing the king. Shortly thereafter, the Babylonians defeated the Egyptians, and Judah became a tax-paying vassal kingdom. A Jewish revolt against them brought the Babylonian army to the gates of Jerusalem, who spared the city that surrendered, while exiling the elite of the nation. Later, after the Jews rebelled again, the Babylonians conquered Judah, destroyed Jerusalem and exiled the entire nation to Babylon.

Babylonian soldier (archer on horse)
wall tablet

TIME LINE

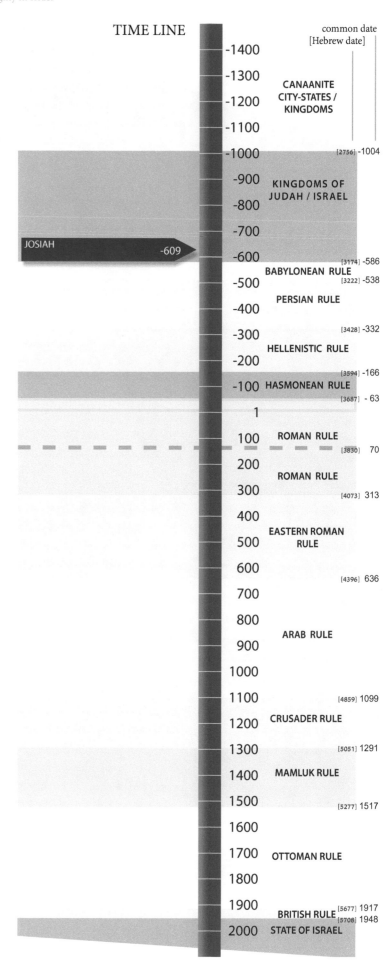

common date
[Hebrew date]

-1400
-1300
-1200 CANAANITE CITY-STATES / KINGDOMS
-1100
[2756] -1004
-1000
-900 KINGDOMS OF JUDAH / ISRAEL
-800
-700
JOSIAH -609
-600
[3174] -586
BABYLONEAN RULE
[3222] -538
-500
PERSIAN RULE
-400
[3428] -332
-300
HELLENISTIC RULE
-200
[3594] -166
-100 HASMONEAN RULE
[3687] - 63
1
100 ROMAN RULE
[3830] 70
200 ROMAN RULE
300
[4073] 313
400
EASTERN ROMAN RULE
500
600
[4396] 636
700
800
ARAB RULE
900
1000
1100
[4859] 1099
CRUSADER RULE
1200
1300
[5051] 1291
1400 MAMLUK RULE
1500
[5277] 1517
1600
1700 OTTOMAN RULE
1800
1900
[5677] 1917
BRITISH RULE
[5708] 1948
2000 STATE OF ISRAEL

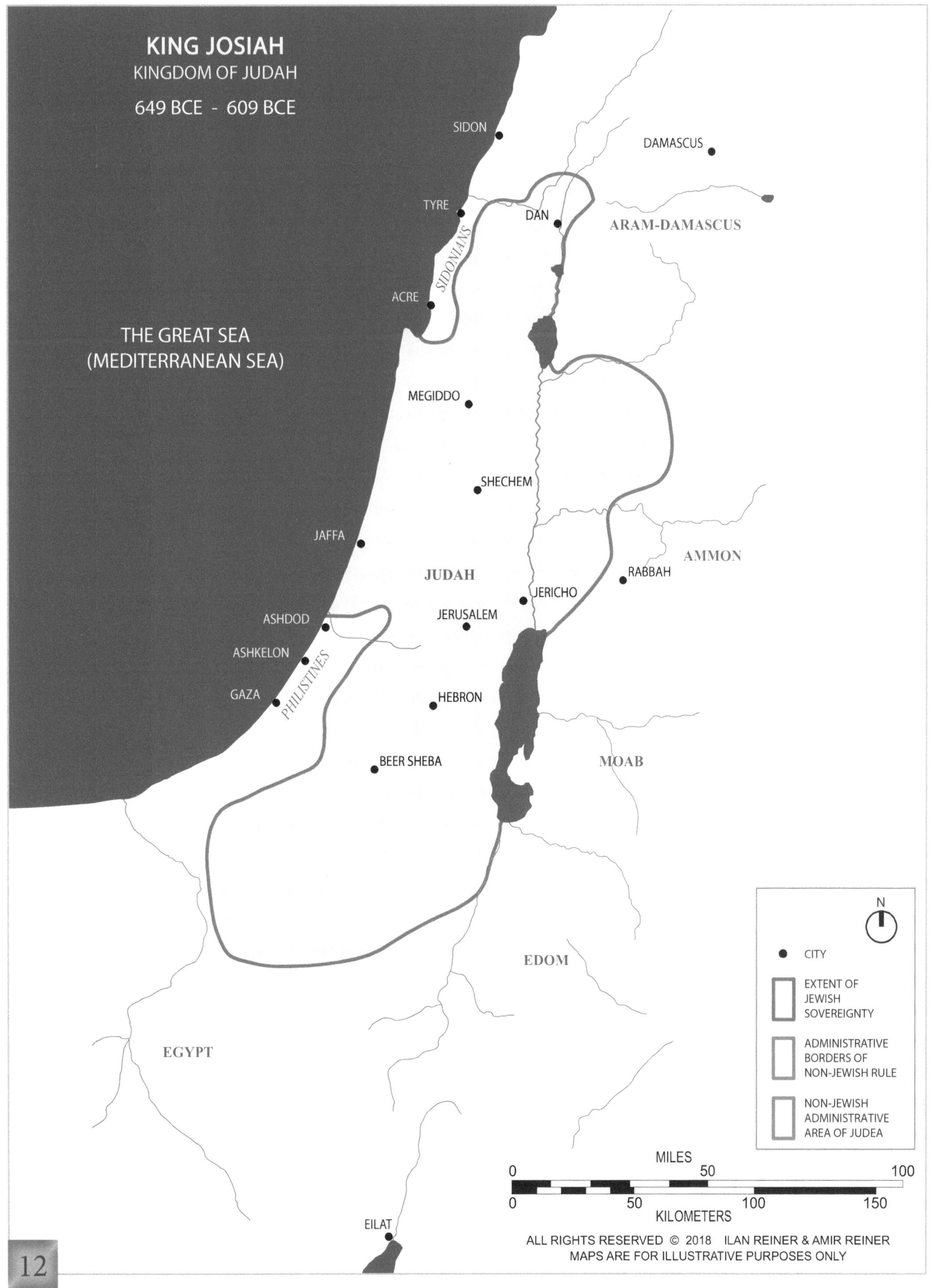
KING JOSIAH
KINGDOM OF JUDAH
649 BCE - 609 BCE
SIDON
DAMASCUS
TYRE
DAN
ARAM-DAMASCUS
SIDONIANS
ACRE
THE GREAT SEA
(MEDITERRANEAN SEA)
MEGIDDO
SHECHEM
JAFFA
AMMON
JUDAH
RABBAH
JERICHO
JERUSALEM
ASHDOD
ASHKELON
PHILISTINES
GAZA
HEBRON
BEER SHEBA
MOAB
EDOM
EGYPT
EILAT
N
CITY
EXTENT OF JEWISH SOVEREIGNTY
ADMINISTRATIVE BORDERS OF NON-JEWISH RULE
NON-JEWISH ADMINISTRATIVE AREA OF JUDEA
MILES
0 50 100
0 50 100 150
KILOMETERS
ALL RIGHTS RESERVED © 2018 ILAN REINER & AMIR REINER
MAPS ARE FOR ILLUSTRATIVE PURPOSES ONLY
12

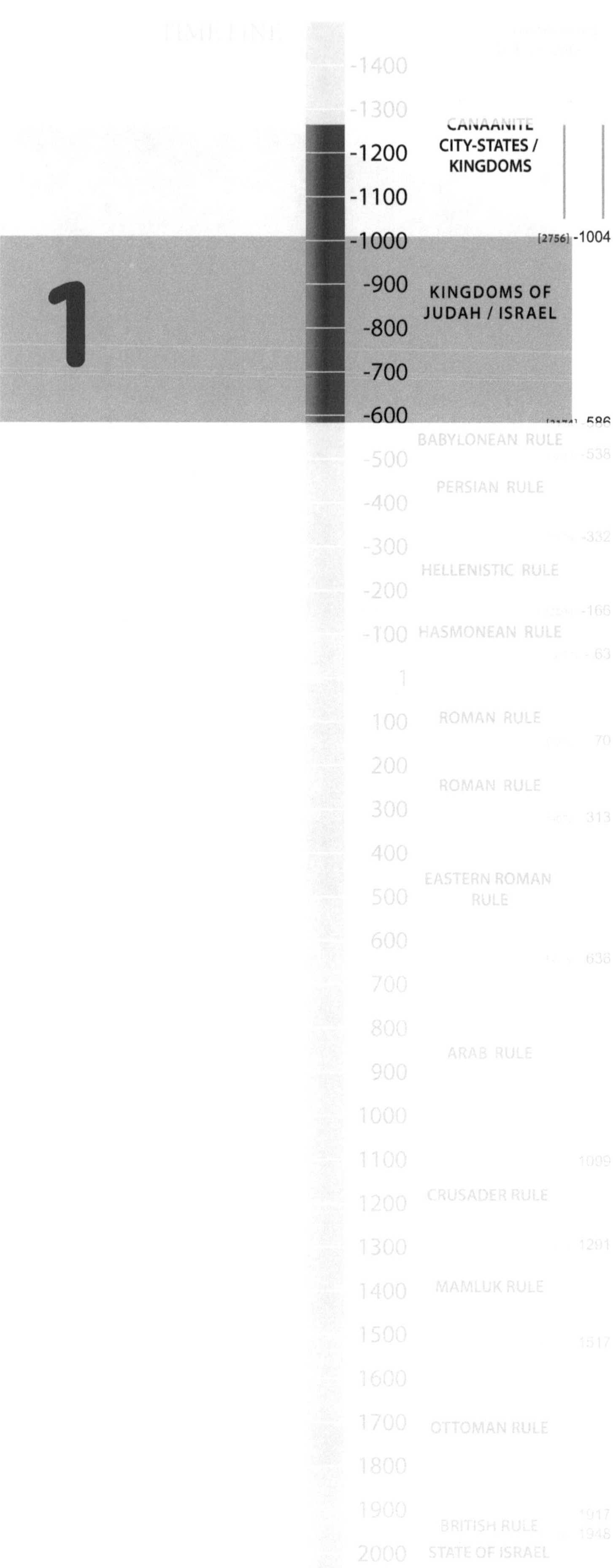
-1400
-1300
CANAANITE
CITY-STATES /
KINGDOMS
-1200
-1100
-1000
[2756] -1004
1
-900
KINGDOMS OF
JUDAH / ISRAEL
-800
-700
-600
586
BABYLONEAN RULE
-500
-538
PERSIAN RULE
-400
-332
-300
HELLENISTIC RULE
-200
-166
-100
HASMONEAN RULE
- 63
1
100
ROMAN RULE
70
200
ROMAN RULE
300
313
400
EASTERN ROMAN
RULE
500
600
636
700
800
ARAB RULE
900
1000
1100
1099
CRUSADER RULE
1200
1300
1291
MAMLUK RULE
1400
1500
1517
1600
1700
OTTOMAN RULE
1800
1900
1917
BRITISH RULE
1948
2000
STATE OF ISRAEL

ENDING OF THE FIRST ERA OF HEBREW RULE IN THE LAND OF ISRAEL

DESTRUCTION OF THE FIRST TEMPLE

-1230 TO -586

The Flight of the Prisoners (After the Destruction of Jerusalem)
By: James Tissot

Neo-Babylonian Kingdom
Exile of Babylon
about 586 BCE to 536 BCE

After conquering the Assyrian Empire, the Babylonians expanded their empire - the Neo- Babylonian Kingdom. To maintain their stability, they had to control all the political entities on the east coast of the Mediterranean. However, despite opposition from great Jewish prophets (2 Kings 24), the kingdom of Judah kept rebelling against the Babylonians, until Babylonian troops swept through the land, devastating all the cities, including the capital Jerusalem, burning down the Temple and exiling the people. For the first time since the exodus from Egypt, the Hebrews were no longer a sovereign nation, and the scattered people now needed to deal with the devastating destruction of their holy city and Temple. The Babylonian culture was very advanced: In architecture, art, astronomy, arithmetic, language and more, and had a profound impact on the Jews in exile in many aspects.

Ruins of the Ancient City of Babylon
Photo credit: Anonymous US Marine in Iraq

TIME LINE

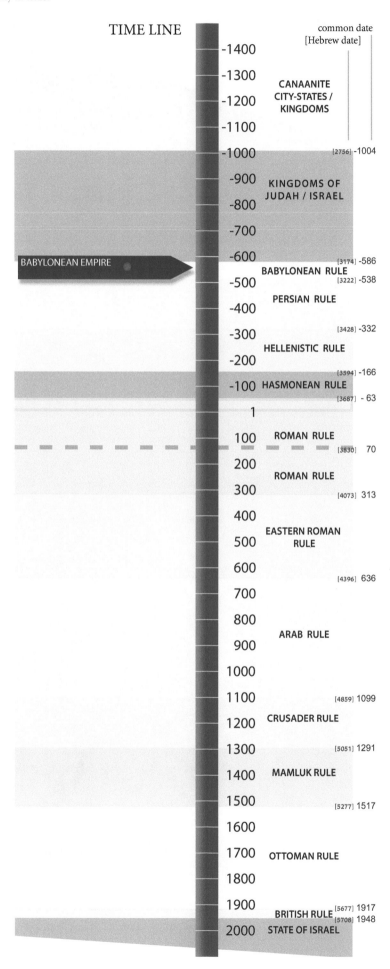

common date
[Hebrew date]

-1400
-1300
-1200
-1100
-1000
-900
-800
-700
-600
-500
-400
-300
-200
-100
1
100
200
300
400
500
600
700
800
900
1000
1100
1200
1300
1400
1500
1600
1700
1800
1900
2000

CANAANITE CITY-STATES / KINGDOMS
[2756] -1004
KINGDOMS OF JUDAH / ISRAEL
BABYLONEAN EMPIRE
[3174] -586
BABYLONEAN RULE
[3222] -538
PERSIAN RULE
[3428] -332
HELLENISTIC RULE
[3594] -166
HASMONEAN RULE
[3687] - 63
ROMAN RULE
[3830] 70
ROMAN RULE
[4073] 313
EASTERN ROMAN RULE
[4396] 636
ARAB RULE
[4859] 1099
CRUSADER RULE
[5051] 1291
MAMLUK RULE
[5277] 1517
OTTOMAN RULE
[5677] 1917
BRITISH RULE
[5708] 1948
STATE OF ISRAEL

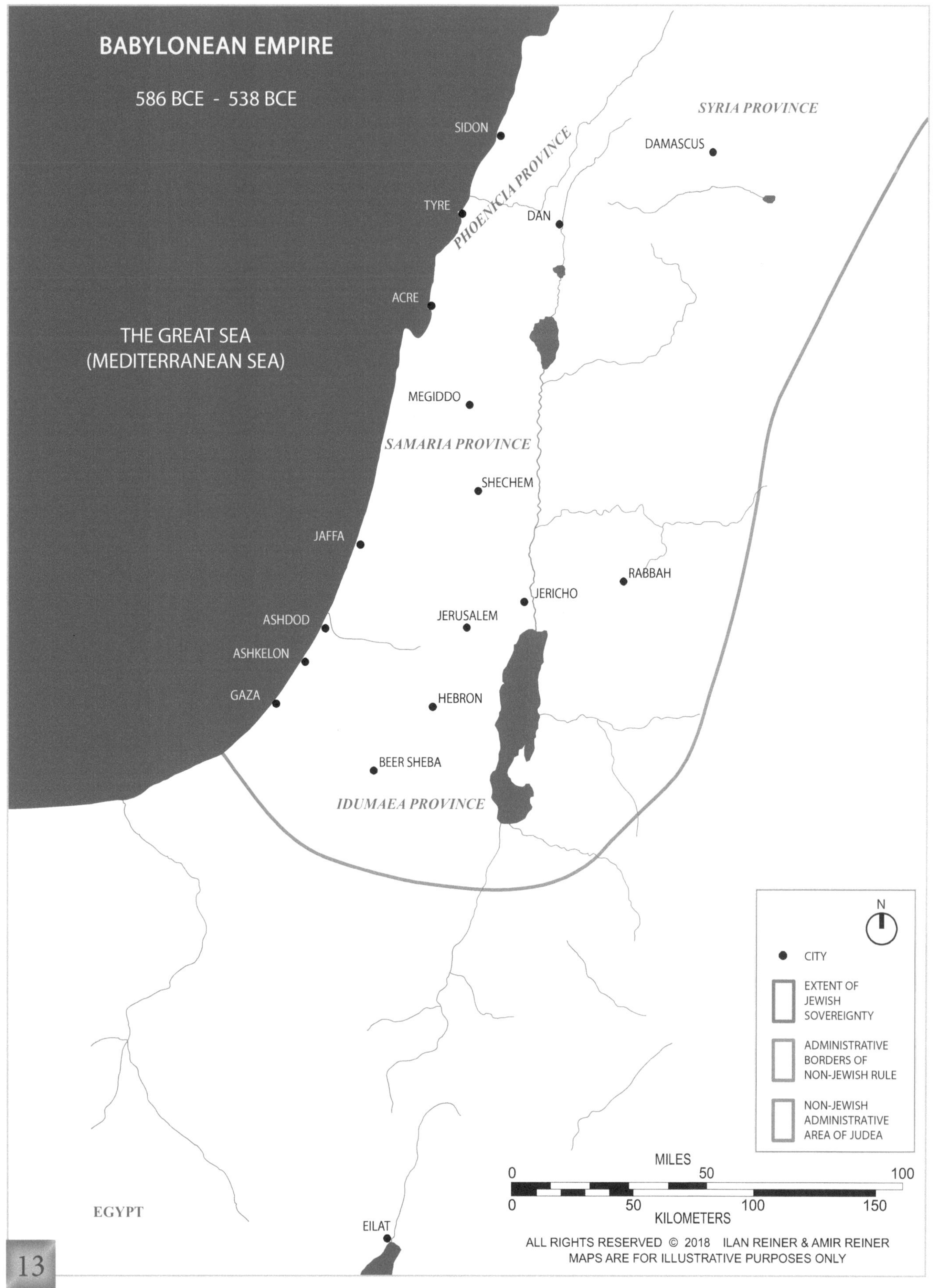

BABYLONEAN EMPIRE
586 BCE - 538 BCE
SYRIA PROVINCE
SIDON
DAMASCUS
PHOENICIA PROVINCE
TYRE
DAN
ACRE
THE GREAT SEA
(MEDITERRANEAN SEA)
MEGIDDO
SAMARIA PROVINCE
SHECHEM
JAFFA
RABBAH
JERICHO
JERUSALEM
ASHDOD
ASHKELON
GAZA
HEBRON
BEER SHEBA
IDUMAEA PROVINCE
N
CITY
EXTENT OF JEWISH SOVEREIGNTY
ADMINISTRATIVE BORDERS OF NON-JEWISH RULE
NON-JEWISH ADMINISTRATIVE AREA OF JUDEA
MILES
0
50
100
0
50
100
150
KILOMETERS
EGYPT
EILAT
ALL RIGHTS RESERVED © 2018 ILAN REINER & AMIR REINER
MAPS ARE FOR ILLUSTRATIVE PURPOSES ONLY
13

Province of Judah (Yehud Medinata)
Persian Achaemenid Empire
about 538 BCE to 332 BCE

Approximately fifty years after the destruction of the temple and Jerusalem, the Babylonian empire was conquered by the rising Persian Achaemenid Empire. The Persian king issued an historical proclamation allowing the Jews to return to the Land of Israel. The general proclamation, addressing all nations, is written on the famous Cyrus Cylinder. This proclamation was part of the Persian doctrine on how to run their empire. But, for the Jews it was also the fulfillment of a prophecy. However, only a few of the Jews answered the call to return home. Those who did, began restoring the cities and started to build a new Temple, within the autonomy that they were granted. The Jewish province under Persian rule was weak demographically and struggling to maintain itself.

Cyrus Cylinder
On display at the British Museum

TIME LINE

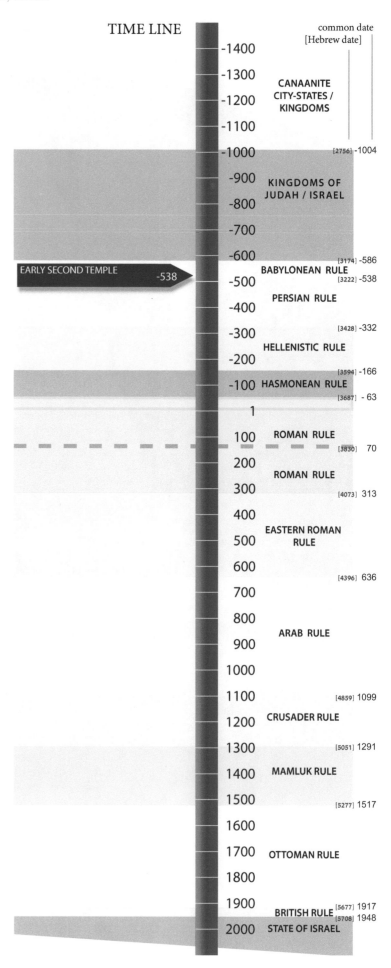

common date
[Hebrew date]

-1400
-1300
-1200 CANAANITE CITY-STATES / KINGDOMS
-1100
-1000 [2756] -1004
-900 KINGDOMS OF JUDAH / ISRAEL
-800
-700
-600 [3174] -586
BABYLONEAN RULE
EARLY SECOND TEMPLE -538
-500 [3222] -538
PERSIAN RULE
-400
-300 [3428] -332
HELLENISTIC RULE
-200
[3594] -166
-100 HASMONEAN RULE
[3687] - 63
1
100 ROMAN RULE
[3830] 70
200 ROMAN RULE
300 [4073] 313
400
500 EASTERN ROMAN RULE
600
[4396] 636
700
800 ARAB RULE
900
1000
1100 [4859] 1099
1200 CRUSADER RULE
1300 [5051] 1291
1400 MAMLUK RULE
1500 [5277] 1517
1600
1700 OTTOMAN RULE
1800
1900 [5677] 1917
BRITISH RULE [5708] 1948
2000 STATE OF ISRAEL

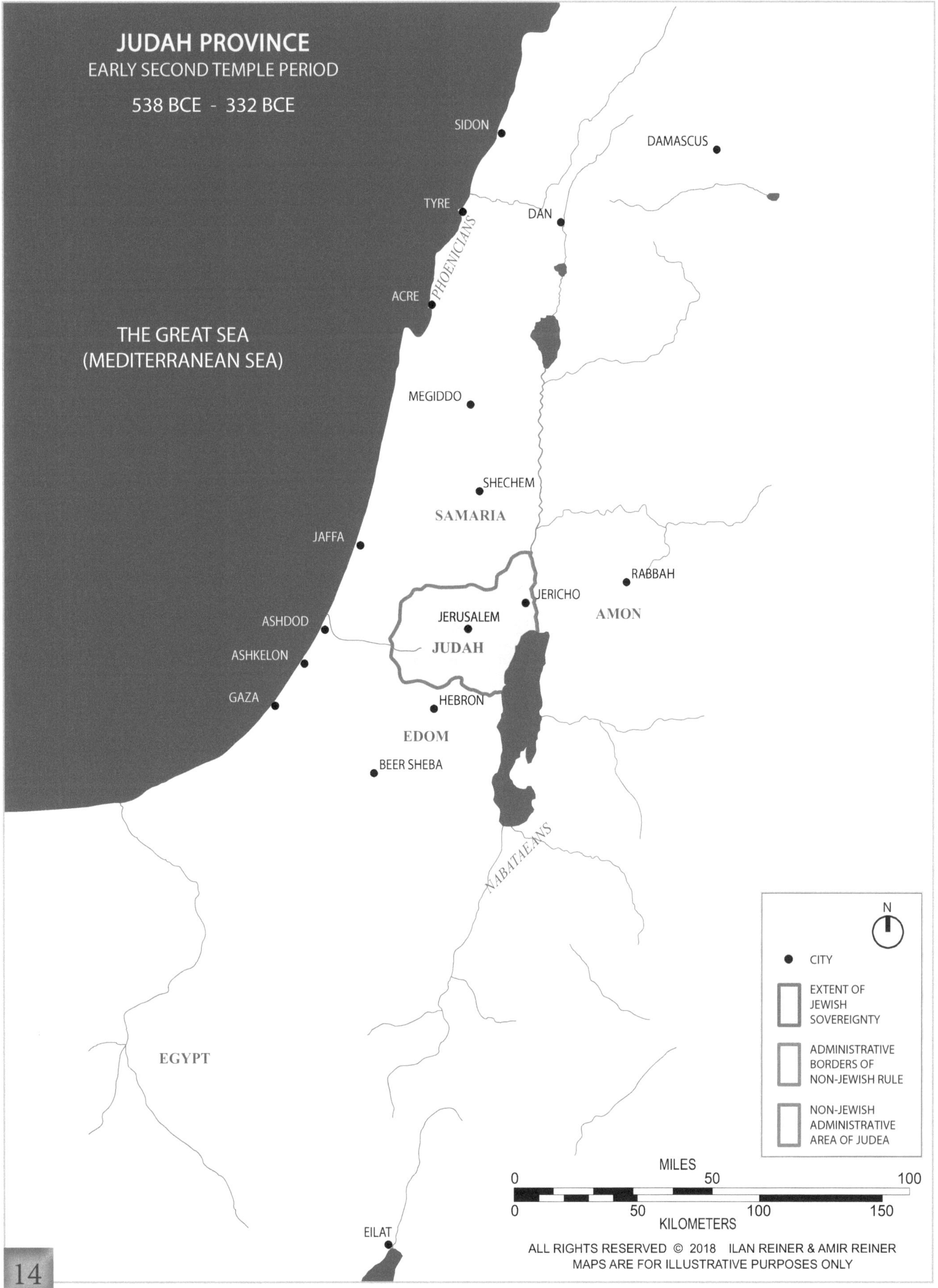
JUDAH PROVINCE
EARLY SECOND TEMPLE PERIOD
538 BCE - 332 BCE
SIDON
DAMASCUS
TYRE
DAN
PHOENICIANS
ACRE
THE GREAT SEA
(MEDITERRANEAN SEA)
MEGIDDO
SHECHEM
SAMARIA
JAFFA
RABBAH
JERICHO
AMON
JERUSALEM
ASHDOD
JUDAH
ASHKELON
GAZA
HEBRON
EDOM
BEER SHEBA
NABATAEANS
N
CITY
EXTENT OF JEWISH SOVEREIGNTY
ADMINISTRATIVE BORDERS OF NON-JEWISH RULE
NON-JEWISH ADMINISTRATIVE AREA OF JUDEA
EGYPT
MILES
0
50
100
0
50
100
150
KILOMETERS
EILAT
ALL RIGHTS RESERVED © 2018 ILAN REINER & AMIR REINER
MAPS ARE FOR ILLUSTRATIVE PURPOSES ONLY
14

Province of Judah
Ptolemaic Dynasty & Seleucid Empire
about 332 BCE to 166 BCE

The Judean province, once part of the Persian Empire, was conquered by Alexander the Great without much resistance, and came under Hellenistic rule and cultural influence. The Ptolemaic Dynasty from Egypt ruled over Judah for about a century, until it was defeated by the Seleucid Empire. Both Hellenistic rulers granted Judah a certain level of autonomy as long as they paid taxes and refrained from any foreign policy. Nor could the Province of Judah maintain an army or have an alliance with any foreign entity. But after about two centuries, tensions rose between the Jewish population and the Seleucid government, due to various governance policies, such as high taxes, restricting Jews from observing their faith and even desecration of the Temple in Jerusalem. Eventually, cultural clashes and religious restrictions forced the Jews into an all out rebellion, led by the Hasmonean family.

The phalanx attacking the center in battle
By: Andre Castaigne {{US-PD}}

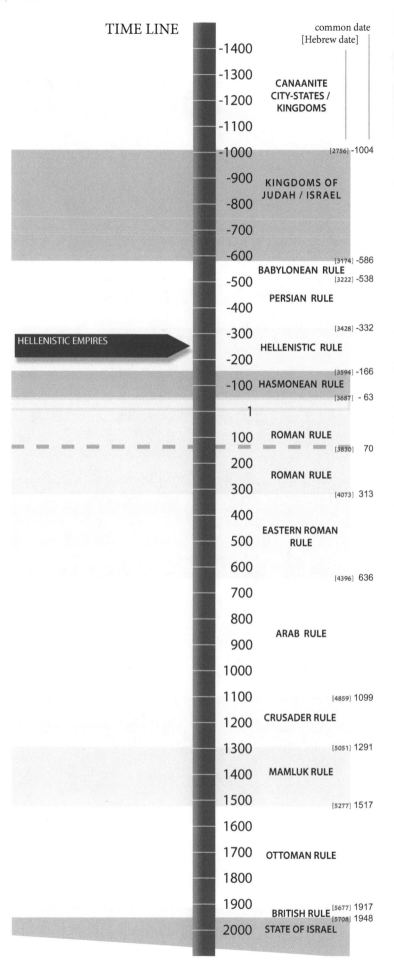

TIME LINE

common date [Hebrew date]

HELLENISTIC EMPIRES

Scale	Period	common date [Hebrew date]
-1400		
-1300	CANAANITE CITY-STATES / KINGDOMS	
-1200		
-1100		
-1000		[2756] -1004
-900	KINGDOMS OF JUDAH / ISRAEL	
-800		
-700		
-600		[3174] -586
	BABYLONEAN RULE	[3222] -538
-500		
-400	PERSIAN RULE	
		[3428] -332
-300	HELLENISTIC RULE	
-200		[3594] -166
-100	HASMONEAN RULE	[3687] - 63
1		
100	ROMAN RULE	[3830] 70
200	ROMAN RULE	
300		[4073] 313
400		
500	EASTERN ROMAN RULE	
600		[4396] 636
700		
800	ARAB RULE	
900		
1000		
1100		[4859] 1099
1200	CRUSADER RULE	
1300		[5051] 1291
1400	MAMLUK RULE	
1500		[5277] 1517
1600		
1700	OTTOMAN RULE	
1800		
1900	BRITISH RULE	[5677] 1917
		[5708] 1948
2000	STATE OF ISRAEL	

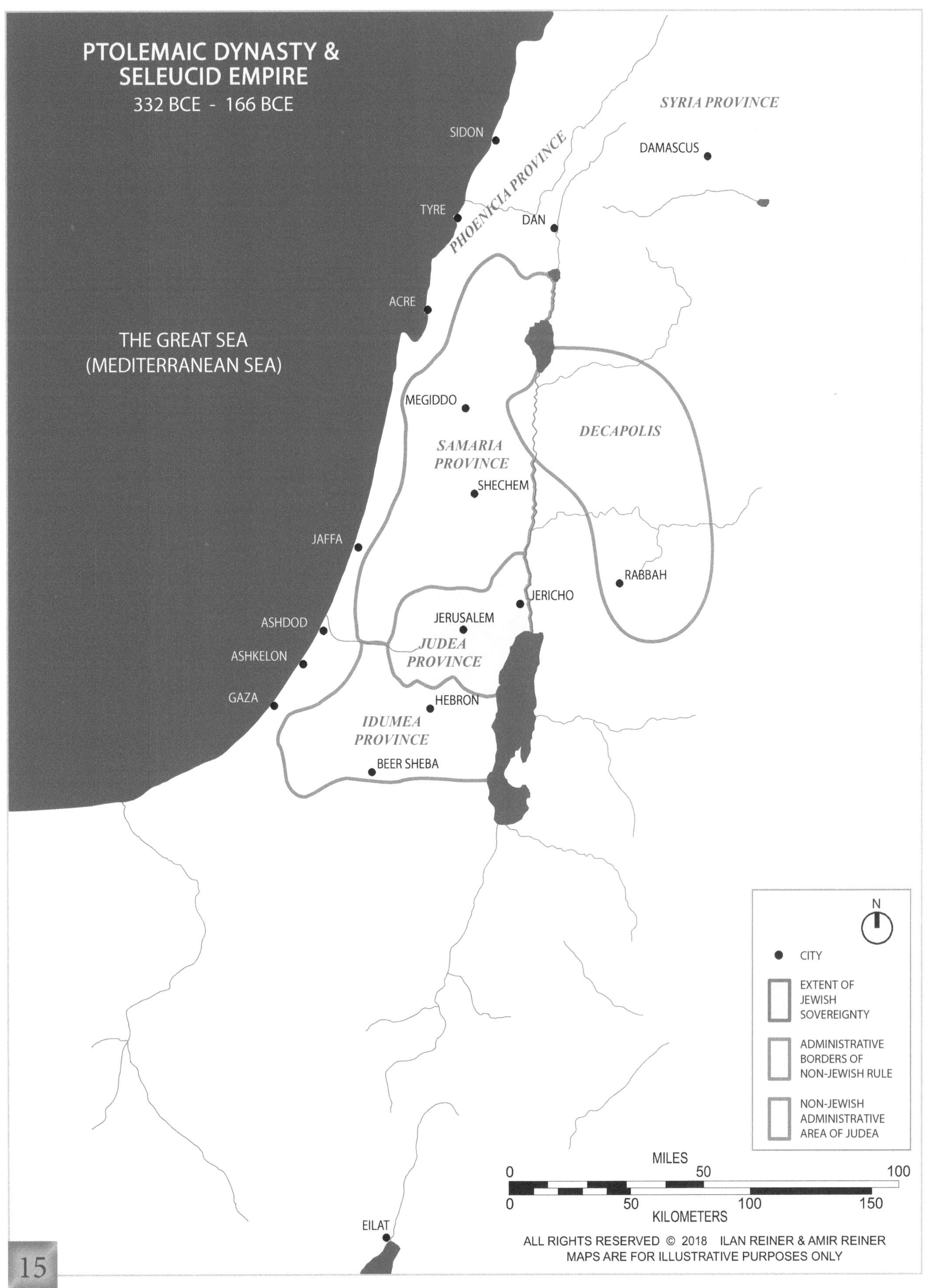
PTOLEMAIC DYNASTY &
SELEUCID EMPIRE
332 BCE - 166 BCE
SYRIA PROVINCE
SIDON
PHOENICIA PROVINCE
DAMASCUS
TYRE
DAN
ACRE
THE GREAT SEA
(MEDITERRANEAN SEA)
MEGIDDO
DECAPOLIS
SAMARIA
PROVINCE
SHECHEM
JAFFA
RABBAH
JERICHO
ASHDOD
JERUSALEM
JUDEA
PROVINCE
ASHKELON
GAZA
HEBRON
IDUMEA
PROVINCE
BEER SHEBA
N
CITY
EXTENT OF
JEWISH
SOVEREIGNTY
ADMINISTRATIVE
BORDERS OF
NON-JEWISH RULE
NON-JEWISH
ADMINISTRATIVE
AREA OF JUDEA
MILES
0
50
100
0
50
100
150
KILOMETERS
EILAT
ALL RIGHTS RESERVED © 2018 ILAN REINER & AMIR REINER
MAPS ARE FOR ILLUSTRATIVE PURPOSES ONLY
15

Beginning of the Second Era of Jewish Rule in the Land of Israel

about 166 BCE to 70 CE

The Second Era of Jewish rule in Israel actually begins when the Jews gained full independence with the Hasmonean revolt, and reestablished the Jewish Kingdom. Later this kingdom came under partial Roman rule and influence as the Hasmonean kings sought an alliance with the rising Roman Empire.

Shortly after, the Romans appointed Herod as the King of Judea. He destroyed the Hasmonean dynasty, established Judea as a kingdom (no longer a Roman province, but still with allegiance to Rome), and then set the path to making Judea a great kingdom. He expanded the boundaries of the Jewish kingdom, built numerous cities, buildings and infrastructures, and practically rebuilt the Temple in Jerusalem.

The Jewish Kingdom enjoyed economic growth and prosperity, despite some civil unrest and disapproval of King Herod. After his death, his descendants were unable to maintain the kingdom, so it fell under Roman rule. As tension grew between the Jewish population and the Roman government, a violent conflict was inevitable. The Jews revolted against the Romans, in what also became an internal Jewish civil war. After four years, Roman legions stormed Jerusalem, destroyed the Temple, burned down the city and exiled many of the Jews to be sold as slaves around the Roman world. This would end the Second Era of Jewish Sovereignty.

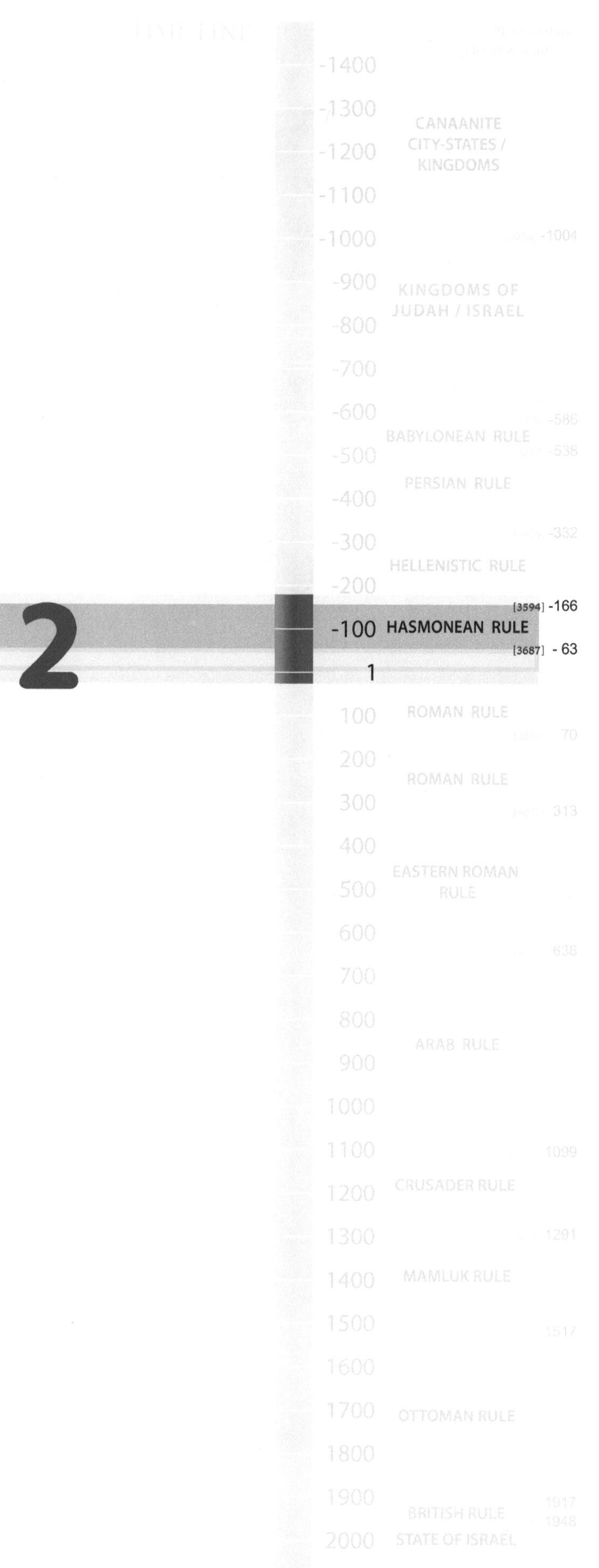

BEGINNING OF THE SECOND ERA OF JEWISH RULE IN THE LAND OF ISRAEL

MACCABEAN REVOLT

-166 TO 70

Maccabees go into Battle
Woodcut by Julius Schnorr von Carolsfeld

Jonathan the Maccabee
Hasmonean Kingdom of Judah
about 160 BCE to 142 BCE

Matityahu and his five sons, known as the Hasmonean, started with a spontaneous uprising against the Seleucid Empire. The main purpose was primarily to gain control over the Judean province and obtain religious and civil autonomy. His son, Judah the Maccabee, became the leader of the Jewish militia and using guerrilla warfare, managed several times to defeat the Seleucid armies sent to suppress the revolt. He even succeeded in conquering Jerusalem, but not the Seleucid fortress within. The success of the revolt is celebrated to this day as the holiday of Hannukkah. After his death in battle, his brother Jonathan was appointed as leader of the revolt. Jonathan had many military and political successes, as he expanded the borders and realm of influence of the Jewish entity, while taking advantage of civil wars and rivalries within the Seleucid Empire.

Judas Maccabee
By: Julius Schnorr von Carolsfeld

TIME LINE

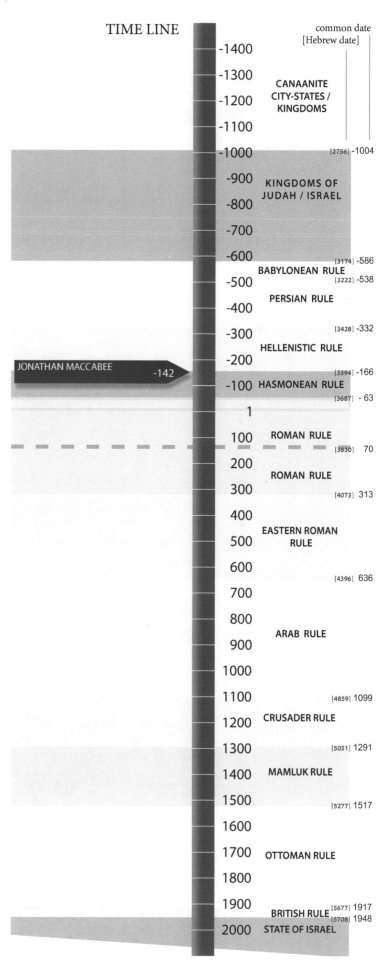

common date
[Hebrew date]

-1400
-1300
-1200
-1100
CANAANITE CITY-STATES / KINGDOMS
[2756] -1004
-1000
-900
-800
-700
-600
KINGDOMS OF JUDAH / ISRAEL
[3174] -586
BABYLONEAN RULE
[3222] -538
-500
-400
PERSIAN RULE
[3428] -332
-300
-200
HELLENISTIC RULE
JONATHAN MACCABEE -142
[3594] -166
-100
HASMONEAN RULE
[3687] - 63
1
100
ROMAN RULE
[3830] 70
200
300
ROMAN RULE
[4073] 313
400
500
EASTERN ROMAN RULE
600
[4396] 636
700
800
900
ARAB RULE
1000
1100
[4859] 1099
1200
CRUSADER RULE
1300
[5051] 1291
1400
MAMLUK RULE
1500
[5277] 1517
1600
1700
1800
OTTOMAN RULE
1900
[5677] 1917
BRITISH RULE
[5708] 1948
2000
STATE OF ISRAEL

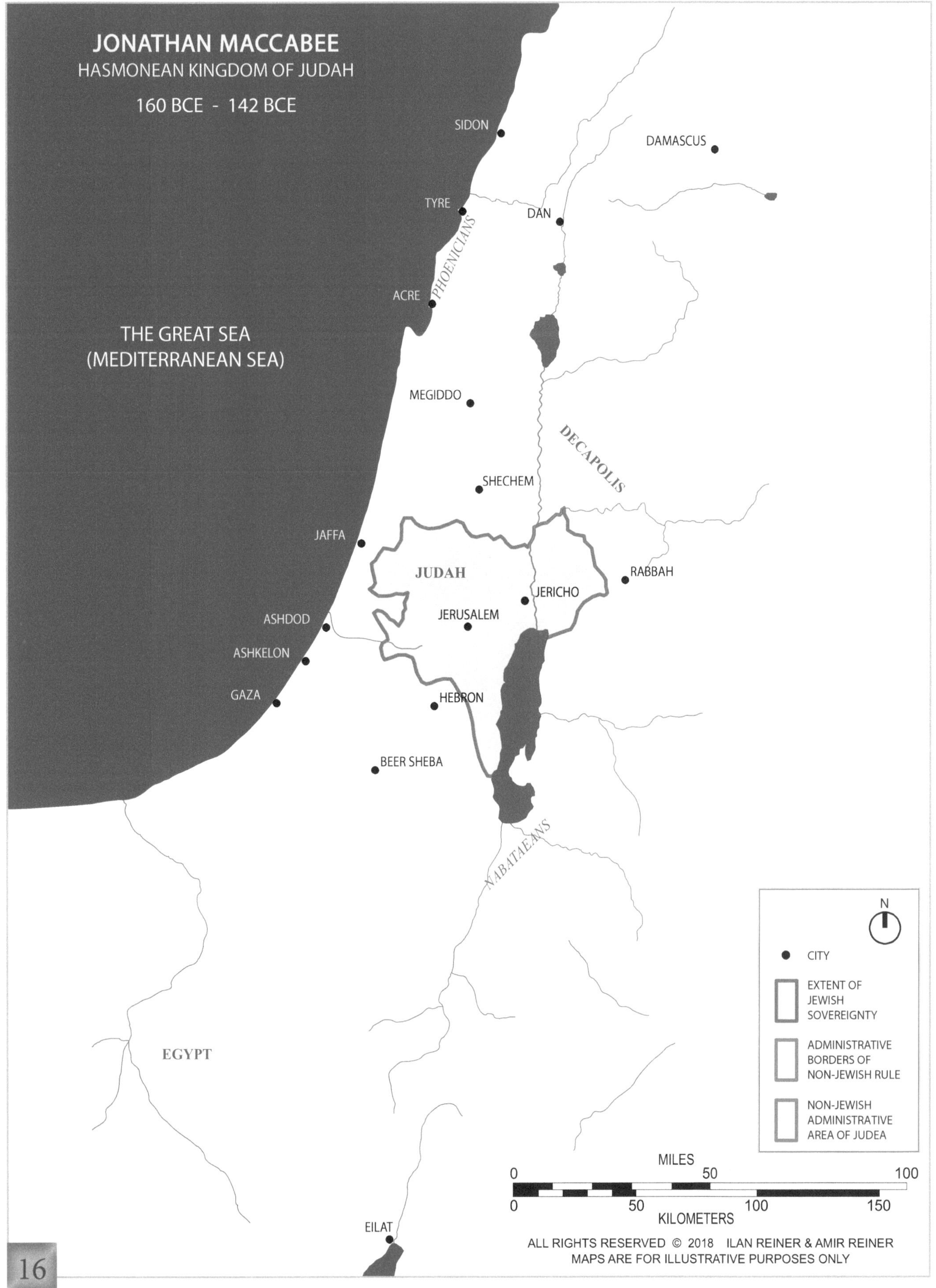
JONATHAN MACCABEE
HASMONEAN KINGDOM OF JUDAH
160 BCE - 142 BCE
THE GREAT SEA
(MEDITERRANEAN SEA)
SIDON
DAMASCUS
TYRE
DAN
PHOENICIANS
ACRE
MEGIDDO
DECAPOLIS
SHECHEM
JAFFA
JUDAH
RABBAH
JERICHO
JERUSALEM
ASHDOD
ASHKELON
GAZA
HEBRON
BEER SHEBA
NABATAEANS
EGYPT
EILAT
N
CITY
EXTENT OF
JEWISH
SOVEREIGNTY
ADMINISTRATIVE
BORDERS OF
NON-JEWISH RULE
NON-JEWISH
ADMINISTRATIVE
AREA OF JUDEA
MILES
0
50
100
0
50
100
150
KILOMETERS
ALL RIGHTS RESERVED © 2018 ILAN REINER & AMIR REINER
MAPS ARE FOR ILLUSTRATIVE PURPOSES ONLY
16

Simon the Maccabee
Hasmonean Kingdom of Judah
about 142 BCE to 135 BCE

Following the deaths of his brothers, Simon (Shimon) was appointed as ruler by the general National Assembly. Taking political advantage of the rivalries to the Seleucid throne, Simon ensured that the land of Judah was formally recognized as an independent sovereignty, a kingdom, for the first time since the destruction of the First Temple. As such, he expanded and secured the borders, as well as conquering Jerusalem completely. He fortified the city and restored its position as the Jewish nation's capital. He secured the city of Jaffa by expelling its Gentile inhabitants and populating it with Jews, thus providing Judah with a direct access to the sea and to her new ally, the Roman Republic. When his right to seize those recent cities was questioned, he replied: "We have neither taken other men's land, nor holden that which appertaineth to others, but the inheritance of our fathers, which our enemies had wrongfully in possession a certain time". Simon also secured the succession of leadership to his descendants, having the National Assembly recognize him as a king, by essence although not by title.

Simon Maccabee Made High Priest
By: Julius Schnorr von Carolsfeld

TIME LINE

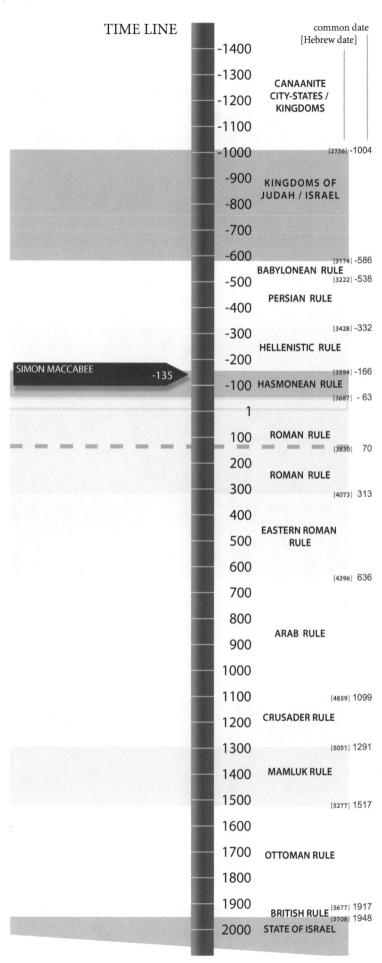

common date
[Hebrew date]

-1400
-1300
-1200
-1100
CANAANITE CITY-STATES / KINGDOMS
-1000 [2756] -1004
-900
-800
-700
KINGDOMS OF JUDAH / ISRAEL
-600 [3174] -586
BABYLONEAN RULE
-500 [3222] -538
PERSIAN RULE
-400
-300 [3428] -332
HELLENISTIC RULE
-200 [3594] -166
SIMON MACCABEE -135
-100 HASMONEAN RULE
[3687] - 63
1
100 ROMAN RULE
[3830] 70
200 ROMAN RULE
300 [4073] 313
400
500 EASTERN ROMAN RULE
600 [4396] 636
700
800
900 ARAB RULE
1000
1100 [4859] 1099
1200 CRUSADER RULE
1300 [5051] 1291
1400 MAMLUK RULE
1500 [5277] 1517
1600
1700 OTTOMAN RULE
1800
1900 BRITISH RULE [5677] 1917
[5708] 1948
2000 STATE OF ISRAEL

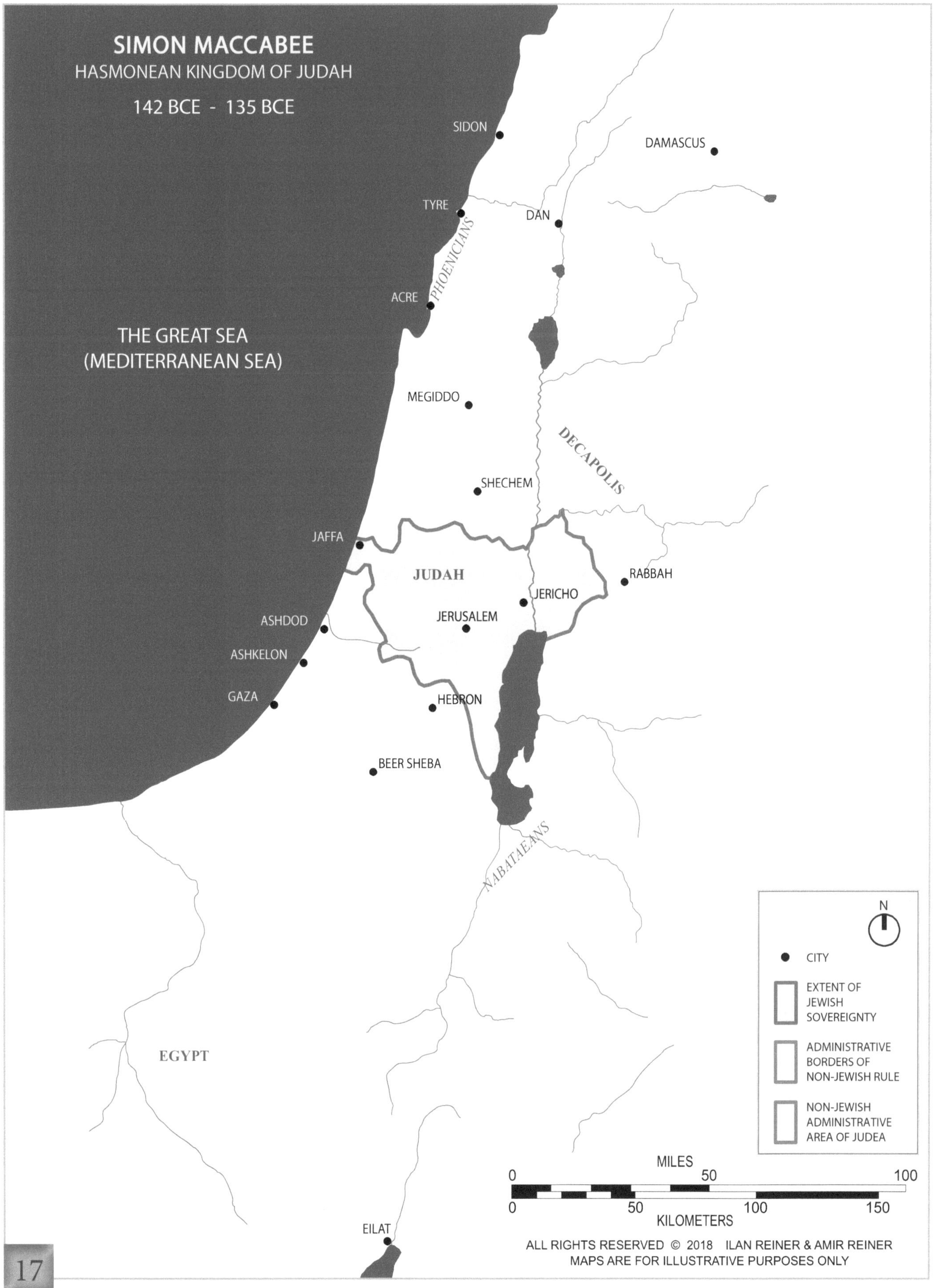
SIMON MACCABEE
HASMONEAN KINGDOM OF JUDAH
142 BCE - 135 BCE
SIDON
DAMASCUS
TYRE
DAN
PHOENICIANS
ACRE
THE GREAT SEA
(MEDITERRANEAN SEA)
MEGIDDO
DECAPOLIS
SHECHEM
JAFFA
JUDAH
RABBAH
JERICHO
JERUSALEM
ASHDOD
ASHKELON
GAZA
HEBRON
BEER SHEBA
NABATAEANS
N
CITY
EXTENT OF JEWISH SOVEREIGNTY
ADMINISTRATIVE BORDERS OF NON-JEWISH RULE
NON-JEWISH ADMINISTRATIVE AREA OF JUDEA
EGYPT
MILES
0
50
100
0
50
100
150
KILOMETERS
EILAT
ALL RIGHTS RESERVED © 2018 ILAN REINER & AMIR REINER
MAPS ARE FOR ILLUSTRATIVE PURPOSES ONLY
17

John Hyrcanus
Hasmonean Kingdom of Judah
about 135 BCE to 104 BCE

The days of John (Yochanan) Hyrcanus were those of conquest and border expansion as well as significant intellectual and spiritual development. He was considered an "ethnarch" (Greek term meaning: "political leader"), approved by the People's Assembly, as well as being the High Priest, as much as he was a king to the people. As such, he conquered several neighboring nations and in the case of the Idumeans in Edom, he converted them to Judaism by force. This was an unprecedented move for a Judean ruler. But, by that he gained more allies and increased the overall Jewish population. All this success primarily resulted from the continuing decline of the Seleucid Empire. The growth in wealth and prosperity also set forth the beginning of socioeconomic differences within the Jewish nation, that would be the catalyst for diverging into different religious sects.

TIME LINE

common date
[Hebrew date]

-1400
-1300
-1200
-1100
-1000
-900
-800
-700
-600
-500
-400
-300
-200
-100
1
100
200
300
400
500
600
700
800
900
1000
1100
1200
1300
1400
1500
1600
1700
1800
1900
2000

CANAANITE CITY-STATES / KINGDOMS
[2756] -1004
KINGDOMS OF JUDAH / ISRAEL
[3174] -586
BABYLONEAN RULE
[3222] -538
PERSIAN RULE
[3428] -332
HELLENISTIC RULE
[3594] -166
HASMONEAN RULE
[3687] - 63
ROMAN RULE
[3830] 70
ROMAN RULE
[4073] 313
EASTERN ROMAN RULE
[4396] 636
ARAB RULE
[4859] 1099
CRUSADER RULE
[5051] 1291
MAMLUK RULE
[5277] 1517
OTTOMAN RULE
[5677] 1917
BRITISH RULE
[5708] 1948
STATE OF ISRAEL

JOHN HYRCANUS -104

Coin with Hebrew inscription: "Yehohanan the High Priest and the Council of the Jews"
Classical Numismatic Group, Inc. http://www.cngcoins.com

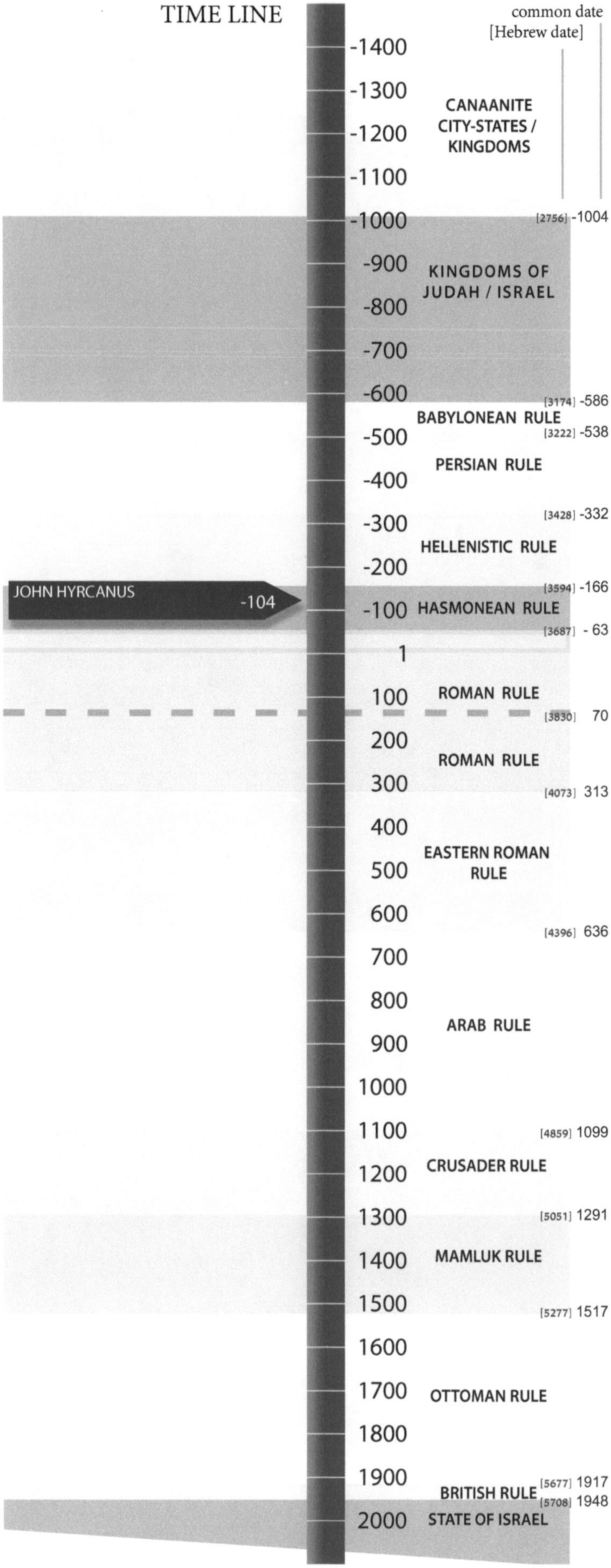

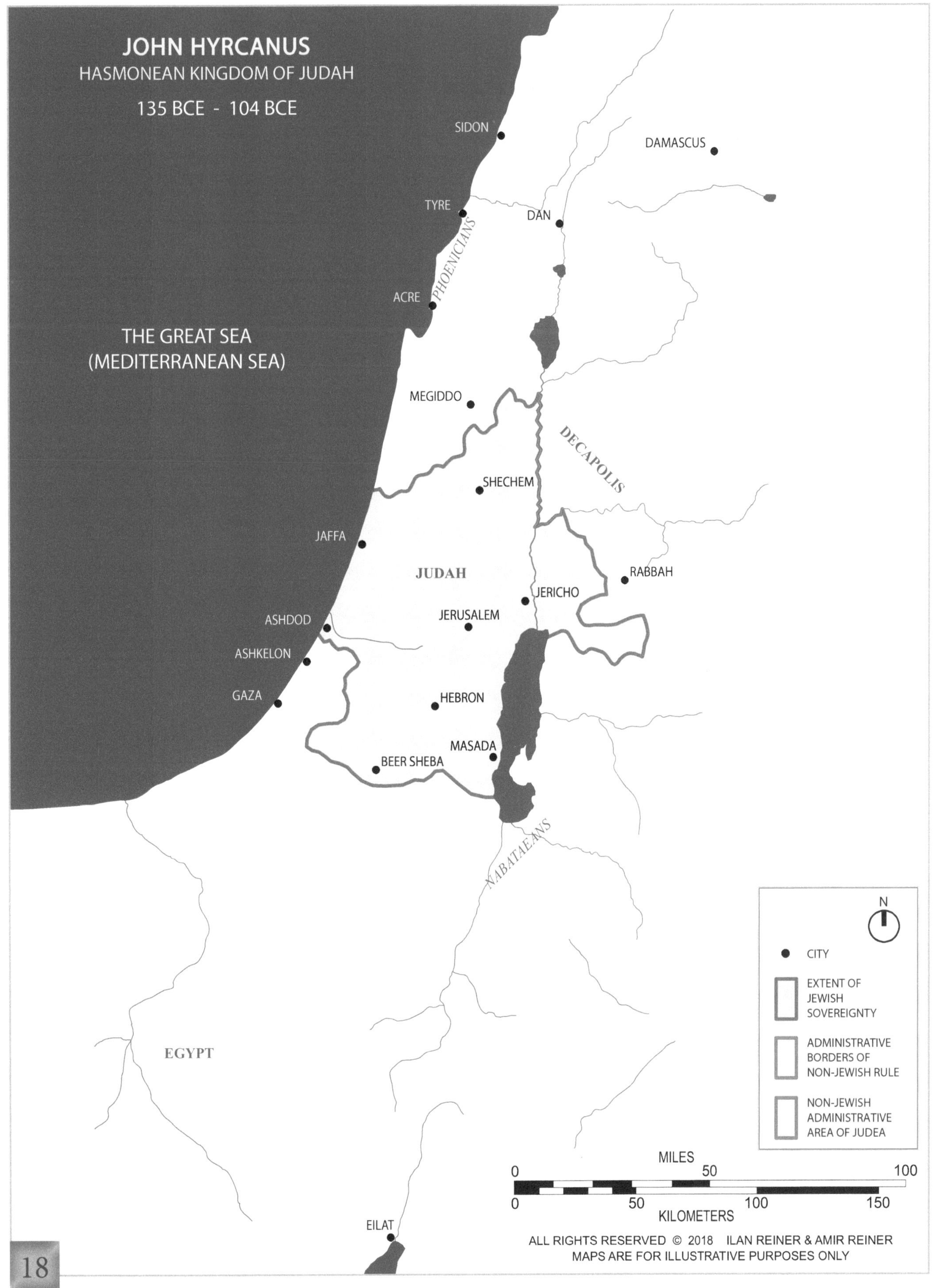
JOHN HYRCANUS
HASMONEAN KINGDOM OF JUDAH
135 BCE - 104 BCE
SIDON
DAMASCUS
TYRE
DAN
PHOENICIANS
ACRE
THE GREAT SEA
(MEDITERRANEAN SEA)
MEGIDDO
DECAPOLIS
SHECHEM
JAFFA
JUDAH
RABBAH
JERICHO
JERUSALEM
ASHDOD
ASHKELON
GAZA
HEBRON
MASADA
BEER SHEBA
NABATAEANS
N
CITY
EXTENT OF JEWISH SOVEREIGNTY
ADMINISTRATIVE BORDERS OF NON-JEWISH RULE
NON-JEWISH ADMINISTRATIVE AREA OF JUDEA
EGYPT
MILES
0
50
100
0
50
100
150
KILOMETERS
EILAT
ALL RIGHTS RESERVED © 2018 ILAN REINER & AMIR REINER
MAPS ARE FOR ILLUSTRATIVE PURPOSES ONLY
18

Judah Aristobulus I
Hasmonean Kingdom of Judah
about 104 BCE to 103 BCE

John Hyrcanus instructed in his will that all government roles would be in the hands of his wife, and his son, Judah Aristobulus, that should be the High Priest. But Judah was not content with that and claimed all roles of governance. He was the first in the Hasmonean dynasty to call himself a "king". He ruled in a Hellenic style and his court was much like that of a Greek court. He murdered his brother who returned victorious from conquering the Galilee and imprisoned his mother until she starved. His army of mercenaries expanded Jewish rule to vast territories of greater Galilee in the north. He passed away from illness after a year on the throne, and his younger brother, Alexander Jannaeus, was his successor.

Possible Model of the Hasmonean Palace in Jerusalem
On display in Israel Museum

TIME LINE

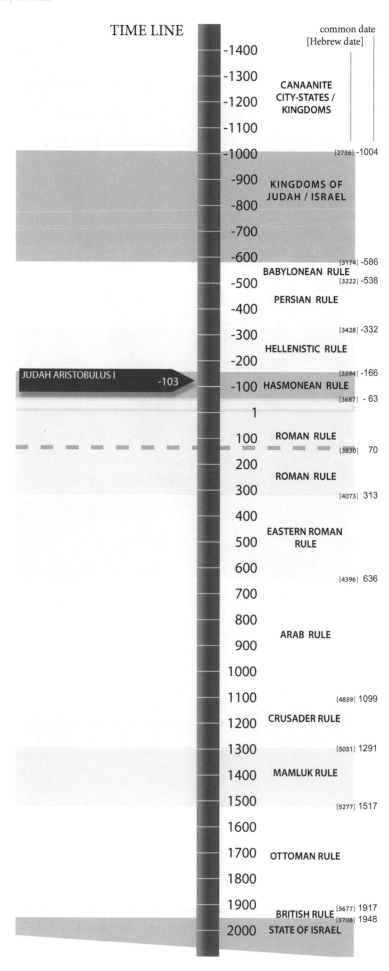

common date
[Hebrew date]

-1400
-1300
-1200
-1100
CANAANITE CITY-STATES / KINGDOMS
-1000 [2756] -1004
-900
-800
-700
KINGDOMS OF JUDAH / ISRAEL
-600 [3174] -586
BABYLONEAN RULE
-500 [3222] -538
PERSIAN RULE
-400
-300 [3428] -332
HELLENISTIC RULE
-200
JUDAH ARISTOBULUS I -103
[3594] -166
-100 HASMONEAN RULE
[3687] - 63
1
100 ROMAN RULE
[3830] 70
200
ROMAN RULE
300 [4073] 313
400
500
EASTERN ROMAN RULE
600
[4396] 636
700
800
ARAB RULE
900
1000
1100 [4859] 1099
1200 CRUSADER RULE
1300 [5051] 1291
1400 MAMLUK RULE
1500 [5277] 1517
1600
1700 OTTOMAN RULE
1800
1900 [5677] 1917
BRITISH RULE [5708] 1948
2000 STATE OF ISRAEL

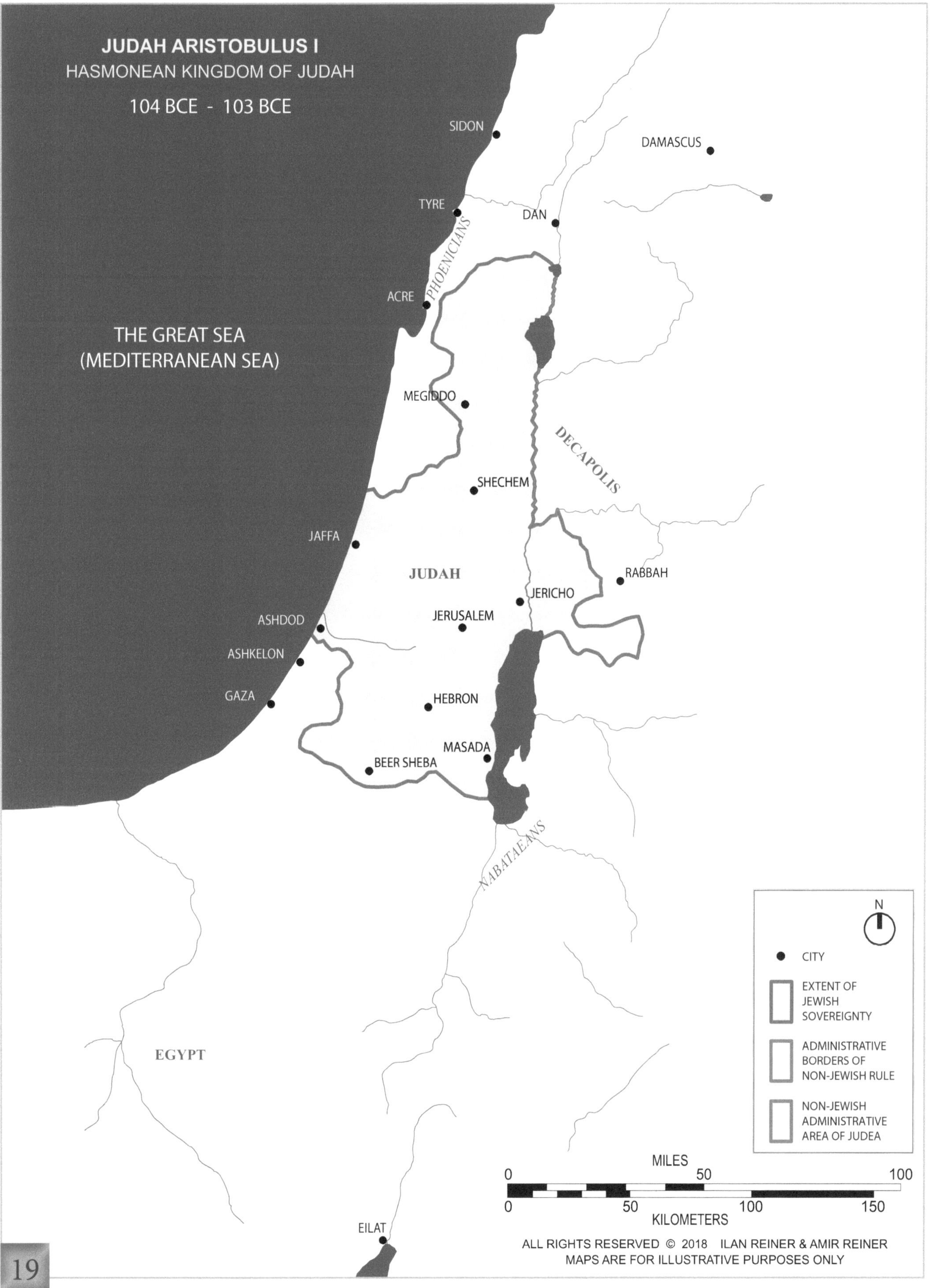
JUDAH ARISTOBULUS I
HASMONEAN KINGDOM OF JUDAH
104 BCE - 103 BCE
SIDON
DAMASCUS
TYRE
DAN
PHOENICIANS
ACRE
THE GREAT SEA
(MEDITERRANEAN SEA)
MEGIDDO
DECAPOLIS
SHECHEM
JAFFA
JUDAH
RABBAH
JERICHO
JERUSALEM
ASHDOD
ASHKELON
GAZA
HEBRON
MASADA
BEER SHEBA
NABATAEANS
N
CITY
EXTENT OF
JEWISH
SOVEREIGNTY
ADMINISTRATIVE
BORDERS OF
NON-JEWISH RULE
NON-JEWISH
ADMINISTRATIVE
AREA OF JUDEA
EGYPT
MILES
0
50
100
0
50
100
150
KILOMETERS
EILAT
ALL RIGHTS RESERVED © 2018 ILAN REINER & AMIR REINER
MAPS ARE FOR ILLUSTRATIVE PURPOSES ONLY
19

Alexander Jannaeus
Hasmonean Kingdom of Judah
about 103 BCE to 76 BCE

Alexander Jannaeus (Yannai) continued his brother's foreign policy and expanded the borders of the Jewish kingdom. He conquered Gaza, Nabatean territories and areas in the Golan. In his many battles, he often used mercenaries and assistance of foreign powers to pressure his enemies. His great success of establishing a strong and secured kingdom was overshadowed by his inability to get along with many of the Jewish leaders at home. He was in constant conflict with many Jewish sages of the Sanhedrin (People's Assembly and High Court), who didn't accept his absolute power. This conflict almost led to a full civil war. Before dying in battle, he advised his wife, Shlomtzion, who rose to the throne after him, to bridge the gap between the monarchy and the Sanhedrin. Her years as queen were marked with peace, as she strengthened the borders and united the people.

Coin with Aramaic inscription "of King Alexander"
Coin courtesy of David Manheim

Illustration of the Sanhedrin
People's Cyclopedia of Universal Knowledge (1883)

TIME LINE

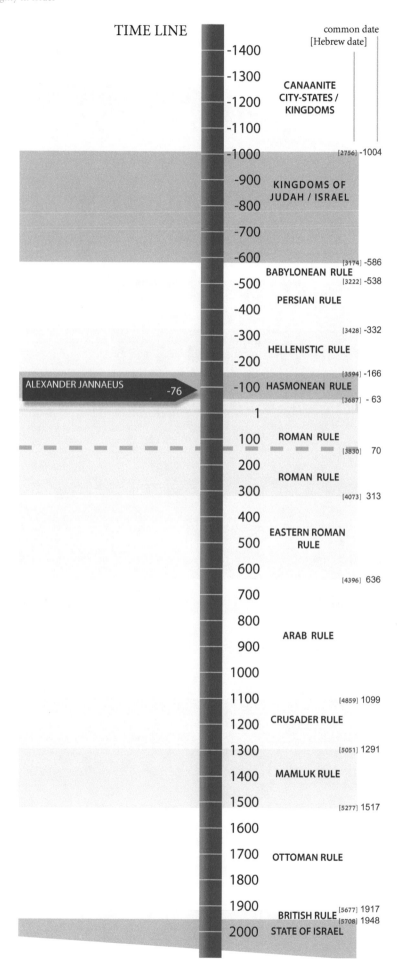

common date
[Hebrew date]

-1400
-1300
-1200
-1100
CANAANITE CITY-STATES / KINGDOMS
-1000 [2756] -1004
-900
KINGDOMS OF JUDAH / ISRAEL
-800
-700
-600 [3174] -586
BABYLONEAN RULE
-500 [3222] -538
PERSIAN RULE
-400
-300 [3428] -332
HELLENISTIC RULE
-200
[3594] -166
ALEXANDER JANNAEUS -76
-100 HASMONEAN RULE
[3687] - 63
1
100 ROMAN RULE
[3830] 70
200
ROMAN RULE
300 [4073] 313
400
EASTERN ROMAN RULE
500
600 [4396] 636
700
800
ARAB RULE
900
1000
1100 [4859] 1099
CRUSADER RULE
1200
1300 [5051] 1291
MAMLUK RULE
1400
1500 [5277] 1517
1600
1700 OTTOMAN RULE
1800
1900 [5677] 1917
BRITISH RULE
[5708] 1948
2000 STATE OF ISRAEL

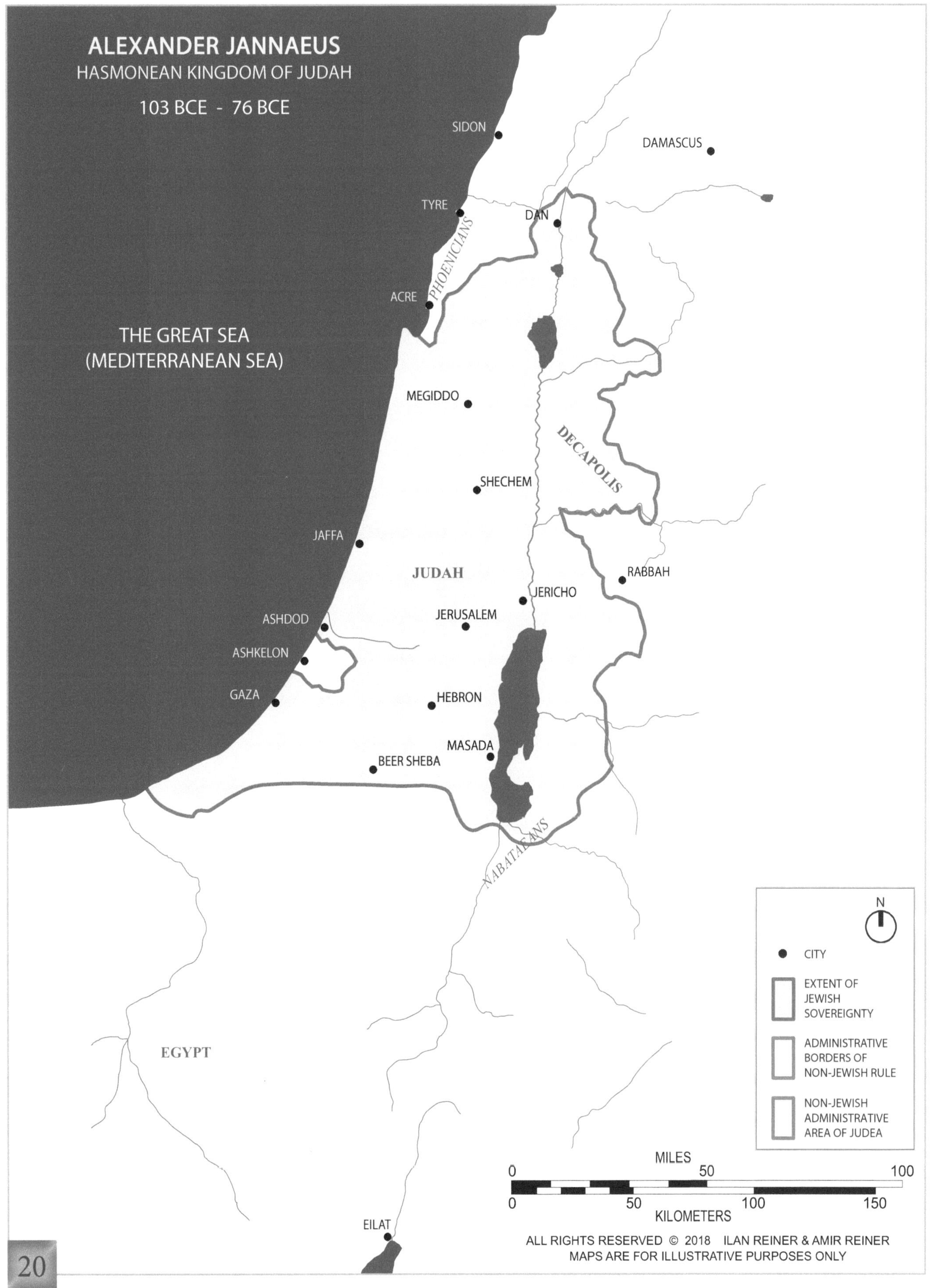

ALEXANDER JANNAEUS
HASMONEAN KINGDOM OF JUDAH
103 BCE - 76 BCE
SIDON
DAMASCUS
TYRE
DAN
PHOENICIANS
ACRE
THE GREAT SEA
(MEDITERRANEAN SEA)
MEGIDDO
DECAPOLIS
SHECHEM
JAFFA
JUDAH
RABBAH
JERICHO
JERUSALEM
ASHDOD
ASHKELON
GAZA
HEBRON
MASADA
BEER SHEBA
NABATAEANS
EGYPT
EILAT
N
CITY
EXTENT OF JEWISH SOVEREIGNTY
ADMINISTRATIVE BORDERS OF NON-JEWISH RULE
NON-JEWISH ADMINISTRATIVE AREA OF JUDEA
MILES
0
50
100
0
50
100
150
KILOMETERS
ALL RIGHTS RESERVED © 2018 ILAN REINER & AMIR REINER
MAPS ARE FOR ILLUSTRATIVE PURPOSES ONLY
20

Roman Rule
Province of Judea
about 63 BCE to 40 BCE

Jews had strong ties with the Roman Empire since the beginning of the Maccabean revolt. The Romans sided with the Jews against the Seleucid Empire until eventually conquering that empire with her expansion east. The heirs to the Jewish Hasmonean kingdom, Hyrcanus II and Aristobulus II, were in conflict regarding who would be king. They turned to Pompey, the Roman general stationed in Syria, who eventually marched into Jerusalem and ended the Hasmonean kingdom by establishing Roman rule. This ended the second era of Jewish independence and full Jewish sovereignty over the land of Israel. Many Jews objected to the conquering force, but many embraced them hoping the land would enjoy peace after troubled times. The Romans brought with them their culture and law, while enhancing public works and infrastructure by constructing roadways and buildings.

Roman Soldiers
Marble, Roman artwork on display at the Louvre

TIME LINE

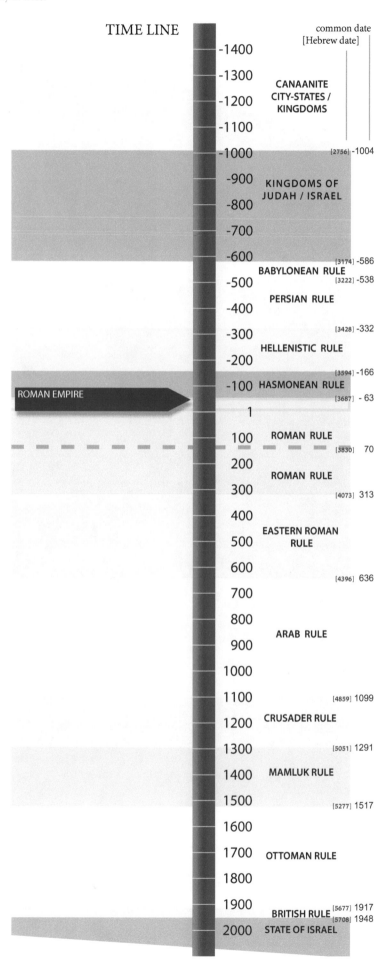

common date
[Hebrew date]

-1400
-1300
-1200
-1100
CANAANITE CITY-STATES / KINGDOMS
-1000
[2756] -1004
-900
-800
KINGDOMS OF JUDAH / ISRAEL
-700
-600
[3174] -586
BABYLONEAN RULE
[3222] -538
-500
PERSIAN RULE
-400
-300
[3428] -332
HELLENISTIC RULE
-200
[3594] -166
-100
HASMONEAN RULE
ROMAN EMPIRE
[3687] - 63
1
100
ROMAN RULE
[3830] 70
200
ROMAN RULE
300
[4073] 313
400
EASTERN ROMAN RULE
500
600
[4396] 636
700
800
ARAB RULE
900
1000
1100
[4859] 1099
CRUSADER RULE
1200
1300
[5051] 1291
MAMLUK RULE
1400
1500
[5277] 1517
1600
1700
OTTOMAN RULE
1800
1900
[5677] 1917
BRITISH RULE
[5708] 1948
2000
STATE OF ISRAEL

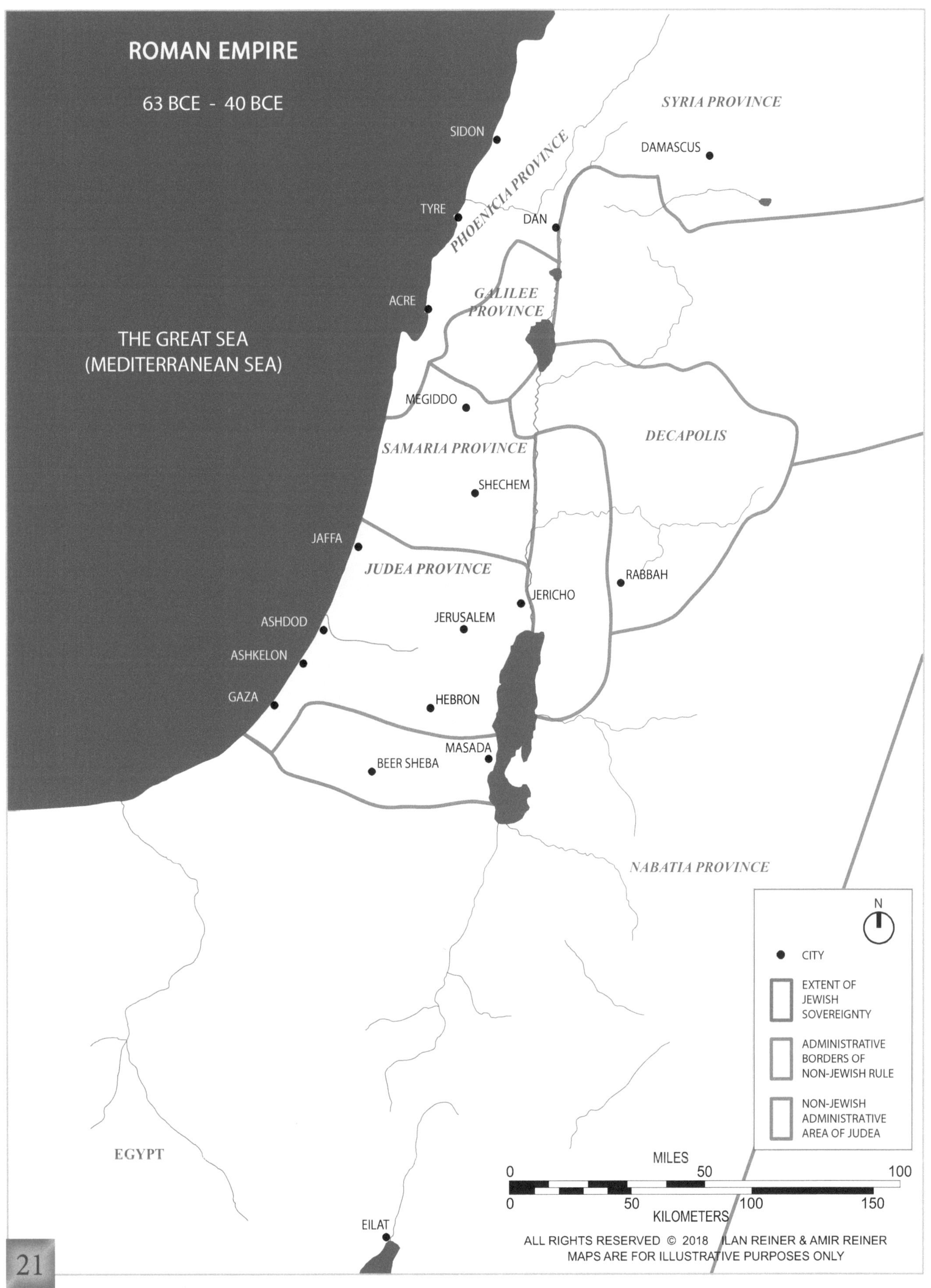
ROMAN EMPIRE
63 BCE - 40 BCE
SYRIA PROVINCE
SIDON
DAMASCUS
PHOENICIA PROVINCE
TYRE
DAN
GALILEE PROVINCE
ACRE
THE GREAT SEA (MEDITERRANEAN SEA)
MEGIDDO
SAMARIA PROVINCE
DECAPOLIS
SHECHEM
JAFFA
JUDEA PROVINCE
RABBAH
JERICHO
ASHDOD
JERUSALEM
ASHKELON
GAZA
HEBRON
MASADA
BEER SHEBA
NABATIA PROVINCE
N
CITY
EXTENT OF JEWISH SOVEREIGNTY
ADMINISTRATIVE BORDERS OF NON-JEWISH RULE
NON-JEWISH ADMINISTRATIVE AREA OF JUDEA
EGYPT
MILES
0 50 100
0 50 100 150
KILOMETERS
EILAT
ALL RIGHTS RESERVED © 2018 ILAN REINER & AMIR REINER
MAPS ARE FOR ILLUSTRATIVE PURPOSES ONLY
21

King Herod
Herodian Kingdom of Judea - Initial Rule
about 43 BCE to 40 BCE

The rise of Herod began with his father, Antipatros, befriending the Romans who in turn appointed him the Procurator of Judea. He then appointed the 25 year old Herod to be governor of the Galilee. This was a time of civil unrest and internal conflict between various factions of the Jewish people. It was during these times when the Roman Empire was changing from a republic to a monarchy, as Julius Caesar seized power and that empire went through civil wars. Four years later, barely escaping Jerusalem alive, Herod convinced the Romans to make him King of Judea (as a Roman client king). Assisted by several legions, he captured Jerusalem and ended the Hasmonean dynasty. Since he owed his allegiance to Rome, he feared for his throne and strengthened the non-Jewish population in Israel.

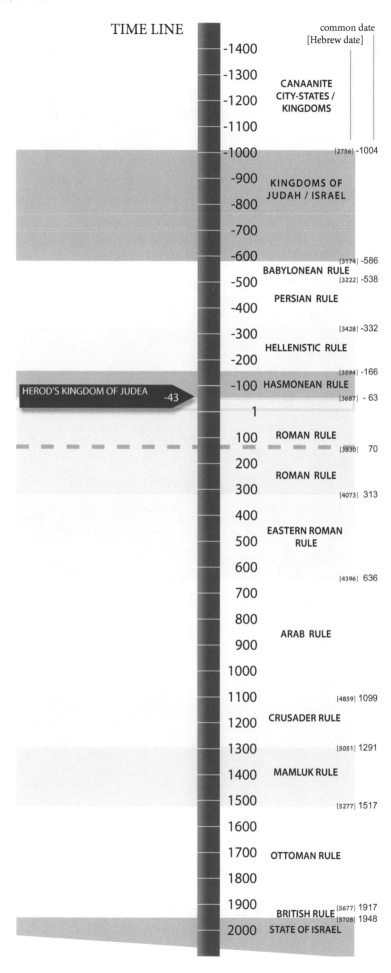

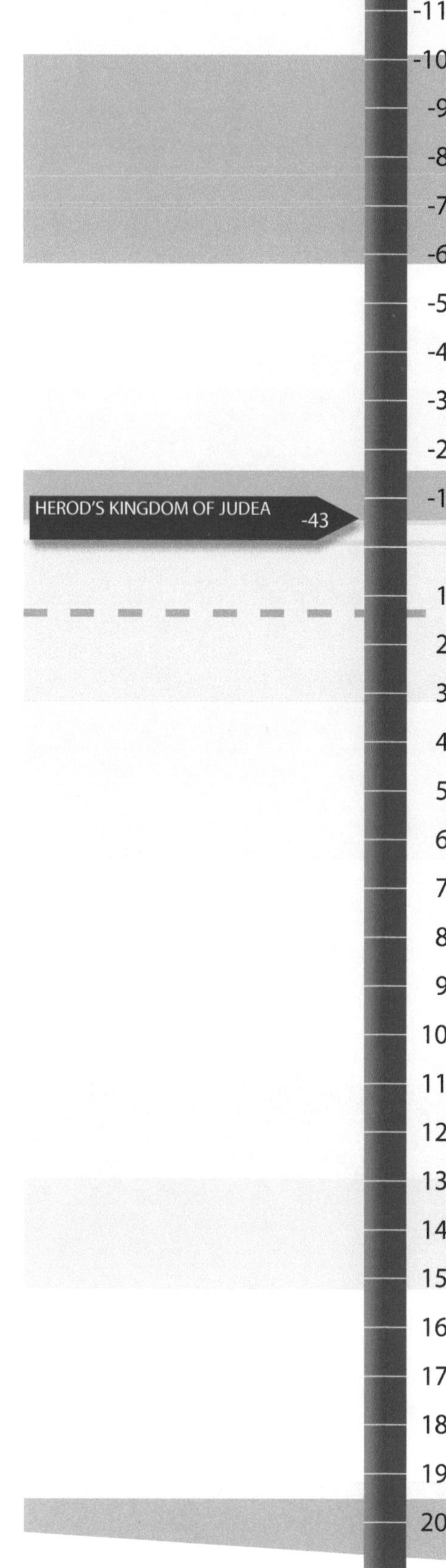

Copper coin of Herod the Great
"Basileus Herodon" and Macedonian sun-symbol

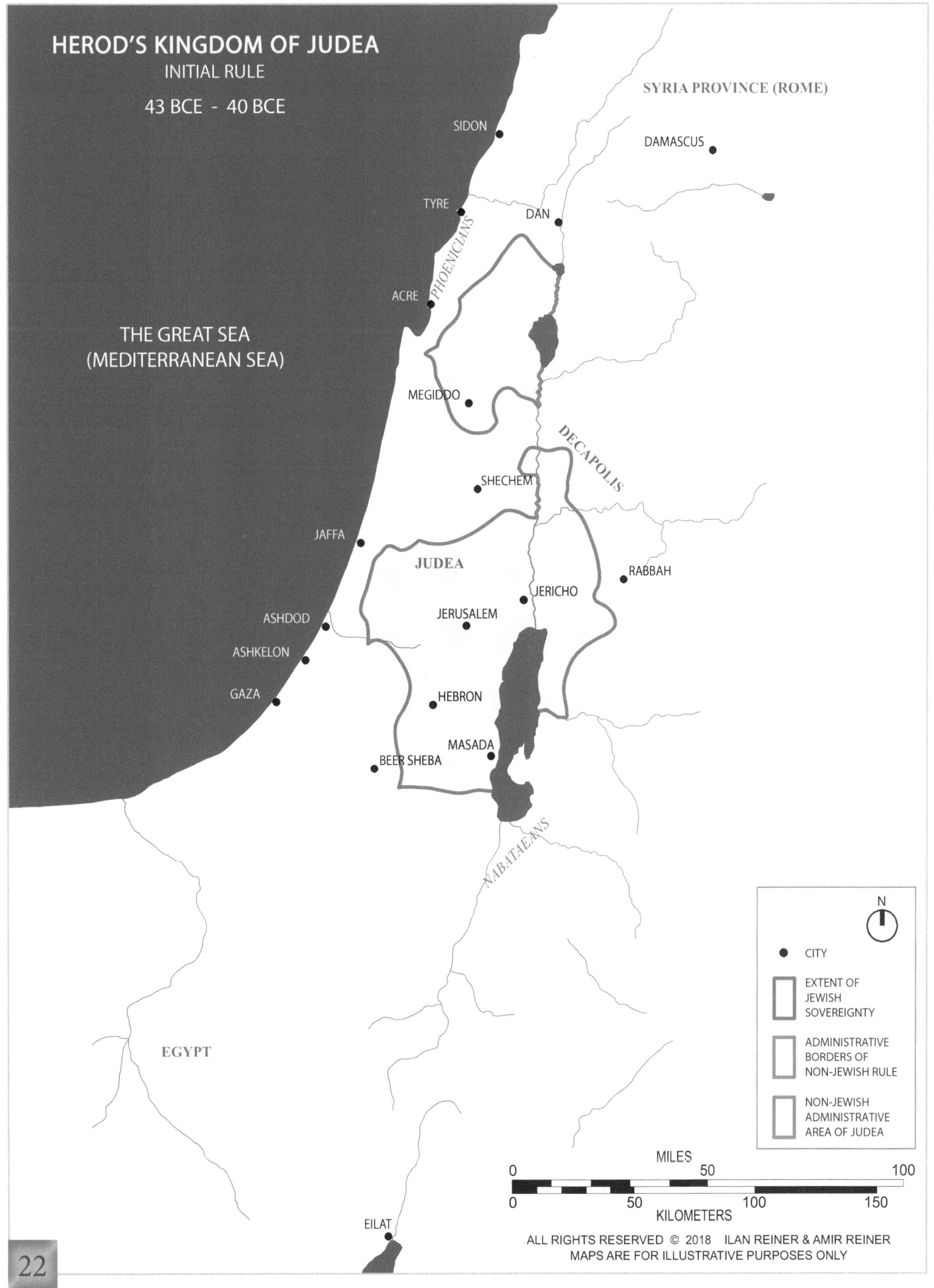
HEROD'S KINGDOM OF JUDEA
INITIAL RULE
43 BCE - 40 BCE
SYRIA PROVINCE (ROME)
SIDON
DAMASCUS
TYRE
DAN
PHOENICIANS
ACRE
THE GREAT SEA
(MEDITERRANEAN SEA)
MEGIDDO
DECAPOLIS
SHECHEM
JAFFA
JUDEA
RABBAH
JERICHO
JERUSALEM
ASHDOD
ASHKELON
GAZA
HEBRON
MASADA
BEER SHEBA
NABATAEANS
N
CITY
EXTENT OF JEWISH SOVEREIGNTY
ADMINISTRATIVE BORDERS OF NON-JEWISH RULE
NON-JEWISH ADMINISTRATIVE AREA OF JUDEA
EGYPT
MILES
0
50
100
0
50
100
150
KILOMETERS
EILAT
22

King Herod

Herodian Kingdom of Judea - Kingdom Expansion

about 40 BCE to 30 BCE

Many Jews disapproved of Herod, because he was a king appointed by Rome, had ended the Hasmonean dynasty and was considered as coming from a family who was not originally Jewish (but converted to Judaism). Hence, in an effort to win the respect and admiration of the Jews, both at home and abroad, he protected Jews across the world, even those outside the Roman Empire. In one case, he provided free grain during drought years. Being as paranoid as he was, he spent a lot on fortification, building forts and sanctuaries to which he could escape in case of a rebellion. Such are Herodion and Masada, which was strengthened based on the existing Hasmonean fortress. These forts included lavish palaces and barracks for his troops. Herod also built many buildings and structures outside of Judea, such as in Antioch and Damascus, to glorify his name among other nations.

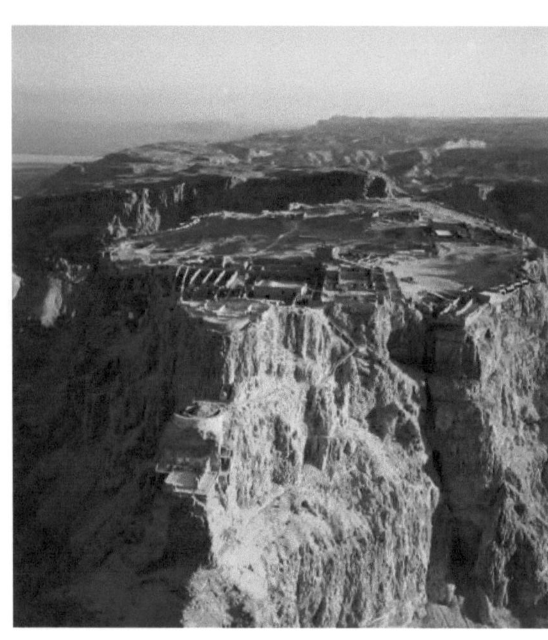

Aerial view of Masada
Photo credit: Andrew Shiva

TIME LINE

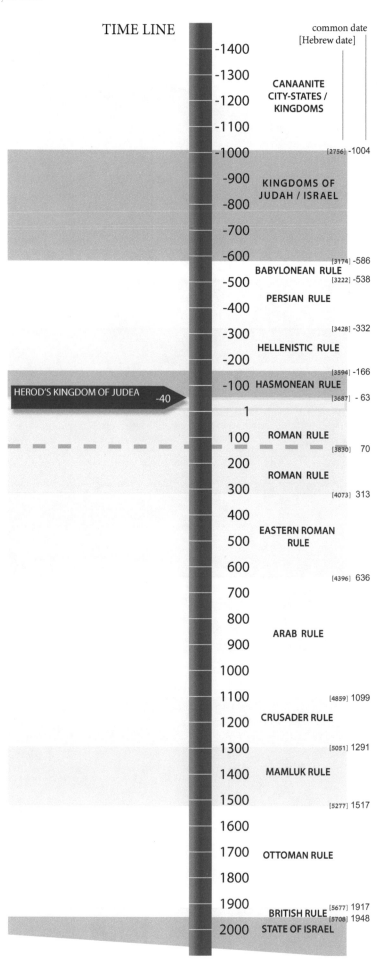

common date
[Hebrew date]

-1400
-1300
-1200
-1100
CANAANITE CITY-STATES / KINGDOMS
[2756] -1004
-1000
-900
-800
-700
KINGDOMS OF JUDAH / ISRAEL
-600
[3174] -586
BABYLONEAN RULE
[3222] -538
-500
PERSIAN RULE
-400
[3428] -332
-300
HELLENISTIC RULE
-200
[3594] -166
-100
HASMONEAN RULE
[3687] - 63
HEROD'S KINGDOM OF JUDEA -40
1
100
ROMAN RULE
[3830] 70
200
ROMAN RULE
300
[4073] 313
400
EASTERN ROMAN RULE
500
600
[4396] 636
700
800
ARAB RULE
900
1000
1100
[4859] 1099
CRUSADER RULE
1200
1300
[5051] 1291
1400
MAMLUK RULE
1500
[5277] 1517
1600
1700
OTTOMAN RULE
1800
1900
[5677] 1917
BRITISH RULE
[5708] 1948
2000
STATE OF ISRAEL

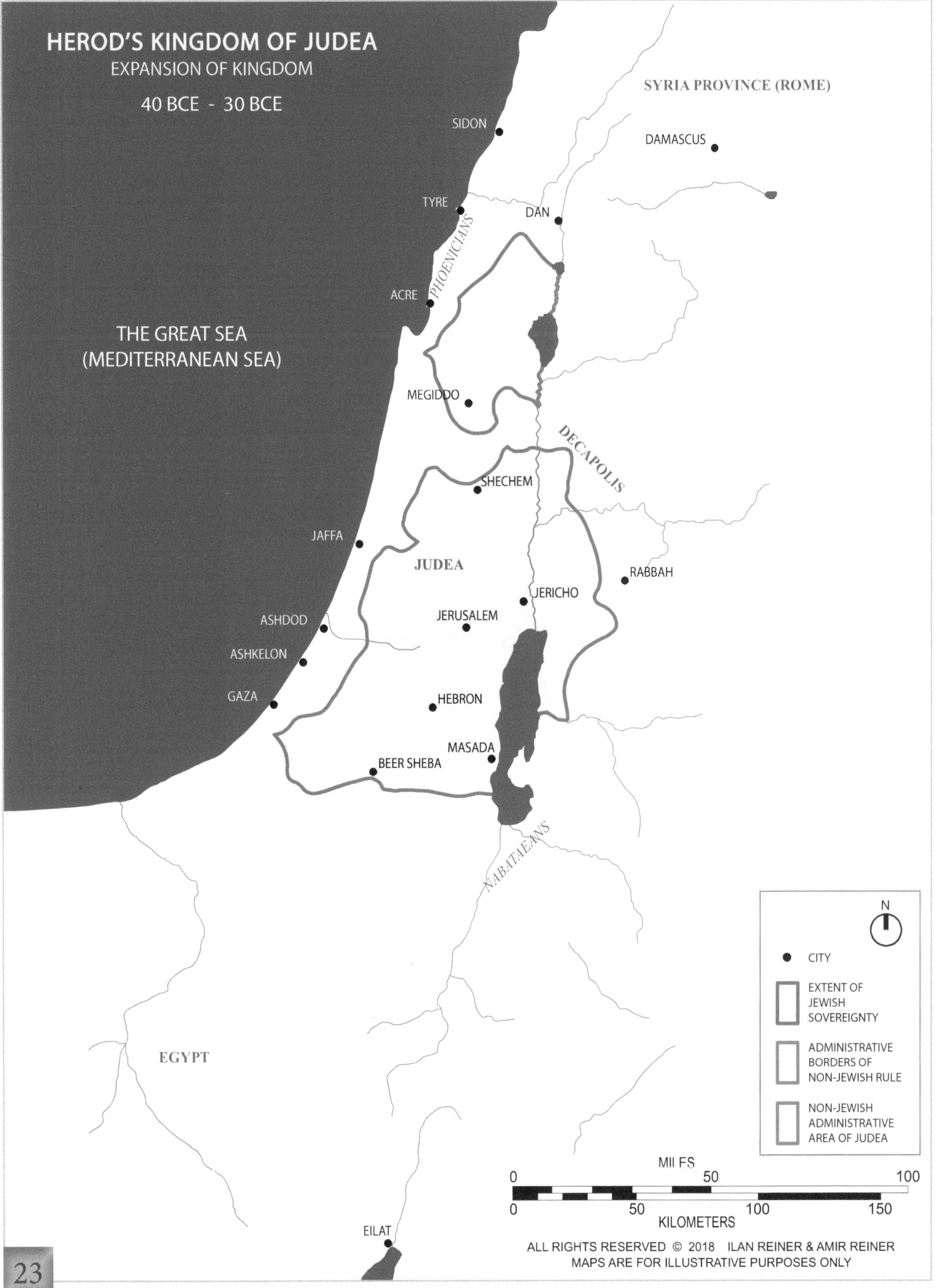
HEROD'S KINGDOM OF JUDEA
EXPANSION OF KINGDOM
40 BCE - 30 BCE
SYRIA PROVINCE (ROME)
SIDON
DAMASCUS
TYRE
DAN
PHOENICIANS
ACRE
THE GREAT SEA
(MEDITERRANEAN SEA)
MEGIDDO
DECAPOLIS
SHECHEM
JAFFA
JUDEA
RABBAH
JERICHO
JERUSALEM
ASHDOD
ASHKELON
GAZA
HEBRON
MASADA
BEER SHEBA
NABATAEANS
EGYPT
EILAT
N
CITY
EXTENT OF JEWISH SOVEREIGNTY
ADMINISTRATIVE BORDERS OF NON-JEWISH RULE
NON-JEWISH ADMINISTRATIVE AREA OF JUDEA
MILES
0
50
100
0
50
100
150
KILOMETERS
ALL RIGHTS RESERVED © 2018 ILAN REINER & AMIR REINER
MAPS ARE FOR ILLUSTRATIVE PURPOSES ONLY

23

King Herod

Herodian Kingdom of Judea - Kingdom Expansion

about 30 BCE to 23 BCE

As Herod gained more power and influence, the borders of his kingdom expanded. The kingdom was no longer split and there was a geographic continuity from the Judean desert in the south up to the Galilee and Lebanon in the north. From the Arabian desert in the east to the Mediterranean Sea in the west. Due to the significance of having direct access to Rome via the sea, Herod built a new city with a modern seaport - Caesarea. This huge city, named in honor of the Roman emperor, had a big port, Roman temples, palaces, theater, hippodrome and other magnificent buildings. This would become the seat of any non-Jewish government, since it was a Roman city.

Ruins of Caesarea
Theater with Harbor in Background

TIME LINE

HEROD'S KINGDOM OF JUDEA -30

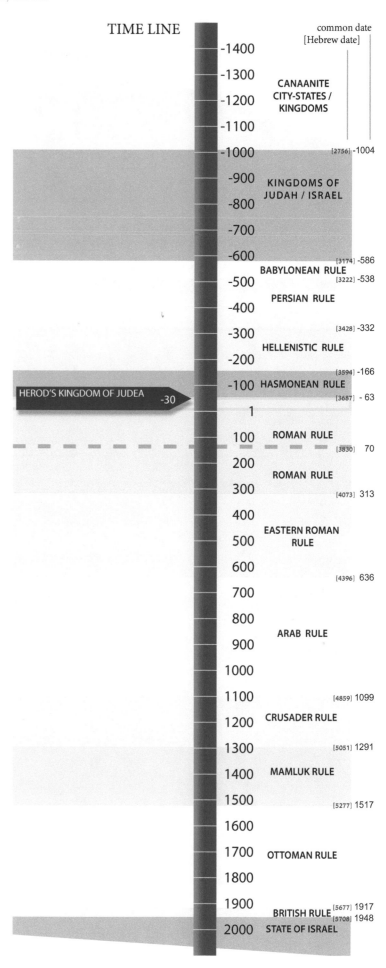

Period	common date [Hebrew date]
CANAANITE CITY-STATES / KINGDOMS	
KINGDOMS OF JUDAH / ISRAEL	[2756] -1004
BABYLONEAN RULE	[3174] -586
PERSIAN RULE	[3222] -538
HELLENISTIC RULE	[3428] -332
HASMONEAN RULE	[3594] -166
ROMAN RULE	[3687] - 63
ROMAN RULE	[3830] 70
EASTERN ROMAN RULE	[4073] 313
ARAB RULE	[4396] 636
CRUSADER RULE	[4859] 1099
MAMLUK RULE	[5051] 1291
OTTOMAN RULE	[5277] 1517
BRITISH RULE	[5677] 1917
STATE OF ISRAEL	[5708] 1948

-1400, -1300, -1200, -1100, -1000, -900, -800, -700, -600, -500, -400, -300, -200, -100, 1, 100, 200, 300, 400, 500, 600, 700, 800, 900, 1000, 1100, 1200, 1300, 1400, 1500, 1600, 1700, 1800, 1900, 2000

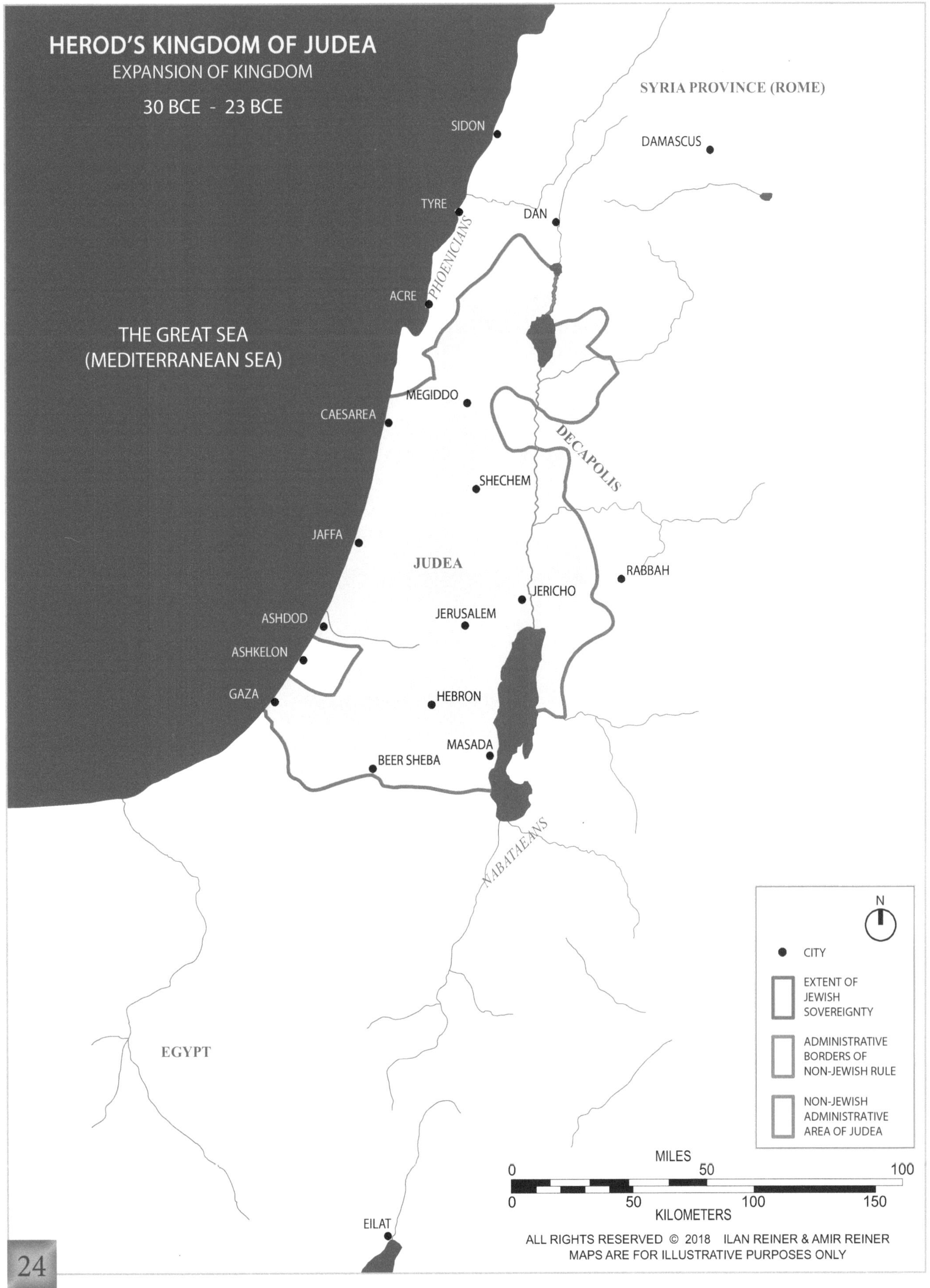
HEROD'S KINGDOM OF JUDEA
EXPANSION OF KINGDOM
30 BCE - 23 BCE
SYRIA PROVINCE (ROME)
SIDON
DAMASCUS
TYRE
DAN
PHOENICIANS
ACRE
THE GREAT SEA
(MEDITERRANEAN SEA)
MEGIDDO
CAESAREA
DECAPOLIS
SHECHEM
JAFFA
JUDEA
RABBAH
JERICHO
JERUSALEM
ASHDOD
ASHKELON
GAZA
HEBRON
MASADA
BEER SHEBA
NABATAEANS
EGYPT
EILAT
N
CITY
EXTENT OF JEWISH SOVEREIGNTY
ADMINISTRATIVE BORDERS OF NON-JEWISH RULE
NON-JEWISH ADMINISTRATIVE AREA OF JUDEA
MILES
0 50 100
0 50 100 150
KILOMETERS
ALL RIGHTS RESERVED © 2018 ILAN REINER & AMIR REINER
MAPS ARE FOR ILLUSTRATIVE PURPOSES ONLY
24

King Herod

Herodian Kingdom of Judea - Kingdom Expansion

about 23 BCE to 20 BCE

The era of Herod's rule was a prosperous time of peace, economic growth and spiritual awareness. Perhaps one of the most significant marks of his reign (from a Jewish standpoint) was the building of the Temple and the associated complex in Jerusalem, which was constructed over decades. It was actually a rebuilding of the existing Second Temple. But, the construction was done in such a way that it was almost considered as a new building. An expanded platform was constructed around the original Temple Mount with supporting buildings of both administrative and religious nature. The Temple halls themselves were elevated and beautified with golden gates, columns and golden decorations. In the Talmud it says that anyone who hasn't seen (Herod's) Temple, hasn't seen a beautiful building in his life. This most marvelous structure epitomizing the Jewish system of faith, sat in the heart of Jerusalem, surrounded by other buildings completed during the reign of Herod.

Model of the Second Temple and Jerusalem
On display in the Israel Museum in Jerusalem

TIME LINE

HEROD'S KINGDOM OF JUDEA -23

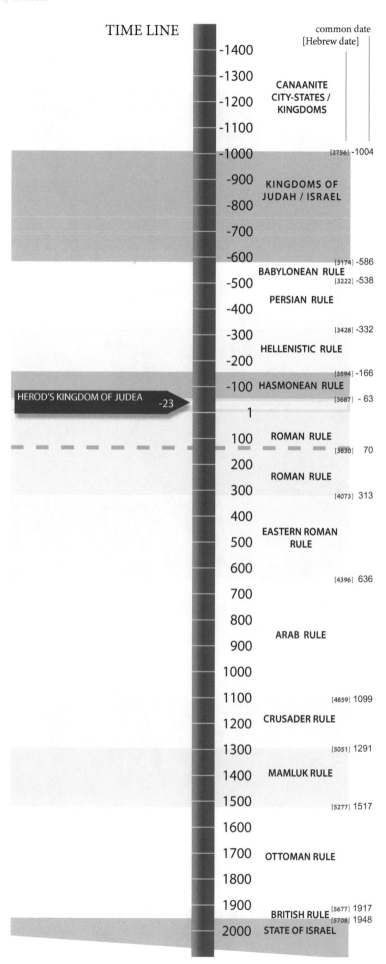

Period	common date [Hebrew date]
CANAANITE CITY-STATES / KINGDOMS	
KINGDOMS OF JUDAH / ISRAEL	[2756] -1004
BABYLONEAN RULE	[3174] -586
PERSIAN RULE	[3222] -538
HELLENISTIC RULE	[3428] -332
HASMONEAN RULE	[3594] -166
ROMAN RULE	[3687] - 63
ROMAN RULE	[3830] 70
EASTERN ROMAN RULE	[4073] 313
ARAB RULE	[4396] 636
CRUSADER RULE	[4859] 1099
MAMLUK RULE	[5051] 1291
OTTOMAN RULE	[5277] 1517
BRITISH RULE	[5677] 1917
STATE OF ISRAEL	[5708] 1948

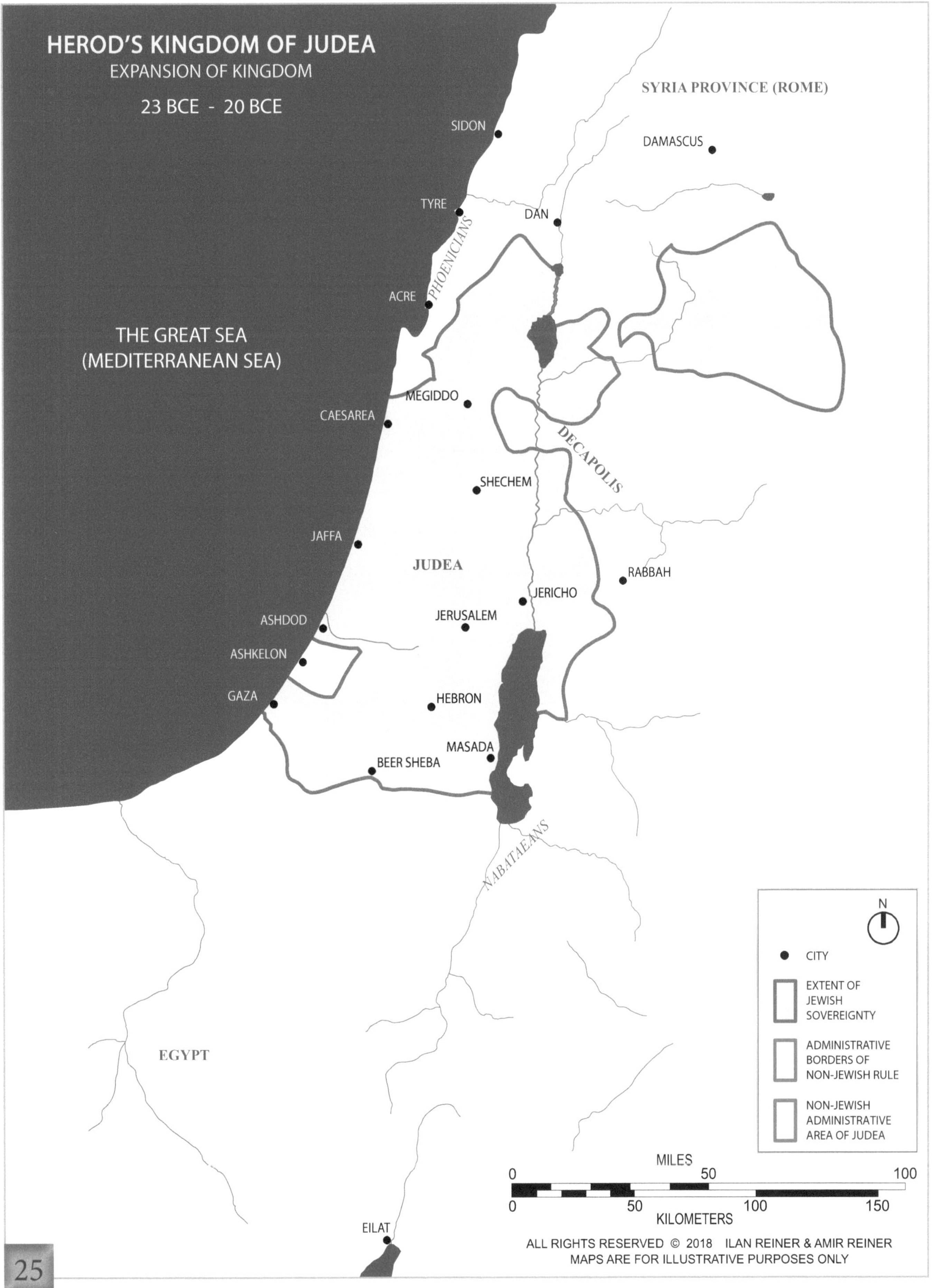
HEROD'S KINGDOM OF JUDEA
EXPANSION OF KINGDOM
23 BCE - 20 BCE
SYRIA PROVINCE (ROME)
SIDON
DAMASCUS
TYRE
DAN
PHOENICIANS
ACRE
THE GREAT SEA
(MEDITERRANEAN SEA)
MEGIDDO
CAESAREA
DECAPOLIS
SHECHEM
JAFFA
JUDEA
RABBAH
JERICHO
JERUSALEM
ASHDOD
ASHKELON
GAZA
HEBRON
MASADA
BEER SHEBA
NABATAEANS
N
CITY
EXTENT OF JEWISH SOVEREIGNTY
ADMINISTRATIVE BORDERS OF NON-JEWISH RULE
NON-JEWISH ADMINISTRATIVE AREA OF JUDEA
EGYPT
MILES
0
50
100
0
50
100
150
KILOMETERS
EILAT
ALL RIGHTS RESERVED © 2018 ILAN REINER & AMIR REINER
MAPS ARE FOR ILLUSTRATIVE PURPOSES ONLY
25

King Herod
Herodian Kingdom of Judea - At her Peak
about 20 BCE to 4 BCE

At the peak of his reign, the kingdom included all of Judah, the coastal regions, areas east of the Jordan river, Galilee and Golan and eastwards. Having a vast kingdom with a diverse population, Herod ruled with terror and great cruelty, especially towards those he suspected that might become his enemies. However, his reign was also marked with significant cultural prosperity and religious renewal. The great Jewish sages, Hillel and Shamai, were active in his times and laid down much of the basis for future Jewish law; the Mishna and the Talmud. Herod was wise to prevent religious tension between Jews and the Romans and other non-Jews. As controversial as his reign was, the magnificence of his monumental buildings are still standing over two millennia later.

View of Herodium (Herod's fort and tomb)
Photo by: Asaf T.

TIME LINE

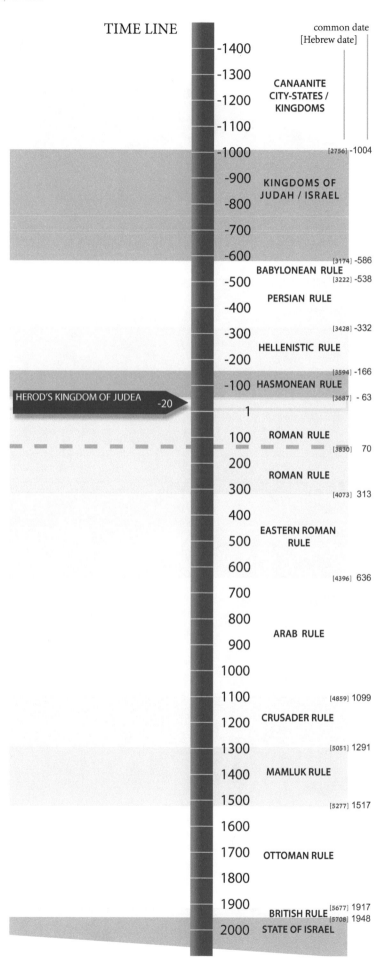

common date
[Hebrew date]

-1400
-1300
-1200
-1100
CANAANITE CITY-STATES / KINGDOMS
[2756] -1004
-1000
-900
-800
-700
-600
KINGDOMS OF JUDAH / ISRAEL
[3174] -586
BABYLONEAN RULE
[3222] -538
-500
-400
PERSIAN RULE
[3428] -332
-300
-200
HELLENISTIC RULE
[3594] -166
-100
HASMONEAN RULE
[3687] - 63
HEROD'S KINGDOM OF JUDEA -20
1
100
ROMAN RULE
[3830] 70
200
300
ROMAN RULE
[4073] 313
400
500
EASTERN ROMAN RULE
600
[4396] 636
700
800
900
1000
ARAB RULE
1100
[4859] 1099
1200
CRUSADER RULE
1300
[5051] 1291
1400
MAMLUK RULE
1500
[5277] 1517
1600
1700
1800
OTTOMAN RULE
1900
[5677] 1917
BRITISH RULE
[5708] 1948
2000
STATE OF ISRAEL

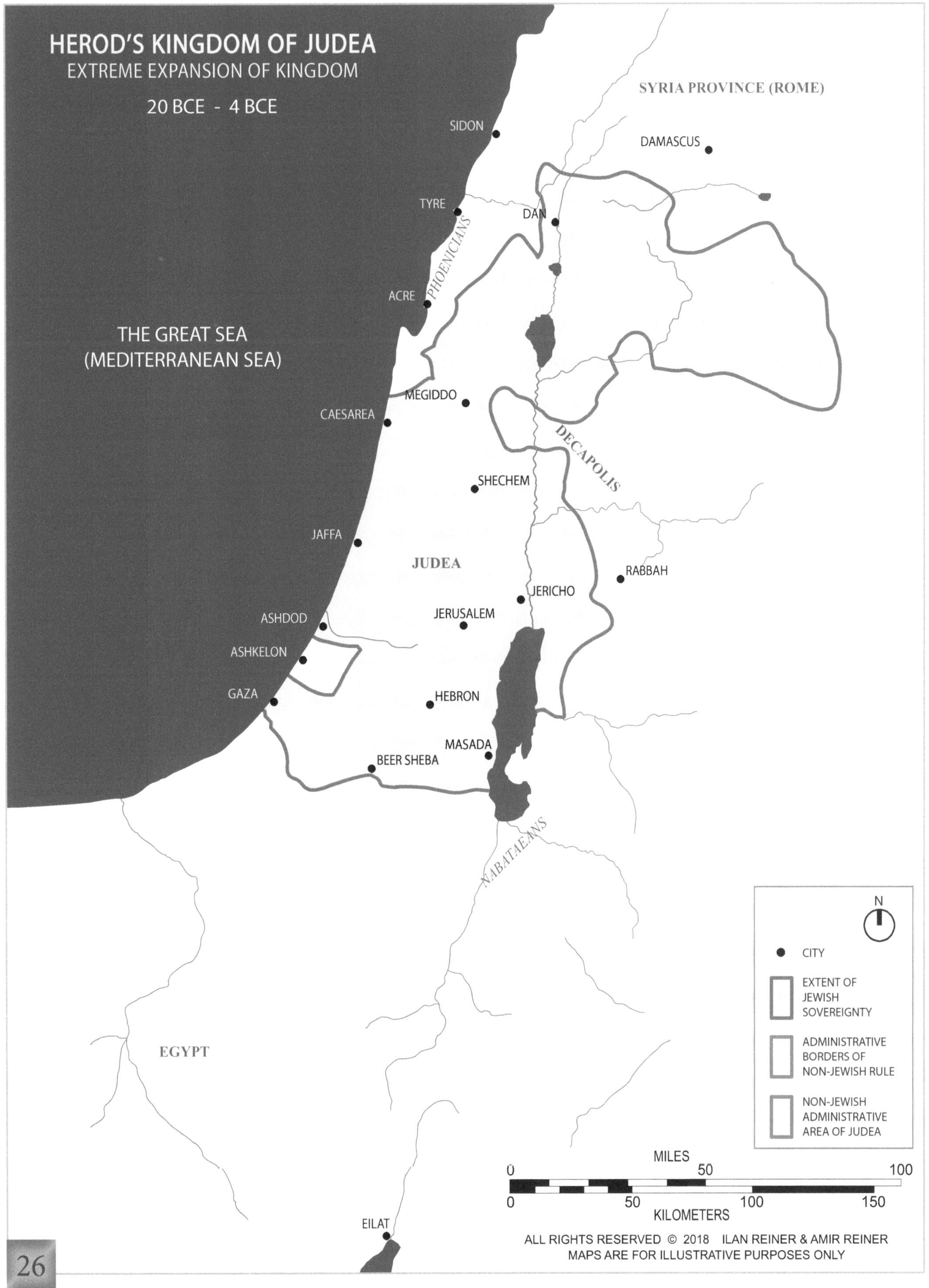
HEROD'S KINGDOM OF JUDEA
EXTREME EXPANSION OF KINGDOM
20 BCE - 4 BCE
SYRIA PROVINCE (ROME)
SIDON
DAMASCUS
TYRE
DAN
PHOENICIANS
ACRE
THE GREAT SEA
(MEDITERRANEAN SEA)
MEGIDDO
CAESAREA
DECAPOLIS
SHECHEM
JAFFA
JUDEA
RABBAH
JERICHO
JERUSALEM
ASHDOD
ASHKELON
GAZA
HEBRON
MASADA
BEER SHEBA
NABATAEANS
EGYPT
EILAT
N
CITY
EXTENT OF JEWISH SOVEREIGNTY
ADMINISTRATIVE BORDERS OF NON-JEWISH RULE
NON-JEWISH ADMINISTRATIVE AREA OF JUDEA
MILES
0 50 100
0 50 100 150
KILOMETERS
ALL RIGHTS RESERVED © 2018 ILAN REINER & AMIR REINER
MAPS ARE FOR ILLUSTRATIVE PURPOSES ONLY
26

Successors of King Herod
Judea At Disarray
about 4 BCE to 6 CE

Civil unrest began towards the end of Herod's days. Upon his death, revolts broke out in several locations, led by army generals as well as Jewish zealots. The Roman governor of Syria, Varus, marched in with several legions, suppressing the rebellions, capturing cities and crucifying thousands.

As matters calmed, Roman Emperor Augustus Caesar decided to honor King Herod's will to some degree. Herod's great kingdom was divided between three princes.

Herod Archelaus was to be named ethnarch (which is of lesser degree than king), and rule over Judaea, Samaria and Idumaea, with the port cities of Ceasaria and Jaffa. Herod Antipas was appointed governor of Galilee and of Peraer, east of the Jordan River. Herod Philip was made governor of Ituraea. Some cities preferred direct Roman rule and were transferred to the governor of Syria.

This transition didn't go smoothly and riots were constantly put down, provoking even greater unrest. The New Testament records (in the Gospel of Matthew) that Joseph took his family to Nazareth in Galilee, rather than stay in Judaea, because life under Archelaus had become insecure and risky. After a decade, Archelaus was exiled.

Recreation of Roman Legion marching
Photo by: Judith M.

TIME LINE

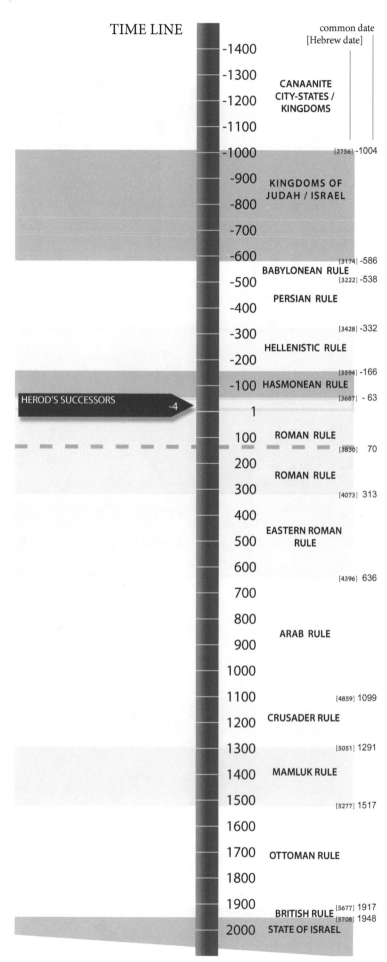

common date
[Hebrew date]

-1400 · -1300 · -1200 · -1100 — CANAANITE CITY-STATES / KINGDOMS

[2756] -1004

-1000 · -900 · -800 · -700 · -600 — KINGDOMS OF JUDAH / ISRAEL

[3174] -586

BABYLONEAN RULE

[3222] -538

-500 · -400 — PERSIAN RULE

[3428] -332

-300 · -200 — HELLENISTIC RULE

[3594] -166

-100 — HASMONEAN RULE

[3687] - 63

HERODS SUCCESSORS -4

1 · 100 — ROMAN RULE

[3830] 70

200 · 300 — ROMAN RULE

[4073] 313

400 · 500 · 600 — EASTERN ROMAN RULE

[4396] 636

700 · 800 · 900 · 1000 — ARAB RULE

[4859] 1099

1100 · 1200 — CRUSADER RULE

[5051] 1291

1300 · 1400 · 1500 — MAMLUK RULE

[5277] 1517

1600 · 1700 · 1800 · 1900 — OTTOMAN RULE

[5677] 1917

BRITISH RULE

[5708] 1948

2000 — STATE OF ISRAEL

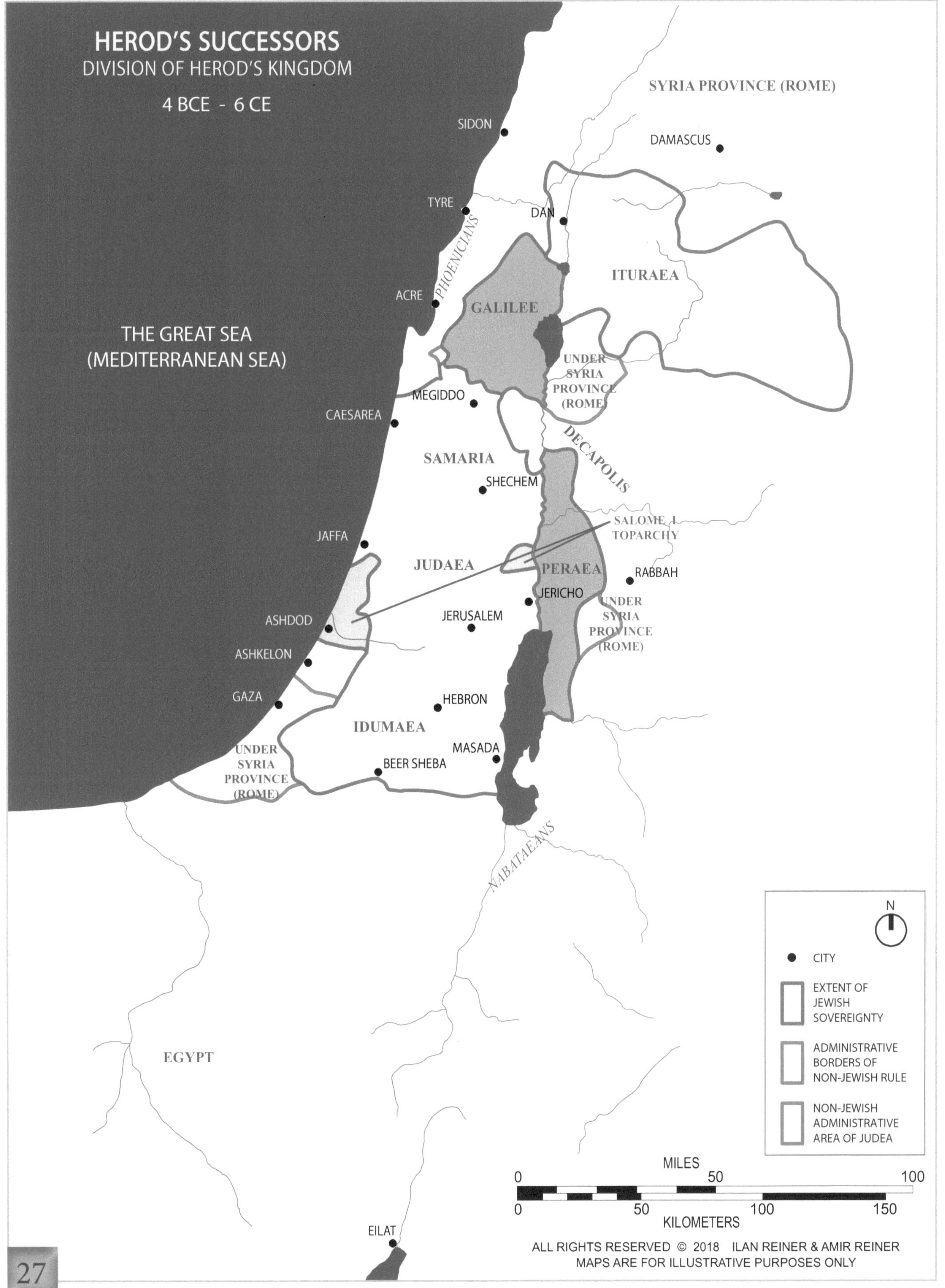
HEROD'S SUCCESSORS
DIVISION OF HEROD'S KINGDOM
4 BCE - 6 CE
SYRIA PROVINCE (ROME)
SIDON
DAMASCUS
TYRE
DAN
PHOENICIANS
ITURAEA
ACRE
GALILEE
THE GREAT SEA
(MEDITERRANEAN SEA)
UNDER SYRIA PROVINCE (ROME)
MEGIDDO
CAESAREA
DECAPOLIS
SAMARIA
SHECHEM
SALOME I TOPARCHY
JAFFA
JUDAEA
PERAEA
RABBAH
JERICHO
UNDER SYRIA PROVINCE (ROME)
ASHDOD
JERUSALEM
ASHKELON
GAZA
HEBRON
IDUMAEA
MASADA
UNDER SYRIA PROVINCE (ROME)
BEER SHEBA
NABATAEANS
N
CITY
EXTENT OF JEWISH SOVEREIGNTY
ADMINISTRATIVE BORDERS OF NON-JEWISH RULE
NON-JEWISH ADMINISTRATIVE AREA OF JUDEA
EGYPT
MILES
0
50
100
0
50
100
150
KILOMETERS
EILAT
ALL RIGHTS RESERVED © 2018 ILAN REINER & AMIR REINER
MAPS ARE FOR ILLUSTRATIVE PURPOSES ONLY
27

Roman Rule
Province of Judea
about 6 CE to 66 CE

After Herod's death, his kingdom was divided among his sons, who became tetrarchs ("rulers of a quarter part"). They ruled so badly that they were dismissed by the Roman emperors after an appeal from their own population. Judea became part of a larger Roman province, called Iudaea, which was formed by combining Judea proper with Samaria and Idumea (Edom). Iudaea province did not include many regions that were part of Herod's kingdom, such as the Galilee and the Golan. The importance of this province was not its revenue, but rather that it controlled the land and coastal sea routes to the "bread basket" Egypt and was a border province against the Parthian Empire (in the area of today's Iran and Iraq) because of the Jewish connections to Babylonia, since the Babylonian exile. The capital of this province was Caesarea, not Jerusalem.

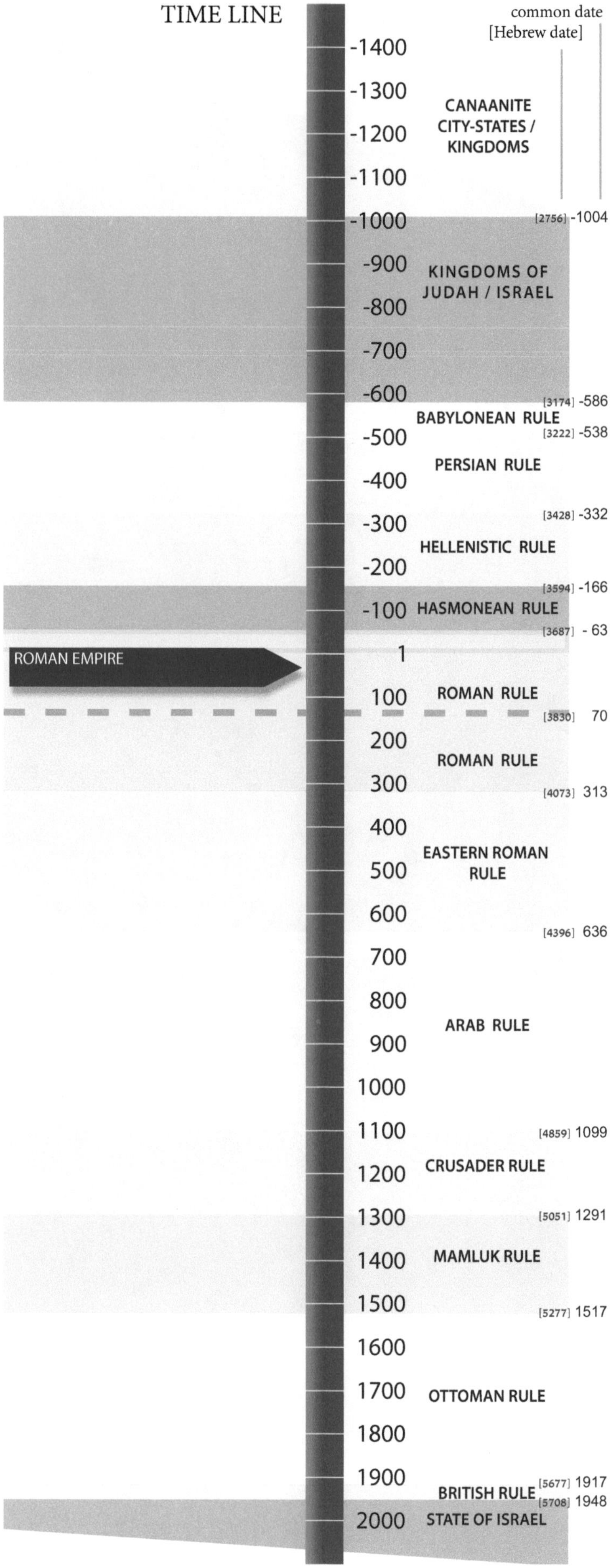

Coin of Marcus Ambivulus, Roman Prefect to Judea
Itamar Atzmon's collection

TIME LINE

common date
[Hebrew date]

-1400
-1300
CANAANITE CITY-STATES / KINGDOMS
-1200
-1100
[2756] -1004
-1000
-900
KINGDOMS OF JUDAH / ISRAEL
-800
-700
-600
[3174] -586
BABYLONEAN RULE
[3222] -538
-500
PERSIAN RULE
-400
[3428] -332
-300
HELLENISTIC RULE
-200
[3594] -166
-100
HASMONEAN RULE
[3687] - 63
ROMAN EMPIRE
1
100
ROMAN RULE
[3830] 70
200
ROMAN RULE
300
[4073] 313
400
EASTERN ROMAN RULE
500
600
[4396] 636
700
800
ARAB RULE
900
1000
1100
[4859] 1099
CRUSADER RULE
1200
[5051] 1291
1300
1400
MAMLUK RULE
1500
[5277] 1517
1600
1700
OTTOMAN RULE
1800
1900
[5677] 1917
BRITISH RULE
[5708] 1948
2000
STATE OF ISRAEL

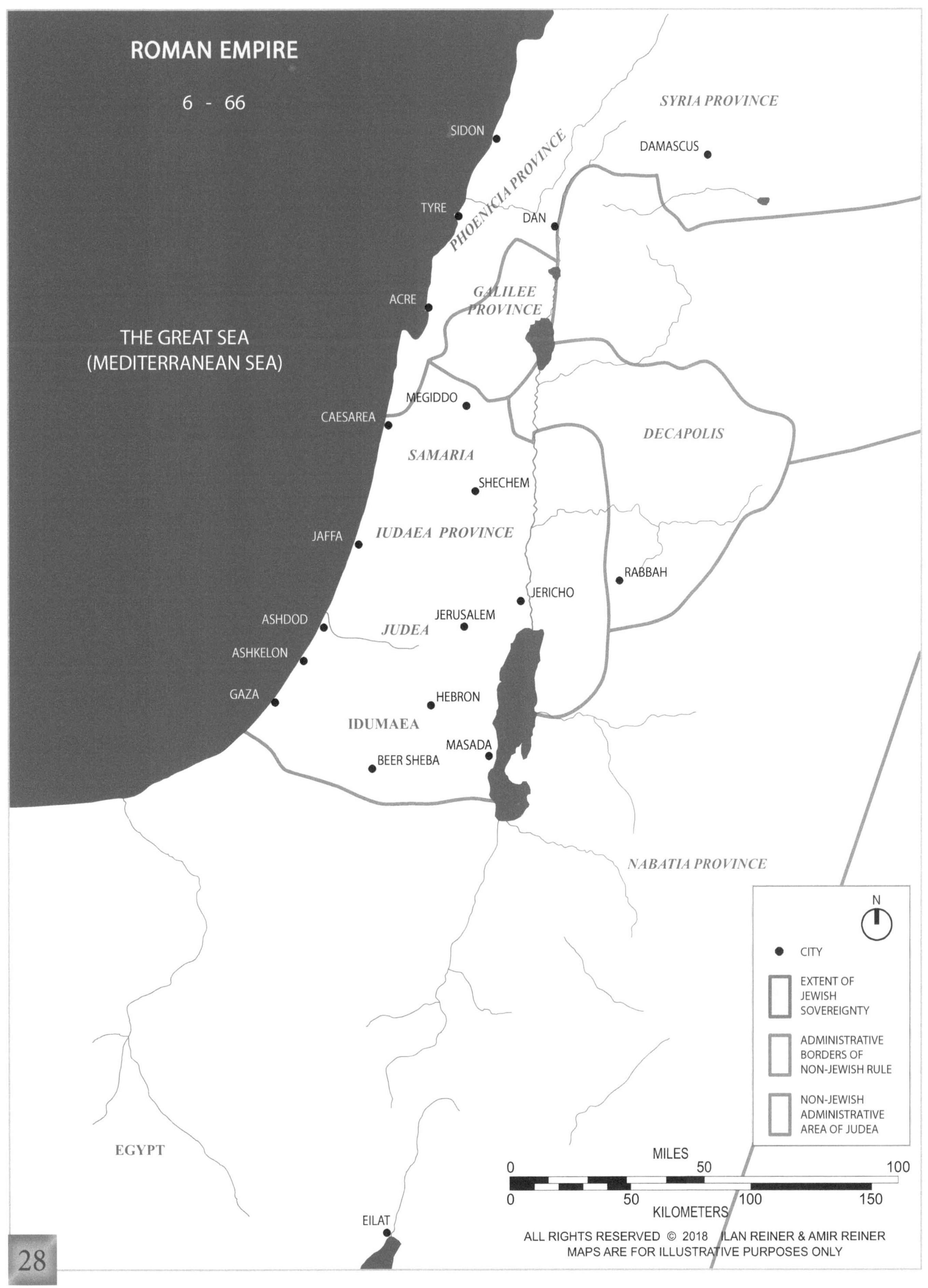
ROMAN EMPIRE
6 - 66
THE GREAT SEA
(MEDITERRANEAN SEA)
SIDON
TYRE
ACRE
CAESAREA
JAFFA
ASHDOD
ASHKELON
GAZA
PHOENICIA PROVINCE
SYRIA PROVINCE
DAMASCUS
DAN
GALILEE
PROVINCE
MEGIDDO
SAMARIA
SHECHEM
DECAPOLIS
IUDAEA PROVINCE
RABBAH
JERICHO
JERUSALEM
JUDEA
HEBRON
IDUMAEA
MASADA
BEER SHEBA
NABATIA PROVINCE
EGYPT
EILAT
N
CITY
EXTENT OF
JEWISH
SOVEREIGNTY
ADMINISTRATIVE
BORDERS OF
NON-JEWISH RULE
NON-JEWISH
ADMINISTRATIVE
AREA OF JUDEA
MILES
0
50
100
0
50
100
150
KILOMETERS
ALL RIGHTS RESERVED © 2018 ILAN REINER & AMIR REINER
MAPS ARE FOR ILLUSTRATIVE PURPOSES ONLY
28

First Jewish - Roman War
Extreme Expansion of the Revolt
about 66 CE to 68 CE

The Great Jewish Revolt broke out for various reasons. One of the main reasons was the rising tension between the Jewish population and the Roman government. Rome turned Judea into a province under direct Roman rule after the death of King Agrippa I. Clashes with the Roman governor drove some extremists to take up arms, and they defeated several Roman cohortes. When the Jewish leadership understood that there was no way back, they organized the nation and prepared for a full war against Rome. This included assigning military leaders and troops to various districts as well as fortifying cities in Judea and the Galilee. Despite the limited success the Roman army had at first, including breaking briefly into Jerusalem, eventually the Roman army retreated out of Judea. During this retreat, one of the legions was destroyed by the Jewish army.

TIME LINE

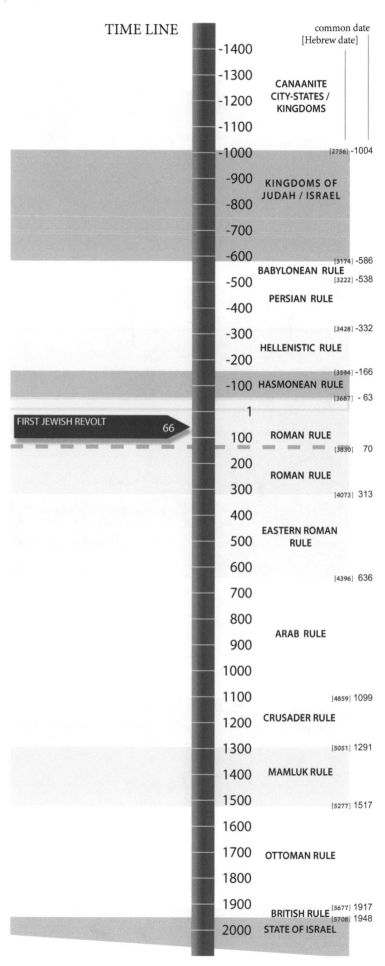

common date
[Hebrew date]

-1400 -1300 -1200 -1100 -1000 -900 -800 -700 -600 -500 -400 -300 -200 -100 1 100 200 300 400 500 600 700 800 900 1000 1100 1200 1300 1400 1500 1600 1700 1800 1900 2000

CANAANITE CITY-STATES / KINGDOMS
[2756] -1004
KINGDOMS OF JUDAH / ISRAEL
[3174] -586
BABYLONEAN RULE
[3222] -538
PERSIAN RULE
[3428] -332
HELLENISTIC RULE
[3594] -166
HASMONEAN RULE
[3687] - 63
FIRST JEWISH REVOLT 66
ROMAN RULE
[3830] 70
ROMAN RULE
[4073] 313
EASTERN ROMAN RULE
[4396] 636
ARAB RULE
[4859] 1099
CRUSADER RULE
[5051] 1291
MAMLUK RULE
[5277] 1517
OTTOMAN RULE
[5677] 1917
BRITISH RULE
[5708] 1948
STATE OF ISRAEL

Roman Soldiers Laying Siege
Temporary life size exhibit in Jerusalem

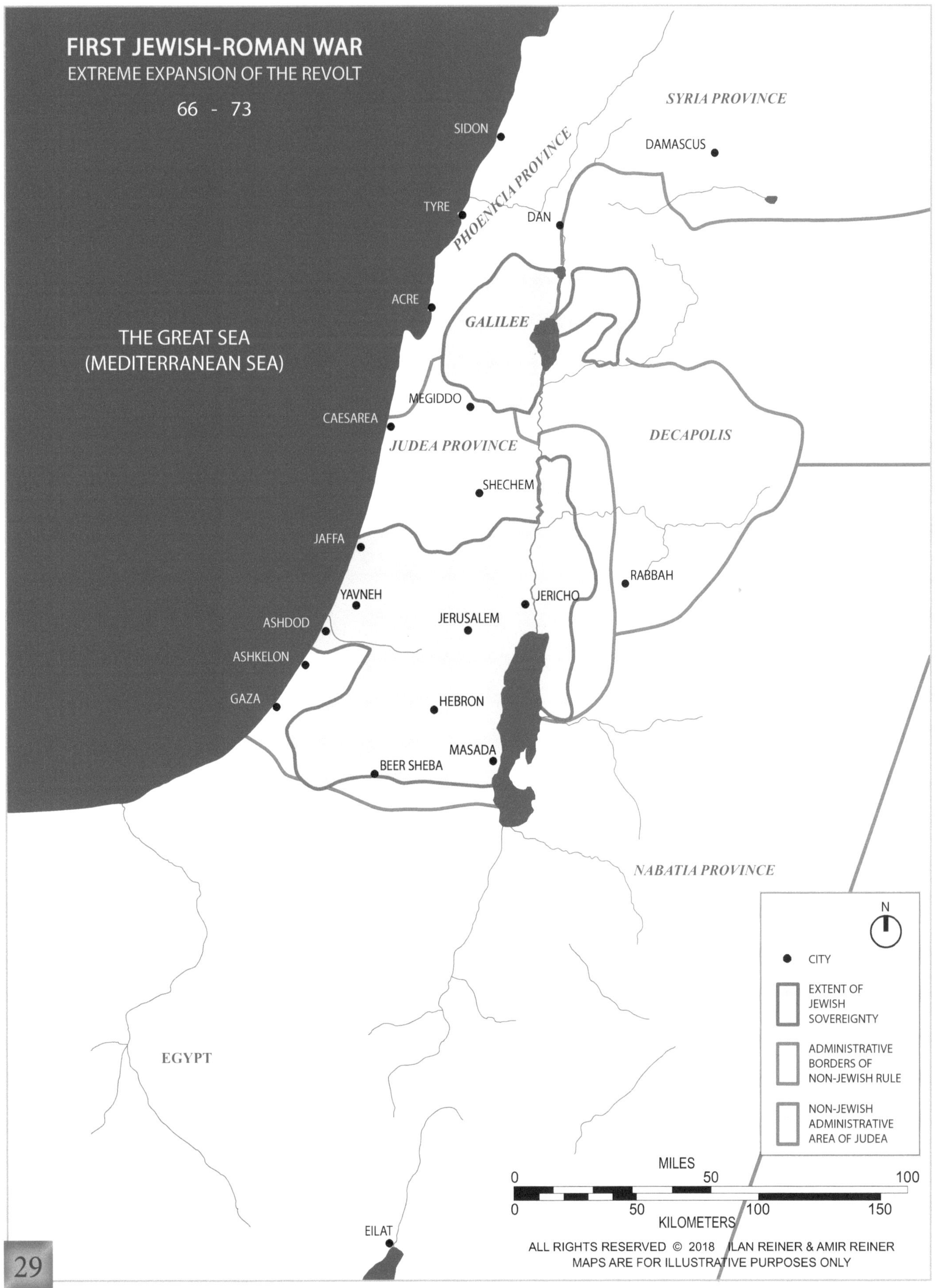
FIRST JEWISH-ROMAN WAR
EXTREME EXPANSION OF THE REVOLT
66 - 73
SIDON
TYRE
PHOENICIA PROVINCE
SYRIA PROVINCE
DAMASCUS
DAN
ACRE
GALILEE
THE GREAT SEA
(MEDITERRANEAN SEA)
MEGIDDO
CAESAREA
JUDEA PROVINCE
DECAPOLIS
SHECHEM
JAFFA
RABBAH
YAVNEH
JERICHO
ASHDOD
JERUSALEM
ASHKELON
GAZA
HEBRON
MASADA
BEER SHEBA
NABATIA PROVINCE
EGYPT
EILAT
N
CITY
EXTENT OF JEWISH SOVEREIGNTY
ADMINISTRATIVE BORDERS OF NON-JEWISH RULE
NON-JEWISH ADMINISTRATIVE AREA OF JUDEA
MILES
0 50 100
0 50 100 150
KILOMETERS
ALL RIGHTS RESERVED © 2018 ILAN REINER & AMIR REINER
MAPS ARE FOR ILLUSTRATIVE PURPOSES ONLY
29

First Jewish - Roman War
Decline of the Revolt
about 68 CE to 70 CE

The Jews, excited and motivated from recent victories, were gathering to organize the revolt. The National Assembly made various appointments of military governors to strengthen and fortify cities throughout Israel. Many of the leaders were of the mainstream, and were trying to calm the zealots and extreme elements. Not long after, a new Roman army entered Israel from both north and south (from Egypt). This army was led by Vespasian and his son Titus. One after the other, the Jewish forts and cities were captured, until the entire Galilee and Golan were taken. In the meantime, various groups of extremist Jews were in the midst of a civil war, trying to gain control of the government as they were unable to decide in which direction to take the newly gained independence. The revolt against the Romans soon turned into an internal Jewish civil war, as the factions depleted much needed food, weapons and resources in Jerusalem.

Gamla, in the Golan, destroyed by the Romans
Ruins of the ancient City of Gamla

TIME LINE

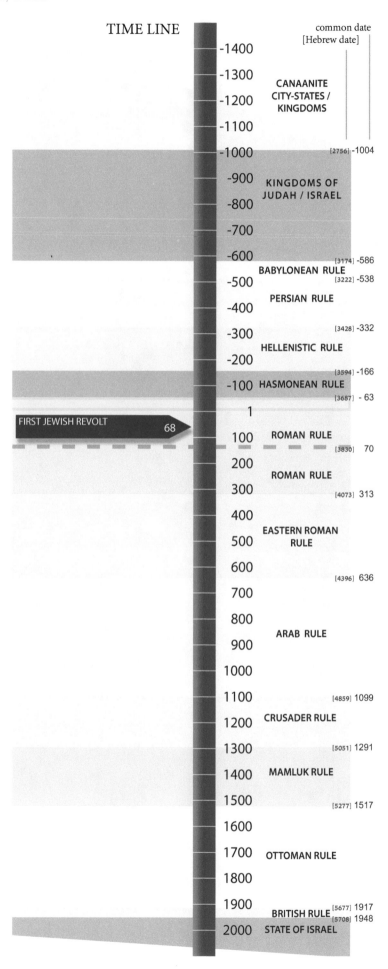

common date
[Hebrew date]

-1400
-1300
CANAANITE CITY-STATES / KINGDOMS
-1200
-1100
[2756] -1004
-1000
-900
KINGDOMS OF JUDAH / ISRAEL
-800
-700
-600
[3174] -586
BABYLONEAN RULE
[3222] -538
-500
PERSIAN RULE
-400
[3428] -332
-300
HELLENISTIC RULE
-200
[3594] -166
-100 HASMONEAN RULE
[3687] - 63
1
FIRST JEWISH REVOLT 68
100 ROMAN RULE
[3830] 70
200
ROMAN RULE
300
[4073] 313
400
EASTERN ROMAN RULE
500
600
[4396] 636
700
800
ARAB RULE
900
1000
1100
[4859] 1099
CRUSADER RULE
1200
1300
[5051] 1291
MAMLUK RULE
1400
1500
[5277] 1517
1600
1700 OTTOMAN RULE
1800
1900
BRITISH RULE [5677] 1917
[5708] 1948
2000 STATE OF ISRAEL

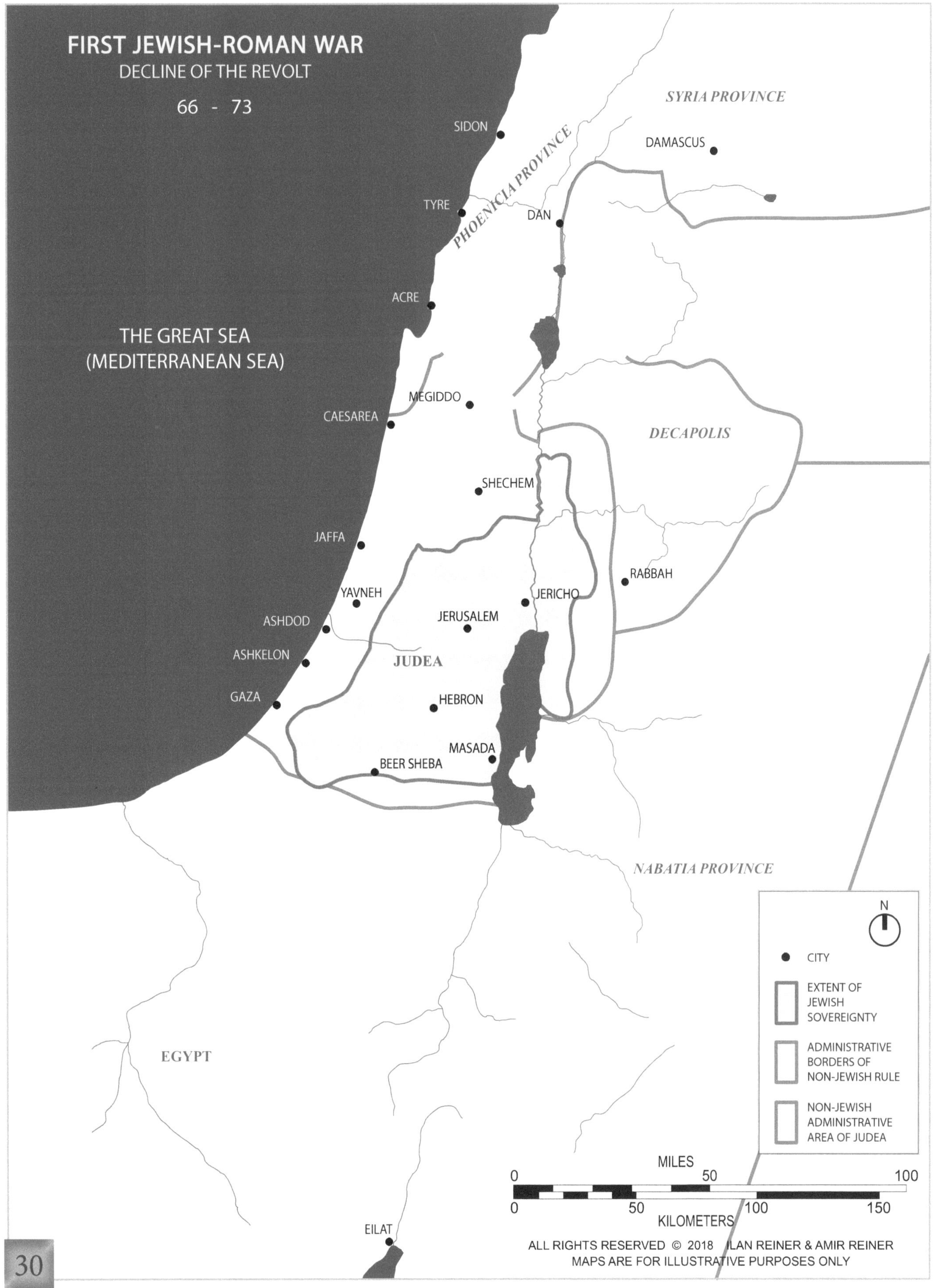
FIRST JEWISH-ROMAN WAR
DECLINE OF THE REVOLT
66 - 73
THE GREAT SEA
(MEDITERRANEAN SEA)
SIDON
TYRE
ACRE
CAESAREA
MEGIDDO
SHECHEM
JAFFA
YAVNEH
ASHDOD
ASHKELON
GAZA
JERUSALEM
JERICHO
HEBRON
MASADA
BEER SHEBA
RABBAH
DAMASCUS
DAN
EILAT
PHOENICIA PROVINCE
SYRIA PROVINCE
DECAPOLIS
JUDEA
NABATIA PROVINCE
EGYPT
N
CITY
EXTENT OF JEWISH SOVEREIGNTY
ADMINISTRATIVE BORDERS OF NON-JEWISH RULE
NON-JEWISH ADMINISTRATIVE AREA OF JUDEA
MILES
0
50
100
0
50
100
150
KILOMETERS
ALL RIGHTS RESERVED © 2018 ILAN REINER & AMIR REINER
MAPS ARE FOR ILLUSTRATIVE PURPOSES ONLY
30

First Jewish - Roman War
End of the Revolt
70 CE to 73 CE

The civil war between the various Jewish factions ended when the Romans approached Jerusalem. Four legions, led by Titus, laid siege on the city, urging the people to surrender in order to spare the city from destruction. The battles went on for months until the Romans broke into the city. Each day they advanced more, slaughtering all that were in their way. Eventually they broke into the Temple mount and burnt down the Second Temple. Many thousands were killed and many more were captured and sold into slavery. Some of the holiest artifacts were brought to Rome and presented as spoils of war. Even then there were Jews still fighting in other fortified locations. The most famous is the one in Masada, where the Jews fought the Romans till the last person. The fall of Masada marked the end of the rebellion.

Sack of Jerusalem
Arch of Titus, Rome, Italy

TIME LINE

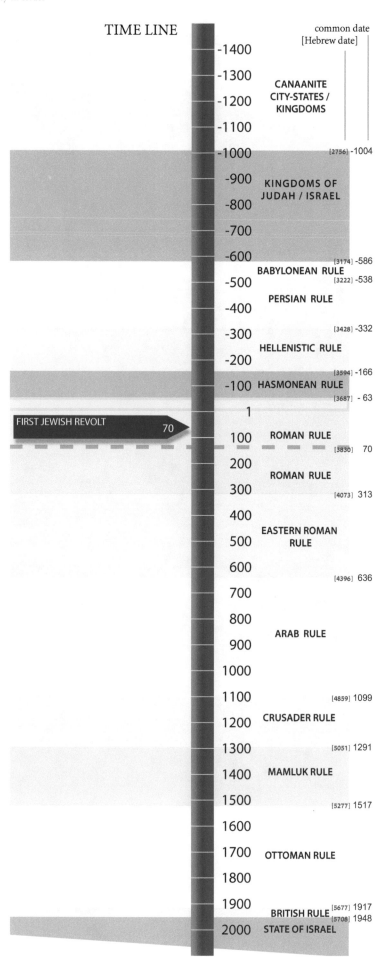

common date [Hebrew date]

-1400, -1300, -1200, -1100: CANAANITE CITY-STATES / KINGDOMS

[2756] -1004

-1000, -900, -800, -700, -600: KINGDOMS OF JUDAH / ISRAEL

[3174] -586

BABYLONEAN RULE

[3222] -538

-500, -400: PERSIAN RULE

[3428] -332

-300, -200: HELLENISTIC RULE

[3594] -166

-100: HASMONEAN RULE

[3687] - 63

1

FIRST JEWISH REVOLT 70

100: ROMAN RULE

[3830] 70

200, 300: ROMAN RULE

[4073] 313

400, 500, 600: EASTERN ROMAN RULE

[4396] 636

700, 800, 900, 1000, 1100: ARAB RULE

[4859] 1099

1200: CRUSADER RULE

[5051] 1291

1300, 1400, 1500: MAMLUK RULE

[5277] 1517

1600, 1700, 1800, 1900: OTTOMAN RULE

[5677] 1917

BRITISH RULE

[5708] 1948

2000: STATE OF ISRAEL

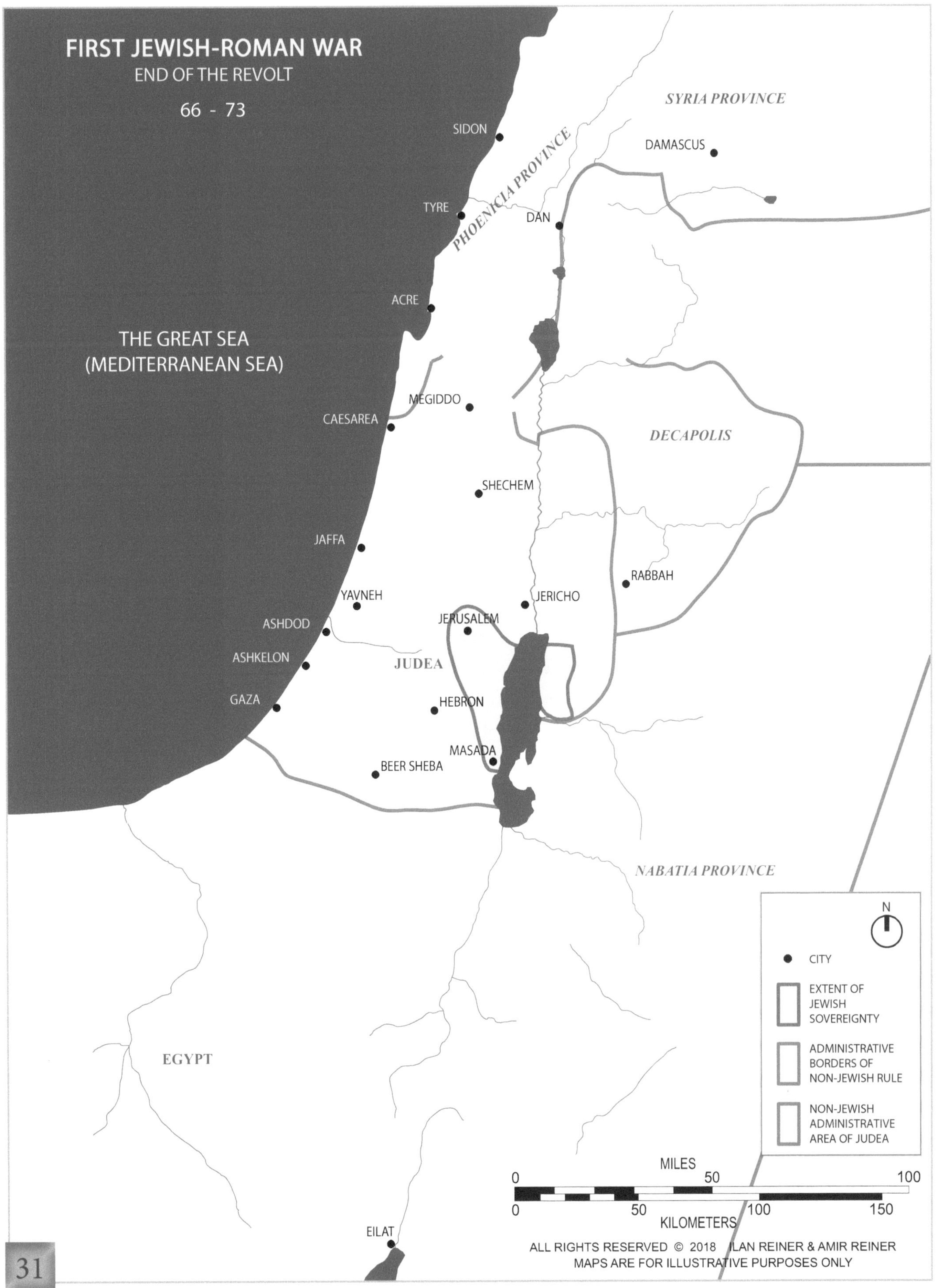
FIRST JEWISH-ROMAN WAR
END OF THE REVOLT
66 - 73
THE GREAT SEA
(MEDITERRANEAN SEA)
SIDON
TYRE
ACRE
CAESAREA
MEGIDDO
SHECHEM
JAFFA
YAVNEH
ASHDOD
ASHKELON
GAZA
JERUSALEM
JERICHO
HEBRON
MASADA
BEER SHEBA
EILAT
DAN
DAMASCUS
RABBAH
PHOENICIA PROVINCE
SYRIA PROVINCE
DECAPOLIS
JUDEA
NABATIA PROVINCE
EGYPT
N
CITY
EXTENT OF JEWISH SOVEREIGNTY
ADMINISTRATIVE BORDERS OF NON-JEWISH RULE
NON-JEWISH ADMINISTRATIVE AREA OF JUDEA
MILES
0
50
100
0
50
100
150
KILOMETERS
ALL RIGHTS RESERVED © 2018 ILAN REINER & AMIR REINER
MAPS ARE FOR ILLUSTRATIVE PURPOSES ONLY
31

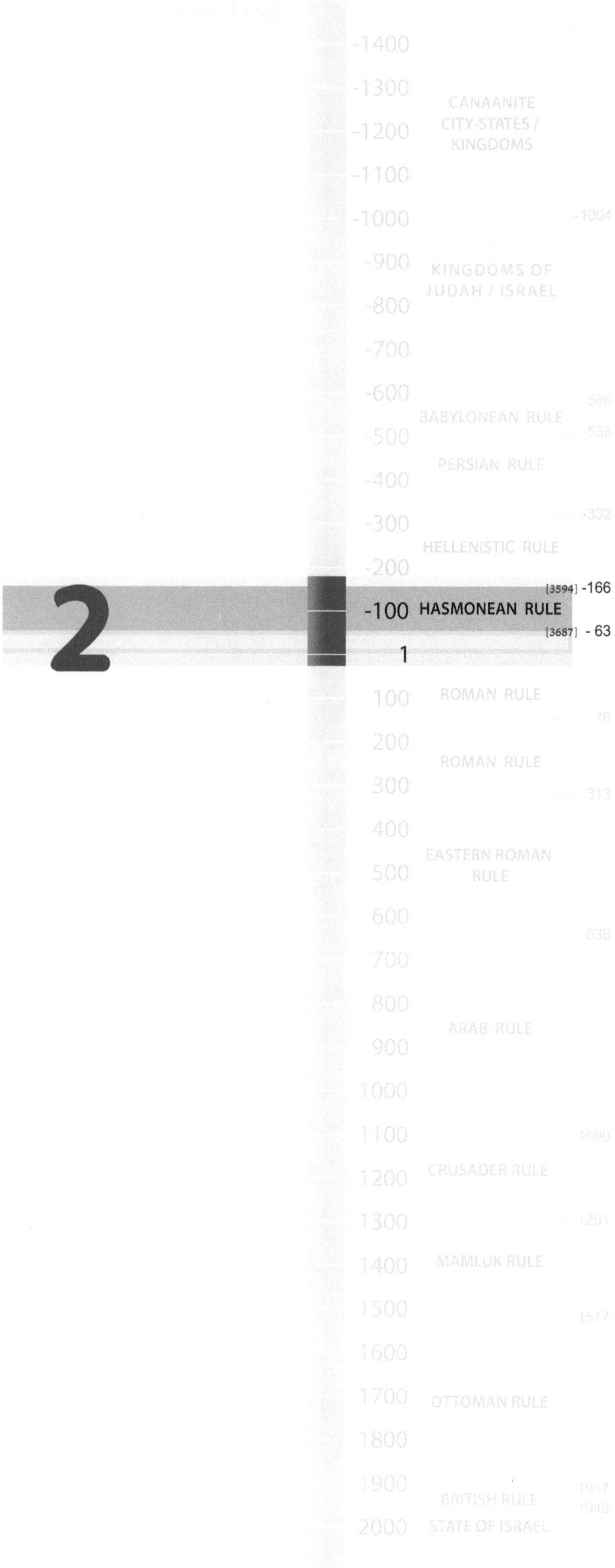

-1400
-1300
-1200 CANAANITE CITY-STATES / KINGDOMS
-1100
-1000 -1004
-900 KINGDOMS OF JUDAH / ISRAEL
-800
-700
-600 -586
BABYLONEAN RULE
-500 -538
PERSIAN RULE
-400
-300 -332
HELLENISTIC RULE
-200

2

[3594] -166
-100 **HASMONEAN RULE**
[3687] - 63
1

100 ROMAN RULE
70
200 ROMAN RULE
300 313
400
500 EASTERN ROMAN RULE
600 638
700
800
900 ARAB RULE
1000
1100 1099
1200 CRUSADER RULE
1300 1291
1400 MAMLUK RULE
1500 1517
1600
1700 OTTOMAN RULE
1800
1900 1917
BRITISH RULE 1948
2000 STATE OF ISRAEL

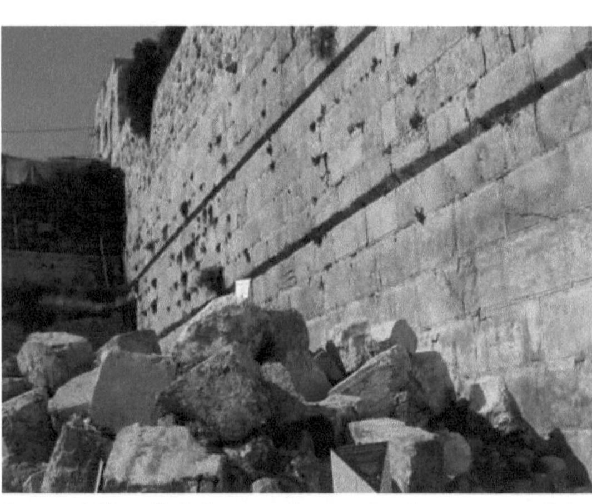

Stones (allegedly) thrown during the destruction of the Temple in Jerusalem remain untouched for 2000 years
Photo by: Dr. Moshe Ra'anan

ENDING OF THE SECOND ERA OF JEWISH RULE IN THE LAND OF ISRAEL

BIG JEWISH REVOLT

-166 TO 70

The Siege and Destruction of Jerusalem by the Romans
By: David Roberts

Roman Rule
Province of Judea
73 CE to 132 CE

Following the failed rebellion, Judea turned from being 'Friend and Ally of the Roman People' to a military occupied imperial procuratorial province, with a full legion camping there permanently. The capital city was Caesarea and many cities were restored as Hellenistic or Roman cities, including the Decapolis cities, such as Rabbah, Gerasa, Scythopolis (Beth-Shean), and others. Despite the many losses, the majority of the population in Israel remained Jewish. Their status was degraded and they were forced to pay a special tax. The spiritual center of Judaism was established in Yavneh (a city along the coastal plain, between Jaffa and Ashdod), headed by Rabbi Ben Zakai. Without a central place of worship, the Jews now faced the huge task and responsibility of adapting the Jewish religious practices and faith to an era without the Temple in Jerusalem in order to perpetuate Judaism in exile, while dispersed throughout the world.

Ruins of an ancient synagogue, built because there was no longer a central temple in Jerusalem

TIME LINE

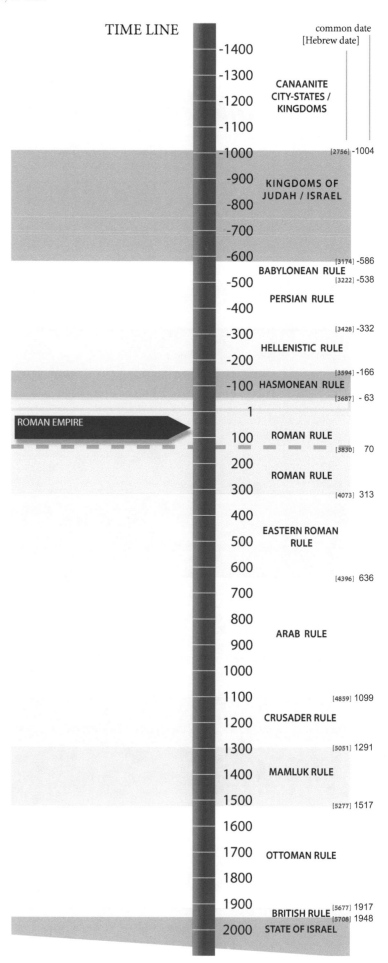

common date [Hebrew date]

ROMAN EMPIRE

Period	Ends at
CANAANITE CITY-STATES / KINGDOMS	[2756] -1004
KINGDOMS OF JUDAH / ISRAEL	[3174] -586
BABYLONEAN RULE	[3222] -538
PERSIAN RULE	[3428] -332
HELLENISTIC RULE	[3594] -166
HASMONEAN RULE	[3687] - 63
ROMAN RULE	[3830] 70
ROMAN RULE	[4073] 313
EASTERN ROMAN RULE	[4396] 636
ARAB RULE	[4859] 1099
CRUSADER RULE	[5051] 1291
MAMLUK RULE	[5277] 1517
OTTOMAN RULE	[5677] 1917
BRITISH RULE	[5708] 1948
STATE OF ISRAEL	

-1400 -1300 -1200 -1100 -1000 -900 -800 -700 -600 -500 -400 -300 -200 -100 1 100 200 300 400 500 600 700 800 900 1000 1100 1200 1300 1400 1500 1600 1700 1800 1900 2000

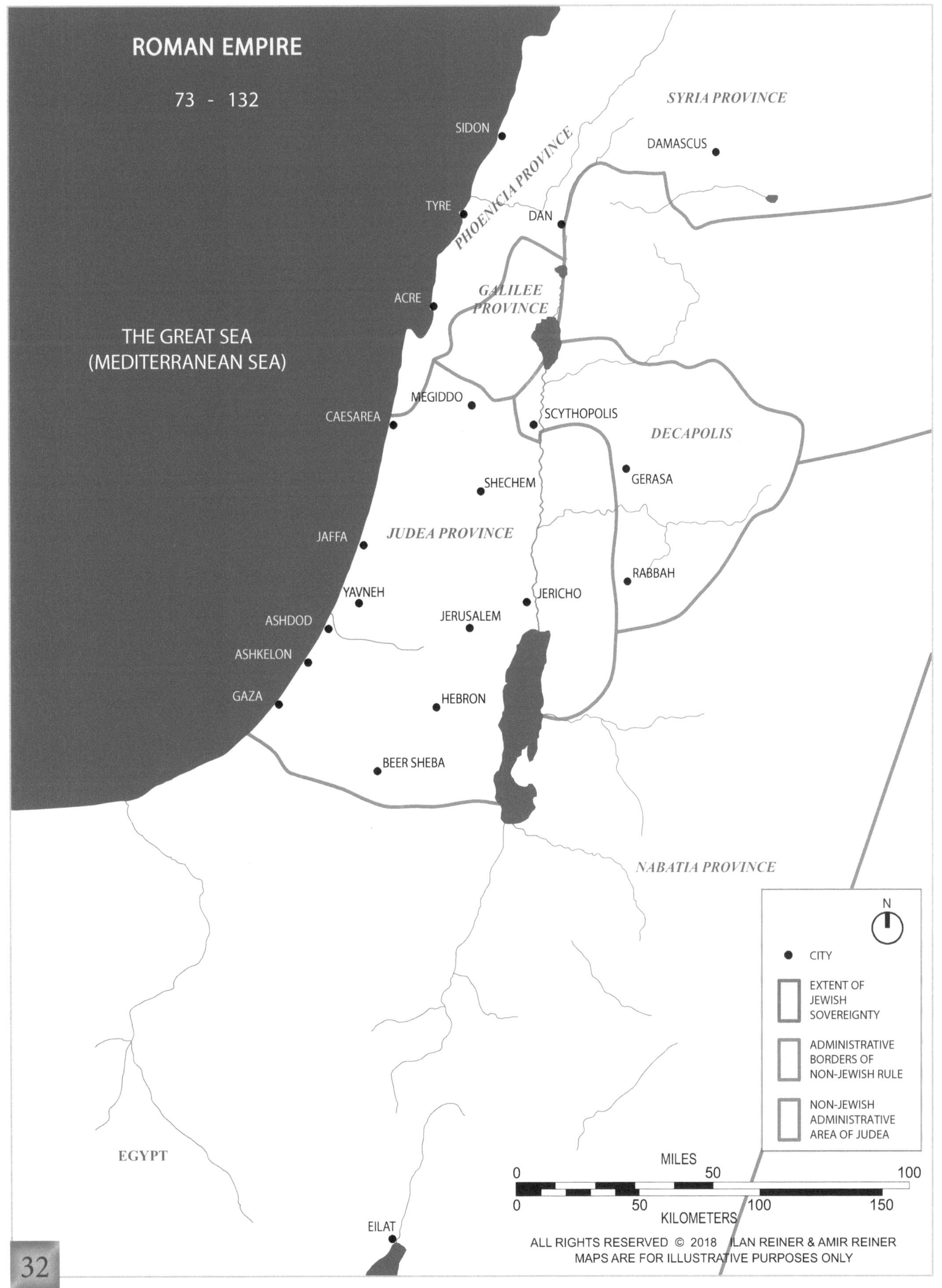
ROMAN EMPIRE
73 - 132
SYRIA PROVINCE
SIDON
DAMASCUS
PHOENICIA PROVINCE
TYRE
DAN
GALILEE PROVINCE
ACRE
THE GREAT SEA (MEDITERRANEAN SEA)
MEGIDDO
CAESAREA
SCYTHOPOLIS
DECAPOLIS
GERASA
SHECHEM
JAFFA
JUDEA PROVINCE
RABBAH
YAVNEH
JERICHO
ASHDOD
JERUSALEM
ASHKELON
GAZA
HEBRON
BEER SHEBA
NABATIA PROVINCE
N
CITY
EXTENT OF JEWISH SOVEREIGNTY
ADMINISTRATIVE BORDERS OF NON-JEWISH RULE
NON-JEWISH ADMINISTRATIVE AREA OF JUDEA
EGYPT
MILES
0
50
100
0
50
100
150
KILOMETERS
EILAT

32

Bar Kochva Revolt
Extreme Expansion of the Revolt

132 CE to 133 CE

The Bar Kochva revolt began with high hopes to restore Jewish independence and sovereignty. But these hopes ended with a violent despair. In times of growing tension between the Jews in Judea and the Roman Empire, the Jews secretly prepared for rebellion. In 132 CE, they launched one of the strongest and deadliest offensives against the Romans. Presumably one or more legions were utterly destroyed as the Romans engaged in battle against the Jewish militia. Under the strong and charismatic leadership of Simon ben Kosiba (who was given the surname Bar Kochva), the Jews captured approximately 50 strongholds in Judea and many other undefended towns and villages, including Jerusalem. Emperor Hadrian ushered more and more legions into Judea, as the Jews declared independence, freed Jerusalem, and minted their own coins that carried such slogans as "Year One of the Freedom of Israel".

Excavated cave used by Bar Kokhva's rebels
Photo by: Udi Steinwell

TIME LINE

ISRAEL - BAR KOCHVA REVOLT 133

-1400, -1300, -1200, -1100, -1000, -900, -800, -700, -600, -500, -400, -300, -200, -100, 1, 100, 200, 300, 400, 500, 600, 700, 800, 900, 1000, 1100, 1200, 1300, 1400, 1500, 1600, 1700, 1800, 1900, 2000

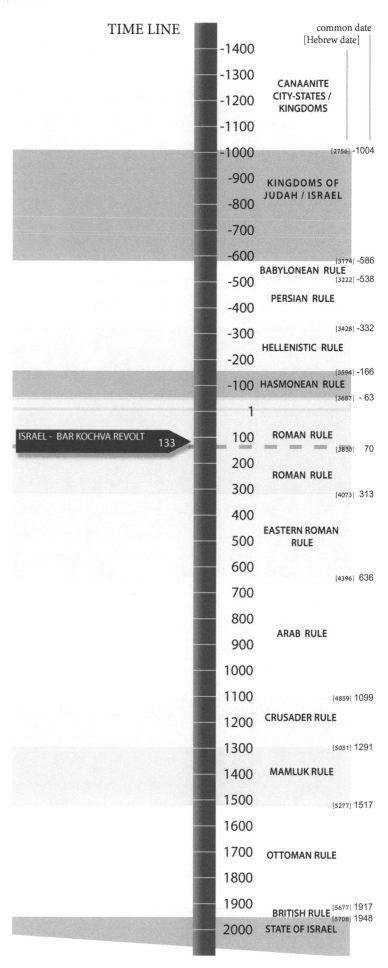

Period	common date [Hebrew date]
CANAANITE CITY-STATES / KINGDOMS	
	[2756] -1004
KINGDOMS OF JUDAH / ISRAEL	
	[3174] -586
BABYLONEAN RULE	
	[3222] -538
PERSIAN RULE	
	[3428] -332
HELLENISTIC RULE	
	[3594] -166
HASMONEAN RULE	
	[3687] - 63
ROMAN RULE	
	[3830] 70
ROMAN RULE	
	[4073] 313
EASTERN ROMAN RULE	
	[4396] 636
ARAB RULE	
	[4859] 1099
CRUSADER RULE	
	[5051] 1291
MAMLUK RULE	
	[5277] 1517
OTTOMAN RULE	
	[5677] 1917
BRITISH RULE	
	[5708] 1948
STATE OF ISRAEL	

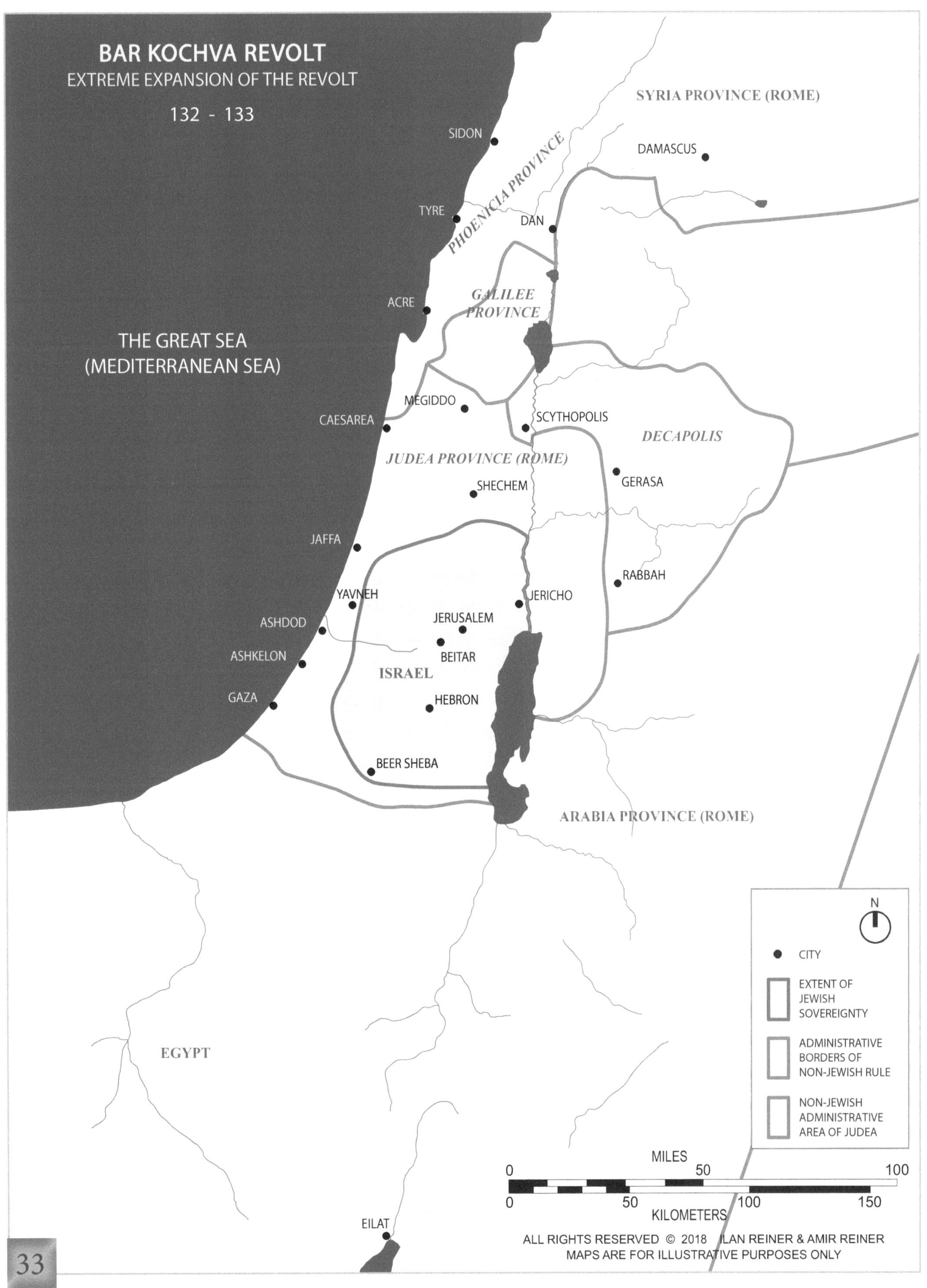
BAR KOCHVA REVOLT
EXTREME EXPANSION OF THE REVOLT
132 - 133
SYRIA PROVINCE (ROME)
SIDON
DAMASCUS
PHOENICIA PROVINCE
TYRE
DAN
GALILEE PROVINCE
ACRE
THE GREAT SEA (MEDITERRANEAN SEA)
MEGIDDO
CAESAREA
SCYTHOPOLIS
DECAPOLIS
JUDEA PROVINCE (ROME)
GERASA
SHECHEM
JAFFA
RABBAH
YAVNEH
JERICHO
ASHDOD
JERUSALEM
BEITAR
ASHKELON
ISRAEL
GAZA
HEBRON
BEER SHEBA
ARABIA PROVINCE (ROME)
N
CITY
EXTENT OF JEWISH SOVEREIGNTY
ADMINISTRATIVE BORDERS OF NON-JEWISH RULE
NON-JEWISH ADMINISTRATIVE AREA OF JUDEA
EGYPT
MILES
0
50
100
0
50
100
150
KILOMETERS
EILAT
ALL RIGHTS RESERVED © 2018 ILAN REINER & AMIR REINER
MAPS ARE FOR ILLUSTRATIVE PURPOSES ONLY
33

Bar Kochva Revolt
Decline of the Revolt
134 CE

In reaction to the Jewish victories, Emperor Hadrian sent into Judea his best generals as well as forces from about a dozen legions, including battalions from Britain. This is probably the only time when the majority of the Roman army was concentrated in one war. The Roman army decided to avoid confronting the Jewish militia in open battle, due to the vast amount of Jewish rebels. Instead, they besieged Jewish fortresses and held back food until the Jews grew weak. Only then did the attack escalate into outright war. Within a year, many fortresses and villages were destroyed and the Jews retreated more and more into the central mountain area.

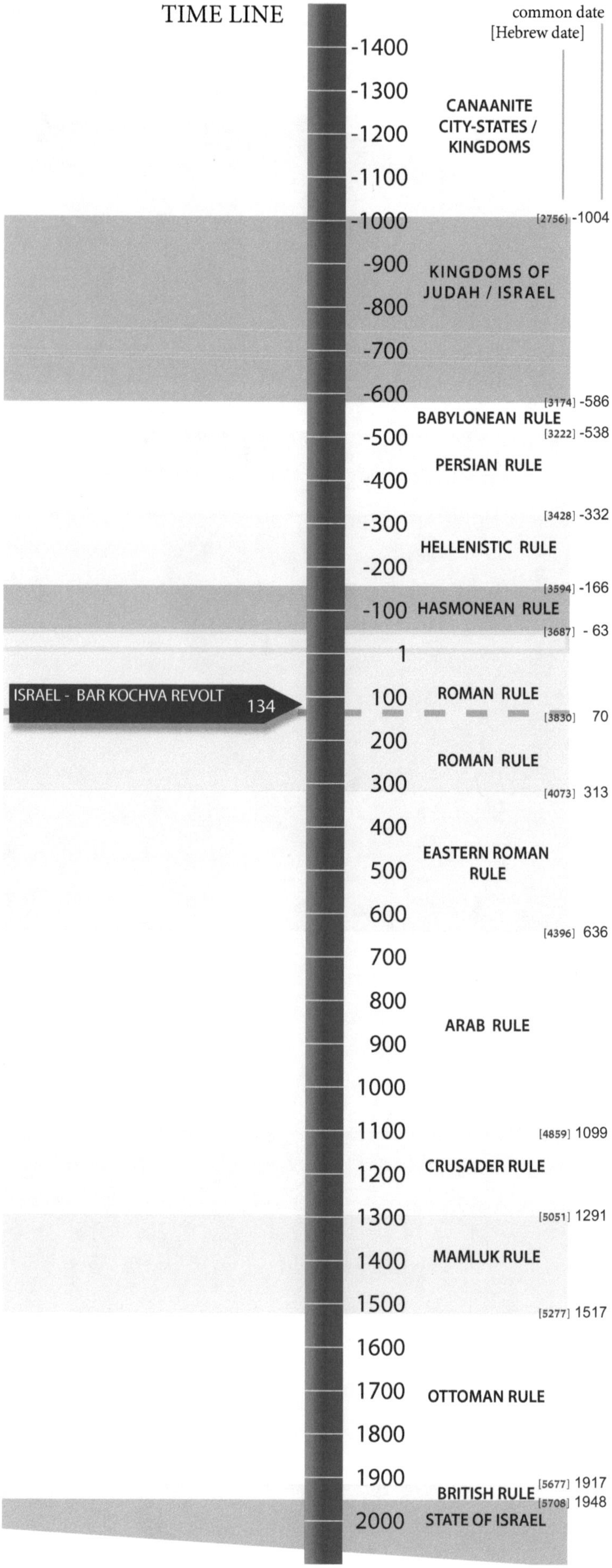

Coin - "Year two to the freedom of Israel"
Photo by: Tallenna Tiedosto

TIME LINE

common date
[Hebrew date]

-1400
-1300
-1200 CANAANITE CITY-STATES / KINGDOMS
-1100
[2756] -1004
-1000
-900 KINGDOMS OF JUDAH / ISRAEL
-800
-700
-600
[3174] -586
BABYLONEAN RULE
[3222] -538
-500
-400 PERSIAN RULE
[3428] -332
-300
-200 HELLENISTIC RULE
[3594] -166
-100 HASMONEAN RULE
[3687] - 63
1
ISRAEL - BAR KOCHVA REVOLT 134
100 ROMAN RULE
[3830] 70
200 ROMAN RULE
300
[4073] 313
400
500 EASTERN ROMAN RULE
600
[4396] 636
700
800
900 ARAB RULE
1000
[4859] 1099
1100
1200 CRUSADER RULE
[5051] 1291
1300
1400 MAMLUK RULE
1500
[5277] 1517
1600
1700 OTTOMAN RULE
1800
1900
[5677] 1917
BRITISH RULE
[5708] 1948
2000 STATE OF ISRAEL

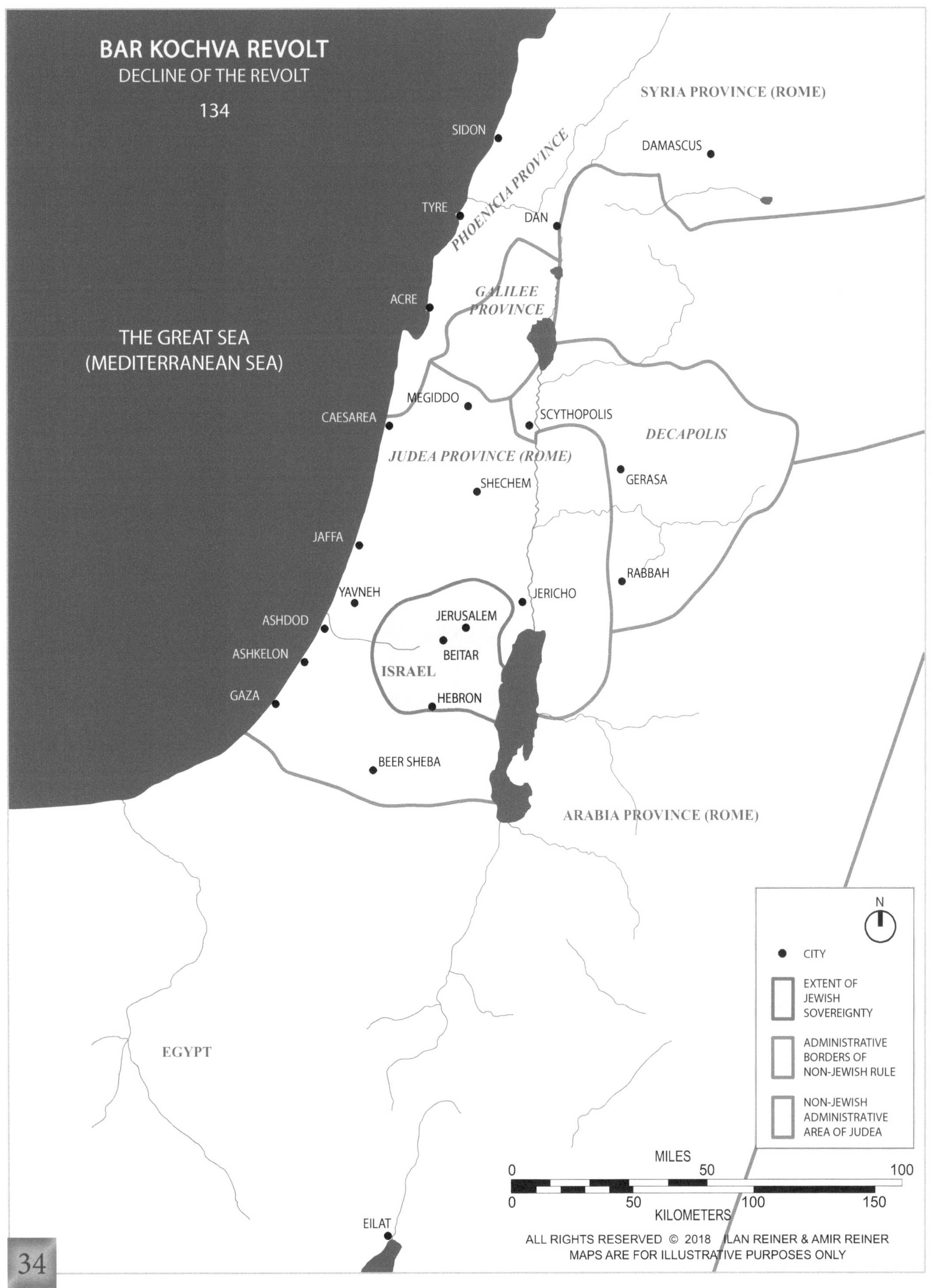
BAR KOCHVA REVOLT
DECLINE OF THE REVOLT
134
SYRIA PROVINCE (ROME)
SIDON
DAMASCUS
PHOENICIA PROVINCE
TYRE
DAN
GALILEE PROVINCE
ACRE
THE GREAT SEA (MEDITERRANEAN SEA)
MEGIDDO
CAESAREA
SCYTHOPOLIS
DECAPOLIS
JUDEA PROVINCE (ROME)
GERASA
SHECHEM
JAFFA
RABBAH
YAVNEH
JERICHO
ASHDOD
JERUSALEM
BEITAR
ASHKELON
ISRAEL
GAZA
HEBRON
BEER SHEBA
ARABIA PROVINCE (ROME)
EGYPT
N
CITY
EXTENT OF JEWISH SOVEREIGNTY
ADMINISTRATIVE BORDERS OF NON-JEWISH RULE
NON-JEWISH ADMINISTRATIVE AREA OF JUDEA
MILES
0
50
100
0
50
100
150
KILOMETERS
EILAT
ALL RIGHTS RESERVED © 2018 ILAN REINER & AMIR REINER
MAPS ARE FOR ILLUSTRATIVE PURPOSES ONLY
34

Bar Kochva Revolt
End of the Revolt
135 CE

Suffering from numerous defeats, Jewish militia forces kept retreating. After Roman troops captured Jerusalem, they prepared for the final battle in Beitar (south of Jerusalem), which was Bar Kochva's main military base and the seat of the Jewish religious leadership. After a long siege, the Romans breached the walls of Beitar and killed the majority of the city's inhabitants. Those who were not killed were sold into slavery. Many Jewish scholars and religious leaders were executed in horrifying ways. The Romans too suffered such heavy casualties, that when sending his written report to the Senate, Hadrian did not use the formal opening commonly reserved for the emperors' military correspondence: "If you and your children are in health, it is well; I and the army are in health."

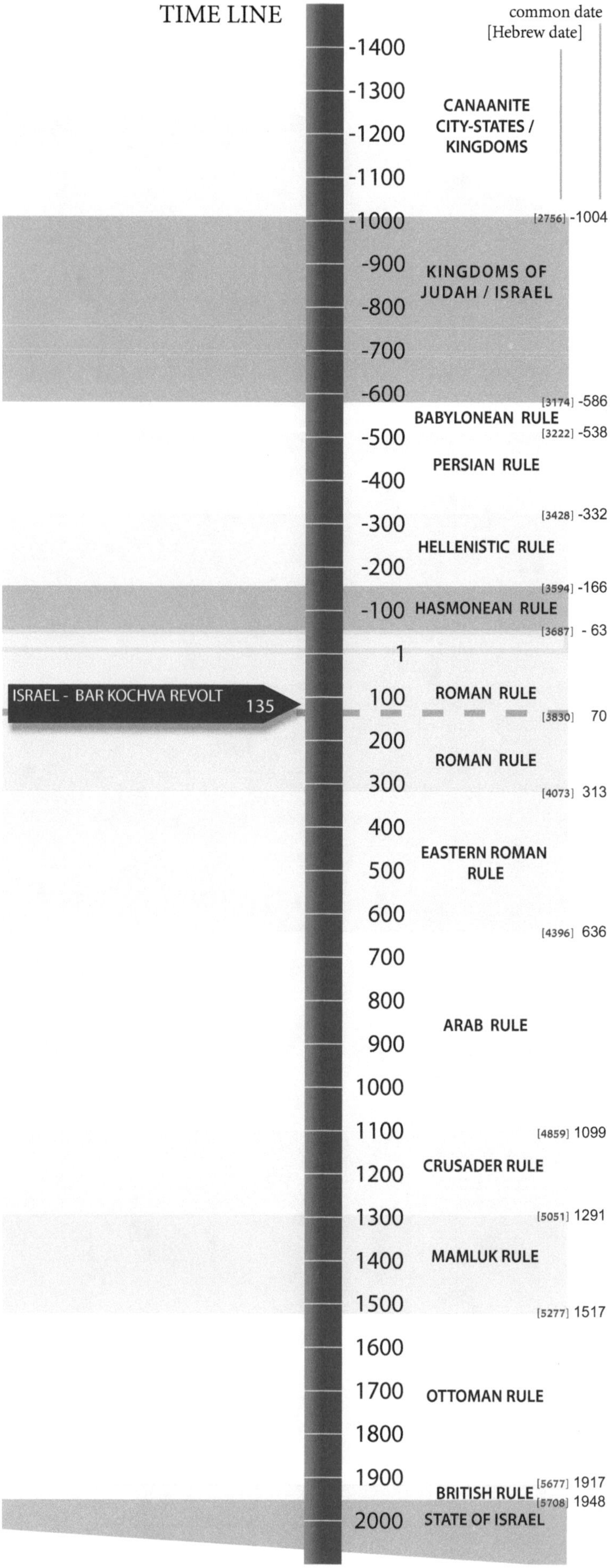

Remains of a Village Destroyed During the Revolt
Photo of Itri Ruins by: Udi Steinwell

TIME LINE

common date
[Hebrew date]

-1400
-1300
-1200
-1100
-1000
-900
-800
-700
-600
-500
-400
-300
-200
-100
1
100
200
300
400
500
600
700
800
900
1000
1100
1200
1300
1400
1500
1600
1700
1800
1900
2000

CANAANITE CITY-STATES / KINGDOMS
[2756] -1004
KINGDOMS OF JUDAH / ISRAEL
[3174] -586
BABYLONEAN RULE
[3222] -538
PERSIAN RULE
[3428] -332
HELLENISTIC RULE
[3594] -166
HASMONEAN RULE
[3687] - 63
ROMAN RULE
[3830] 70
ROMAN RULE
[4073] 313
EASTERN ROMAN RULE
[4396] 636
ARAB RULE
[4859] 1099
CRUSADER RULE
[5051] 1291
MAMLUK RULE
[5277] 1517
OTTOMAN RULE
[5677] 1917
BRITISH RULE
[5708] 1948
STATE OF ISRAEL

ISRAEL - BAR KOCHVA REVOLT 135

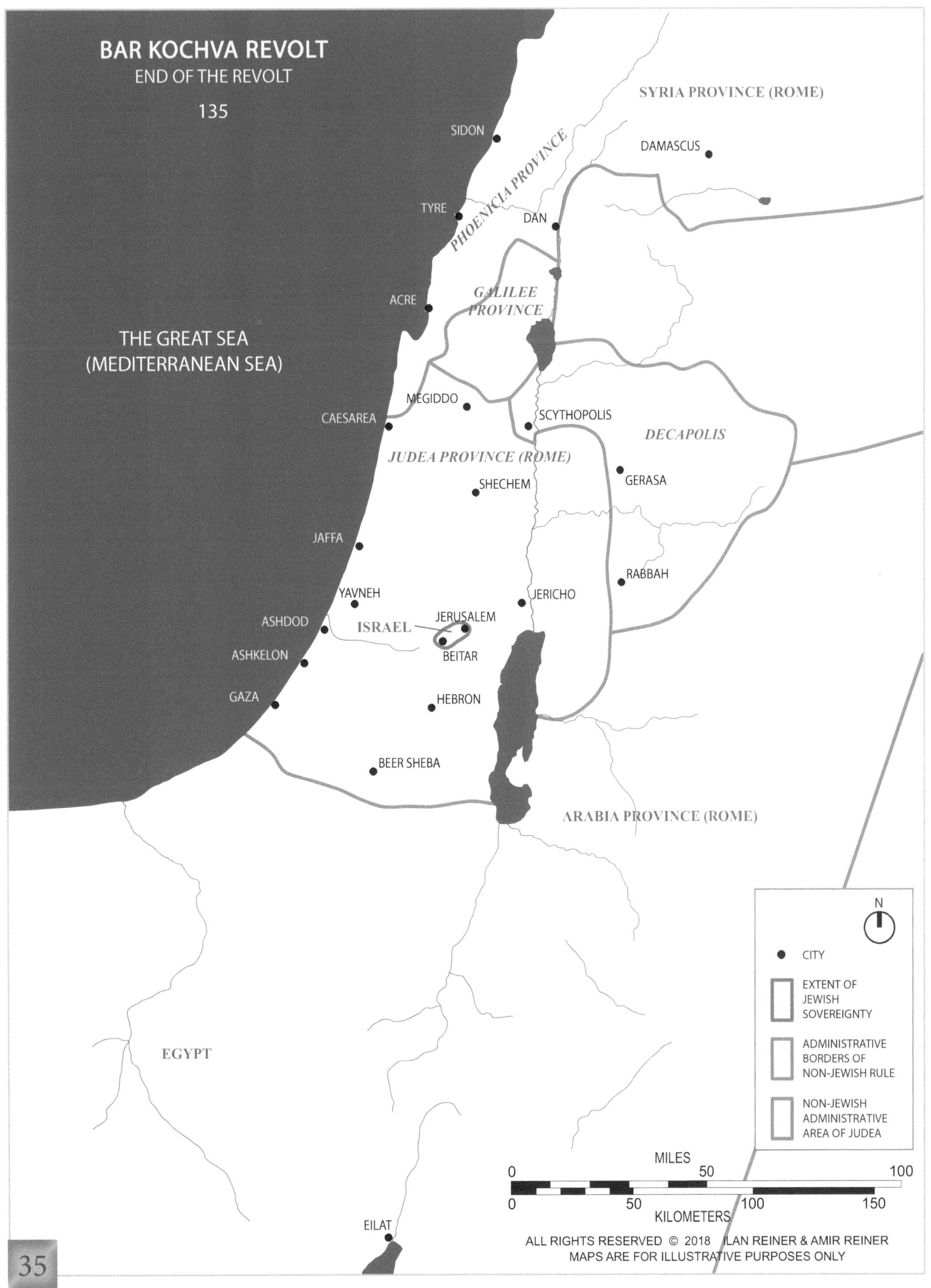
BAR KOCHVA REVOLT
END OF THE REVOLT
135
SYRIA PROVINCE (ROME)
SIDON
DAMASCUS
PHOENICIA PROVINCE
TYRE
DAN
ACRE
GALILEE PROVINCE
THE GREAT SEA
(MEDITERRANEAN SEA)
MEGIDDO
CAESAREA
SCYTHOPOLIS
DECAPOLIS
JUDEA PROVINCE (ROME)
GERASA
SHECHEM
JAFFA
RABBAH
YAVNEH
JERICHO
ASHDOD
ISRAEL
JERUSALEM
BEITAR
ASHKELON
GAZA
HEBRON
BEER SHEBA
ARABIA PROVINCE (ROME)
N
CITY
EXTENT OF JEWISH SOVEREIGNTY
ADMINISTRATIVE BORDERS OF NON-JEWISH RULE
NON-JEWISH ADMINISTRATIVE AREA OF JUDEA
EGYPT
MILES
0
50
100
0
50
100
150
KILOMETERS
EILAT
ALL RIGHTS RESERVED © 2018 ILAN REINER & AMIR REINER
MAPS ARE FOR ILLUSTRATIVE PURPOSES ONLY
35

Roman Rule
Province of Syria Palaestina
135 CE to 313 CE

Following the failed rebellion and the destruction of Jewish life in Judea, the Romans imposed severe restrictions on observance of Jewish Law. Torah scrolls were burned and scholars were killed. Emperor Hadrian built pagan statues and idolatrous temples on the Temple Mount, and renamed the city of Jerusalem as Aelia Capitolina, and the Jews were forbidden to enter. This was the only time in the history of the Roman Empire, that they attempted to erase all memory of Judea and Israel, by renaming the province as Syria Palaestina (after the Philistine people who lived there centuries prior) . For several centuries Jewish life almost ceased to exist in Judea, and instead, concentrated in the Galilee.

Ruins of Beit She'an, a city in the Jordan Valley that flourished during Classical Antiquity period

TIME LINE

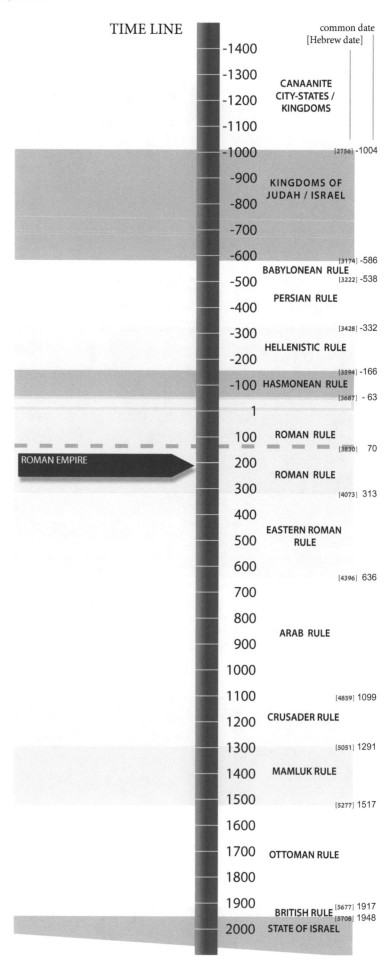

common date
[Hebrew date]

-1400
-1300
-1200
-1100
CANAANITE CITY-STATES / KINGDOMS
[2756] -1004
-1000
-900
-800
-700
KINGDOMS OF JUDAH / ISRAEL
-600
[3174] -586
BABYLONEAN RULE
[3222] -538
-500
PERSIAN RULE
-400
[3428] -332
-300
HELLENISTIC RULE
-200
[3594] -166
-100
HASMONEAN RULE
[3687] - 63
1
100
ROMAN RULE
[3830] 70
ROMAN EMPIRE
200
ROMAN RULE
300
[4073] 313
400
EASTERN ROMAN RULE
500
600
[4396] 636
700
800
ARAB RULE
900
1000
1100
[4859] 1099
CRUSADER RULE
1200
1300
[5051] 1291
1400
MAMLUK RULE
1500
[5277] 1517
1600
1700
OTTOMAN RULE
1800
1900
[5677] 1917
BRITISH RULE
[5708] 1948
2000
STATE OF ISRAEL

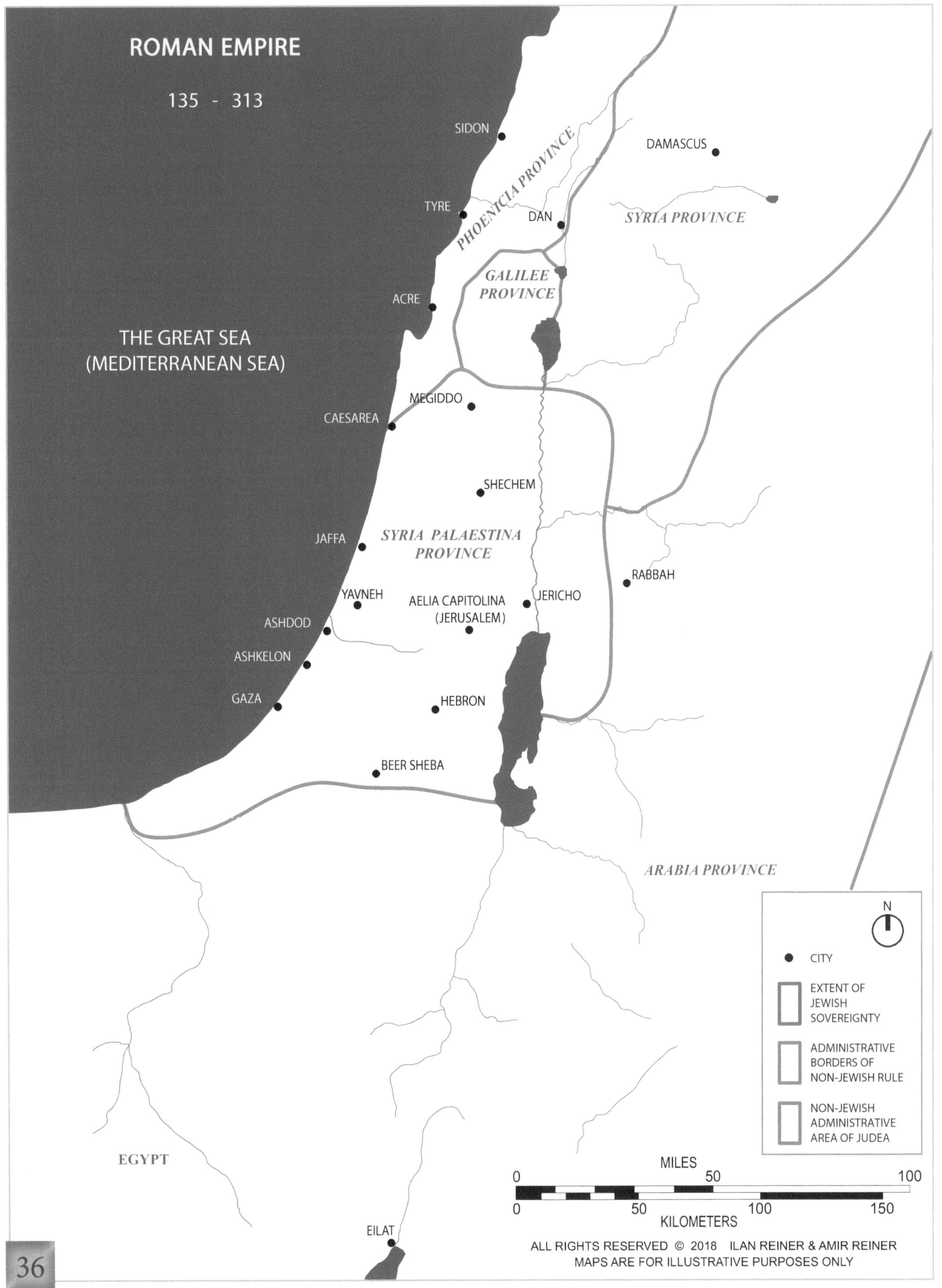
ROMAN EMPIRE
135 - 313
THE GREAT SEA
(MEDITERRANEAN SEA)
SIDON
DAMASCUS
PHOENICIA PROVINCE
TYRE
DAN
SYRIA PROVINCE
GALILEE
PROVINCE
ACRE
MEGIDDO
CAESAREA
SHECHEM
JAFFA
SYRIA PALAESTINA
PROVINCE
RABBAH
YAVNEH
AELIA CAPITOLINA
(JERUSALEM)
JERICHO
ASHDOD
ASHKELON
GAZA
HEBRON
BEER SHEBA
ARABIA PROVINCE
N
CITY
EXTENT OF JEWISH SOVEREIGNTY
ADMINISTRATIVE BORDERS OF NON-JEWISH RULE
NON-JEWISH ADMINISTRATIVE AREA OF JUDEA
EGYPT
MILES
0
50
100
0
50
100
150
KILOMETERS
EILAT
ALL RIGHTS RESERVED © 2018 ILAN REINER & AMIR REINER
MAPS ARE FOR ILLUSTRATIVE PURPOSES ONLY
36

Eastern Roman (Byzantine) Rule
Diocese (Province of) Palaestina Prima
about 313 CE to 636 CE

The rise of Christianity in the Empire also brought uneasy times for the Jews. Although they were generally persecuted to some extent, there were periods in which the government left the Jews alone. This was mainly due to the need to focus attention elsewhere when there was tension and civil unrest in other parts of the Empire. The Jewish population slowly declined over the centuries until it was a minority in the area.

During this era there was prolific building of religious monuments in what the Romans called Palestine. Some of the most important churches and monasteries were built during this era. Several sacred Jewish texts were written in Israel at this time, such as the Jerusalem Talmud and the Passover Haggadah.

Towards the end of the Byzantine era, Jerusalem was conquered by the Persians. Jews enjoyed a privileged status under Persian rule. Christians were persecuted and many churches were destroyed. Throughout the Christian world, Jews were blamed for that. After the Byzantines retook Jerusalem about a decade later, Emperor Heraclius decreed that the Jews of Palestine should be killed. No one was saved except the few who hid or fled.

Page from Medieval Jerusalem Talmud manuscript
Found in the Cairo Genizah

TIME LINE

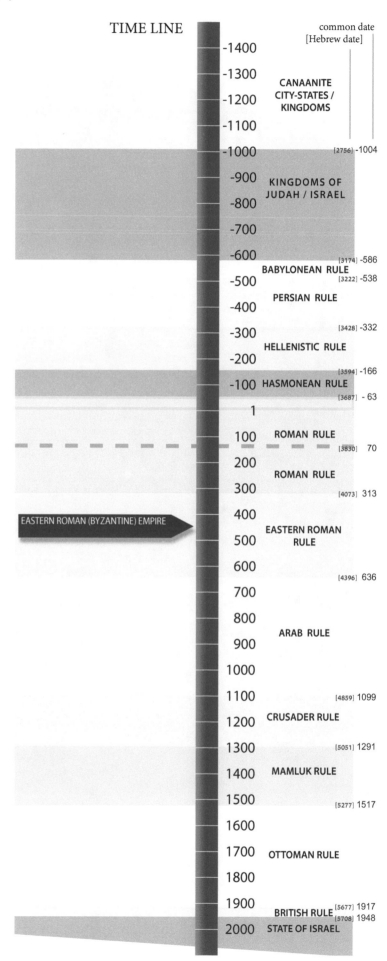

Period	common date [Hebrew date]
CANAANITE CITY-STATES / KINGDOMS	
	[2756] -1004
KINGDOMS OF JUDAH / ISRAEL	
	[3174] -586
BABYLONEAN RULE	
	[3222] -538
PERSIAN RULE	
	[3428] -332
HELLENISTIC RULE	
	[3594] -166
HASMONEAN RULE	
	[3687] - 63
ROMAN RULE	
	[3830] 70
ROMAN RULE	
	[4073] 313
EASTERN ROMAN RULE	
	[4396] 636
ARAB RULE	
	[4859] 1099
CRUSADER RULE	
	[5051] 1291
MAMLUK RULE	
	[5277] 1517
OTTOMAN RULE	
	[5677] 1917
BRITISH RULE	
	[5708] 1948
STATE OF ISRAEL	

Scale: -1400, -1300, -1200, -1100, -1000, -900, -800, -700, -600, -500, -400, -300, -200, -100, 1, 100, 200, 300, 400, 500, 600, 700, 800, 900, 1000, 1100, 1200, 1300, 1400, 1500, 1600, 1700, 1800, 1900, 2000

EASTERN ROMAN (BYZANTINE) EMPIRE

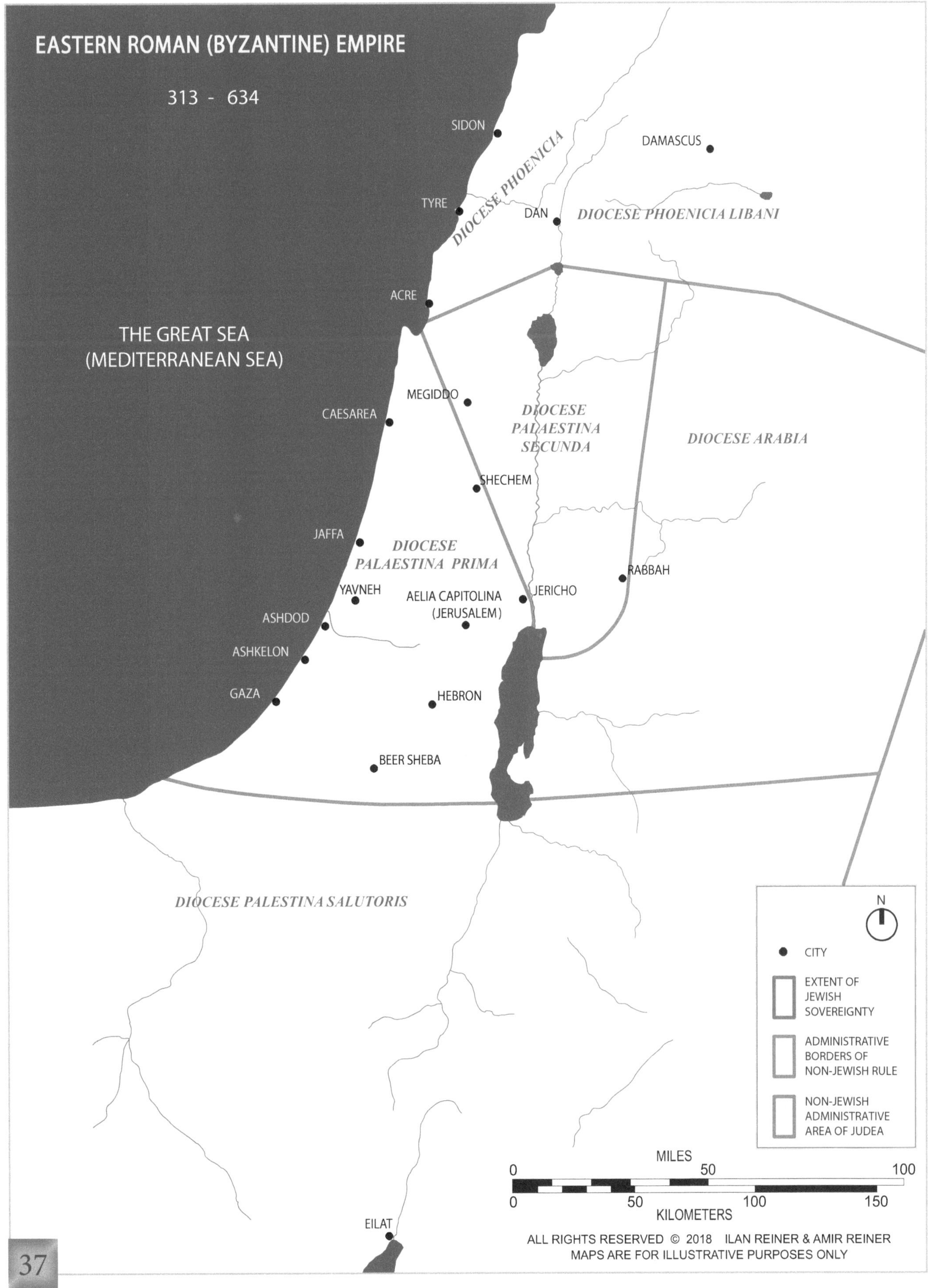

EASTERN ROMAN (BYZANTINE) EMPIRE
313 - 634
SIDON
DAMASCUS
DIOCESE PHOENICIA
TYRE
DAN
DIOCESE PHOENICIA LIBANI
ACRE
THE GREAT SEA
(MEDITERRANEAN SEA)
MEGIDDO
CAESAREA
DIOCESE
PALAESTINA
SECUNDA
DIOCESE ARABIA
SHECHEM
JAFFA
DIOCESE
PALAESTINA PRIMA
RABBAH
YAVNEH
AELIA CAPITOLINA
(JERUSALEM)
JERICHO
ASHDOD
ASHKELON
GAZA
HEBRON
BEER SHEBA
DIOCESE PALESTINA SALUTORIS
N
CITY
EXTENT OF
JEWISH
SOVEREIGNTY
ADMINISTRATIVE
BORDERS OF
NON-JEWISH RULE
NON-JEWISH
ADMINISTRATIVE
AREA OF JUDEA
MILES
0
50
100
0
50
100
150
KILOMETERS
EILAT

37

Arab Rule
Jund Filastin
about 636 CE to 1099 CE

In the mid 7th century, many Arab tribes in the Saudi desert united under a new religion called Islam. They set forth in waves of conquests, defeated the Byzantine Empire, and established a vast Arab Caliphate. The Muslim conquest of Palestine was a gradual process. During that time, many Arabs moved to Palestine, and clashed with the local Jewish population, who were the majority. Despite various restrictions, the Jews were tolerated and even respected under Muslim rule: They were allowed to have their own autonomous religious and civil institutions as long as they paid their taxes. In the late 7th century, Umayyad Caliph Abd al-Malik constructed the Dome of the Rock shrine on the Temple Mount. Jews consider it to be built where the Temple once stood. The Dome is built around a rock, which the Jews consider to be the Foundation Stone, which was in the Holy of Holies in the Temple. A second building, the Al-Aqsa Mosque, was also erected on the Temple Mount a few years later. Between the 7th and 11th centuries, Jewish scribes located in Galilee and Jerusalem, established the Masoretic Text, the final text of the Hebrew Bible.

Dome of the Rock shrine
Temple Mount, Jerusalem

TIME LINE

-1400, -1300, -1200, -1100, -1000, -900, -800, -700, -600, -500, -400, -300, -200, -100, 1, 100, 200, 300, 400, 500, 600, 700, 800, 900, 1000, 1100, 1200, 1300, 1400, 1500, 1600, 1700, 1800, 1900, 2000

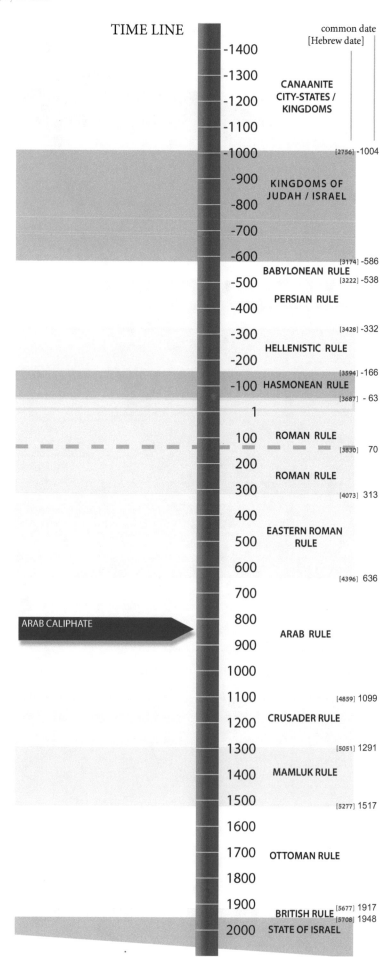

Period	common date [Hebrew date]
CANAANITE CITY-STATES / KINGDOMS	
	[2756] -1004
KINGDOMS OF JUDAH / ISRAEL	
	[3174] -586
BABYLONEAN RULE	
	[3222] -538
PERSIAN RULE	
	[3428] -332
HELLENISTIC RULE	
	[3594] -166
HASMONEAN RULE	
	[3687] - 63
ROMAN RULE	
	[3830] 70
ROMAN RULE	
	[4073] 313
EASTERN ROMAN RULE	
	[4396] 636
ARAB RULE	
	[4859] 1099
CRUSADER RULE	
	[5051] 1291
MAMLUK RULE	
	[5277] 1517
OTTOMAN RULE	
	[5677] 1917
BRITISH RULE	
	[5708] 1948
STATE OF ISRAEL	

ARAB CALIPHATE

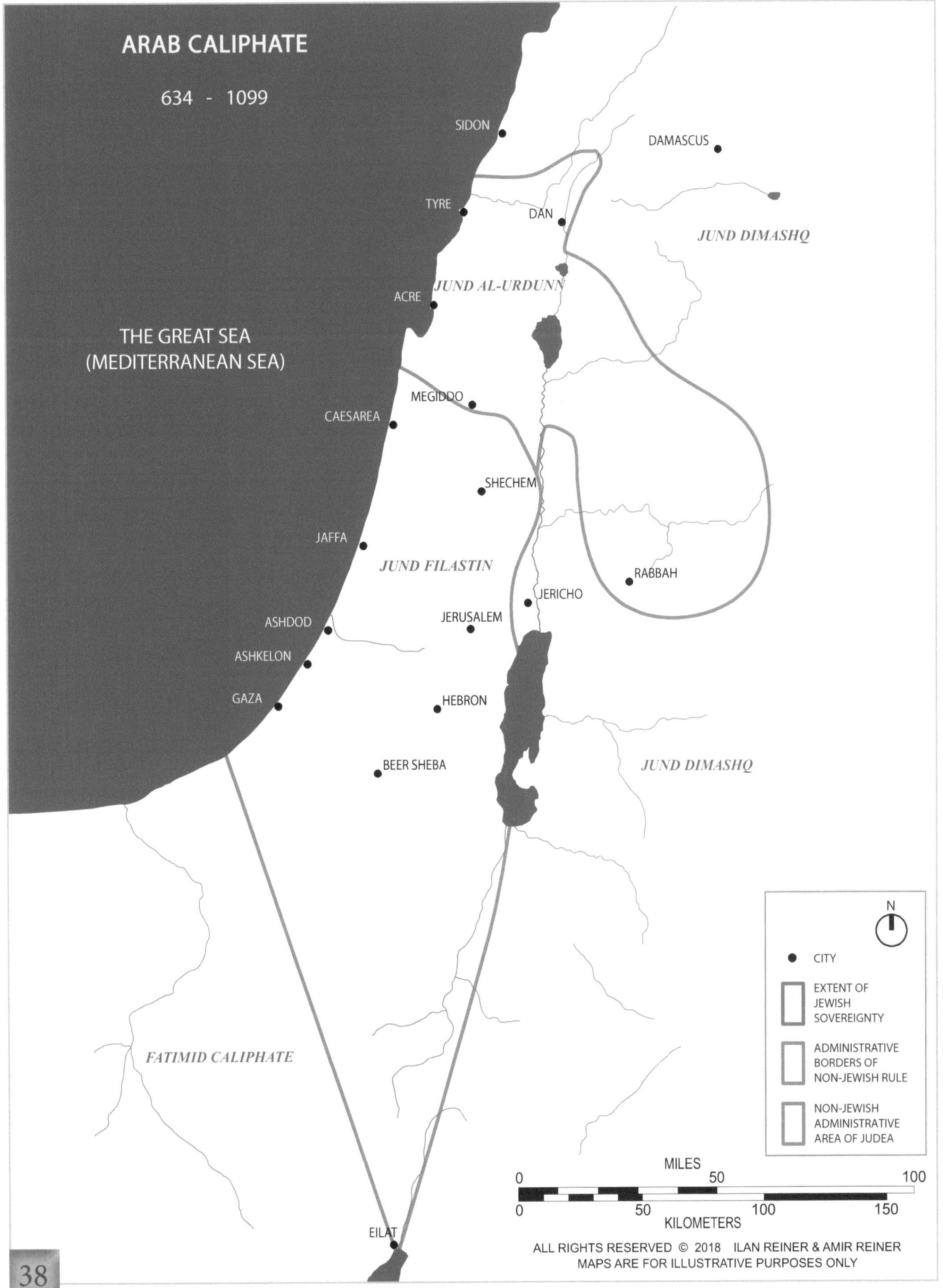
ARAB CALIPHATE
634 - 1099
SIDON
DAMASCUS
TYRE
DAN
JUND DIMASHQ
JUND AL-URDUNN
ACRE
THE GREAT SEA
(MEDITERRANEAN SEA)
MEGIDDO
CAESAREA
SHECHEM
JAFFA
JUND FILASTIN
RABBAH
JERICHO
JERUSALEM
ASHDOD
ASHKELON
GAZA
HEBRON
BEER SHEBA
JUND DIMASHQ
N
CITY
EXTENT OF JEWISH SOVEREIGNTY
ADMINISTRATIVE BORDERS OF NON-JEWISH RULE
NON-JEWISH ADMINISTRATIVE AREA OF JUDEA
FATIMID CALIPHATE
MILES
0
50
100
0
50
100
150
KILOMETERS
EILAT
ALL RIGHTS RESERVED © 2018 ILAN REINER & AMIR REINER
MAPS ARE FOR ILLUSTRATIVE PURPOSES ONLY
38

Kingdom of Jerusalem
Christian (Crusader) Rule
about 1099 CE to 1291 CE

The Church's call to free Jerusalem from Muslim hands led thousands of knights and common soldiers in several Crusades to the Holy Land. On their way, they annihilated hundreds of Jewish communities in Europe until they arrived at the gates of Jerusalem in 1099. On the conquered land, the crusaders established the Kingdom of Jerusalem, with numerous fortresses and supply stations to protect against the Arab attacks. Less than a century after her establishment, the Christian Kingdom fell following defeat by Arab forces, led by the Ayyubid Sultan, Saladin, who defeated the Crusaders in the Battle of Hattin. A second attempt to establish a Christian kingdom decades later lasted only for a short period of time. Some Christian orders still have land and property in Israel today, dating back to the times of the Crusades.

Capture of Jerusalem during the First Crusade, 1099
Unidentified late medieval illustration

TIME LINE

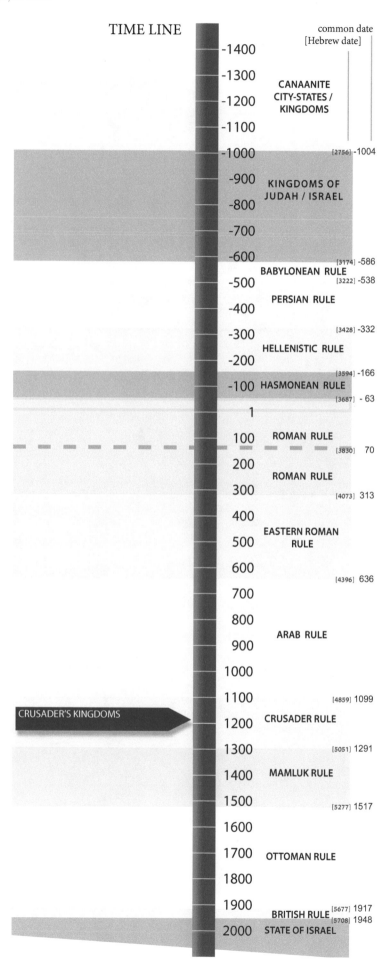

common date
[Hebrew date]

-1400
-1300
-1200
-1100
CANAANITE CITY-STATES / KINGDOMS
[2756] -1004
-1000
-900
-800
-700
KINGDOMS OF JUDAH / ISRAEL
-600
[3174] -586
BABYLONEAN RULE
[3222] -538
-500
PERSIAN RULE
-400
[3428] -332
-300
HELLENISTIC RULE
-200
[3594] -166
-100
HASMONEAN RULE
[3687] - 63
1
100
ROMAN RULE
[3830] 70
200
ROMAN RULE
300
[4073] 313
400
EASTERN ROMAN RULE
500
600
[4396] 636
700
800
ARAB RULE
900
1000
1100
[4859] 1099
CRUSADER'S KINGDOMS
CRUSADER RULE
1200
1300
[5051] 1291
1400
MAMLUK RULE
1500
[5277] 1517
1600
1700
OTTOMAN RULE
1800
1900
[5677] 1917
BRITISH RULE
[5708] 1948
2000
STATE OF ISRAEL

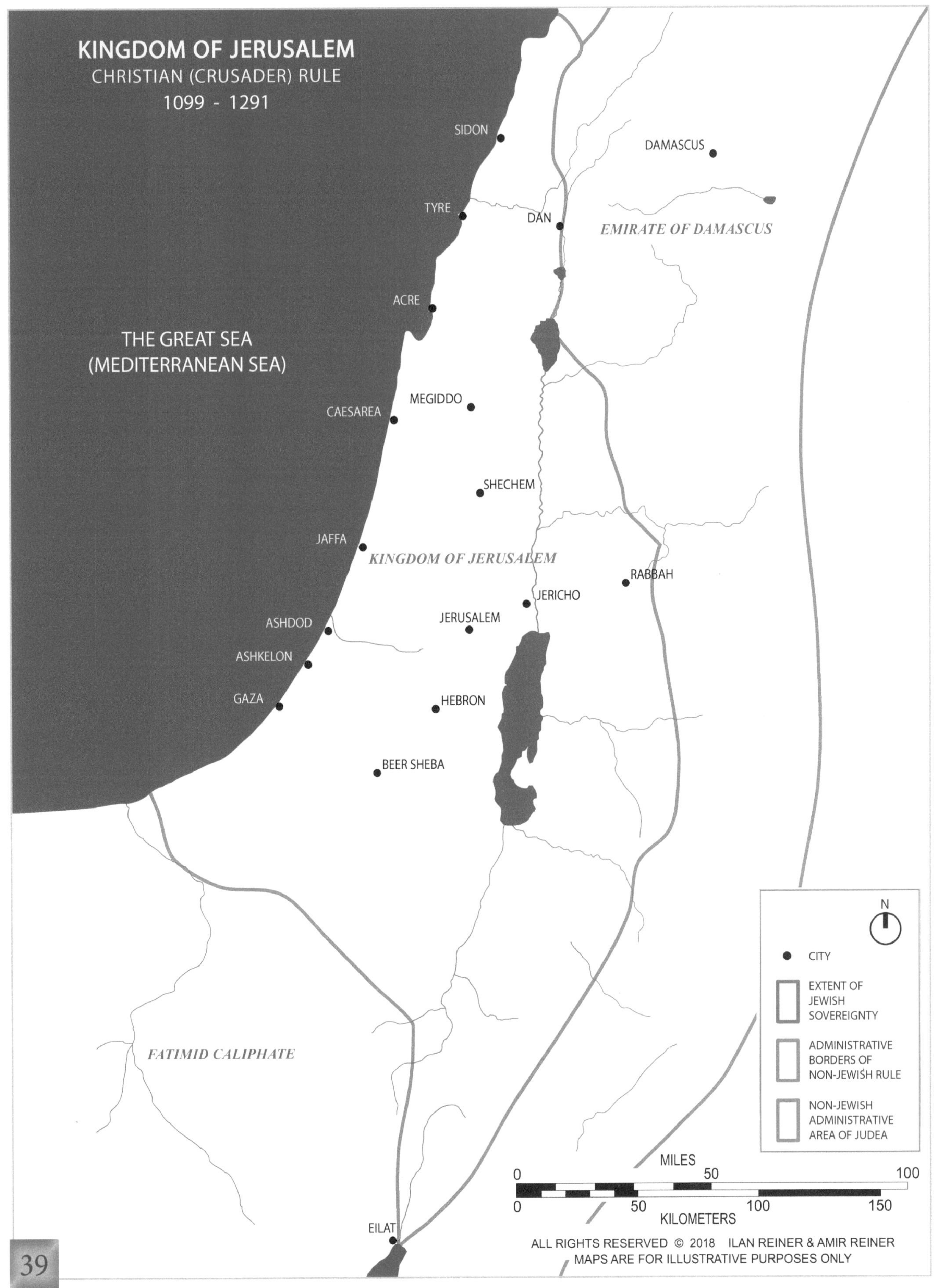
KINGDOM OF JERUSALEM
CHRISTIAN (CRUSADER) RULE
1099 - 1291
SIDON
DAMASCUS
TYRE
DAN
EMIRATE OF DAMASCUS
ACRE
THE GREAT SEA
(MEDITERRANEAN SEA)
MEGIDDO
CAESAREA
SHECHEM
JAFFA
KINGDOM OF JERUSALEM
RABBAH
JERICHO
JERUSALEM
ASHDOD
ASHKELON
GAZA
HEBRON
BEER SHEBA
FATIMID CALIPHATE
EILAT
N
CITY
EXTENT OF JEWISH SOVEREIGNTY
ADMINISTRATIVE BORDERS OF NON-JEWISH RULE
NON-JEWISH ADMINISTRATIVE AREA OF JUDEA
MILES
0
50
100
0
50
100
150
KILOMETERS
ALL RIGHTS RESERVED © 2018 ILAN REINER & AMIR REINER
MAPS ARE FOR ILLUSTRATIVE PURPOSES ONLY
39

Mamluk Sultanate Rule
Damascus Wilayah
about 1291 CE to 1517 CE

The Mamluks, a Muslim (non-Arab) people who took over Egypt, began their expansion north during the middle of the 13th century. For them, Israel was just a land between Egypt and Syria, as well as being the site of holy cities mentioned in the Quran. Mamluk rulers called the Jews to settle in Israel and offered them protection and religious freedom. In addition to Jews who lived there for generations, many new Jewish immigrants arrived. Some Jews came from Europe due to persecution and some came from Spain, following the expulsion of the Jews from Spain in 1492. Much of the Jewish population living in Israel was supported by Jewish communities in Europe.

Three Mamelukes with lances on horseback
By: Daniel Hopfer

TIME LINE

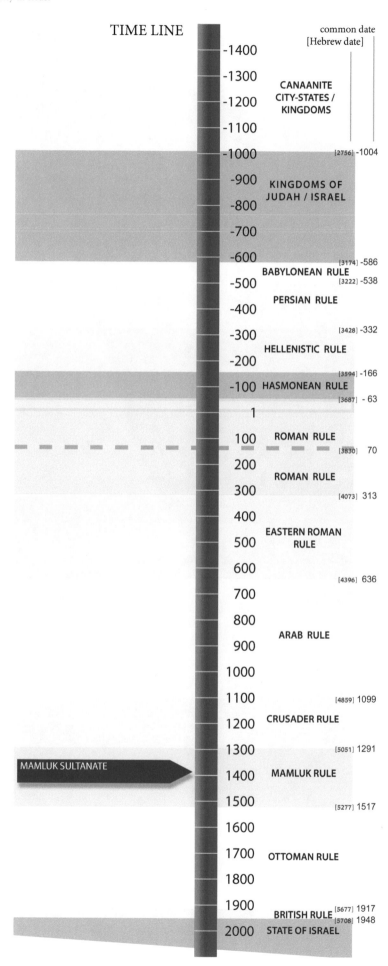

common date
[Hebrew date]

-1400
-1300
-1200
-1100
CANAANITE CITY-STATES / KINGDOMS
[2756] -1004
-1000
-900
-800
-700
KINGDOMS OF JUDAH / ISRAEL
-600
[3174] -586
BABYLONEAN RULE
[3222] -538
-500
-400
PERSIAN RULE
[3428] -332
-300
-200
HELLENISTIC RULE
[3594] -166
-100
HASMONEAN RULE
[3687] - 63
1
100
ROMAN RULE
[3830] 70
200
300
ROMAN RULE
[4073] 313
400
500
600
EASTERN ROMAN RULE
[4396] 636
700
800
900
1000
ARAB RULE
1100
[4859] 1099
1200
CRUSADER RULE
[5051] 1291
1300
1400
MAMLUK SULTANATE
MAMLUK RULE
1500
[5277] 1517
1600
1700
1800
OTTOMAN RULE
1900
[5677] 1917
BRITISH RULE
[5708] 1948
2000
STATE OF ISRAEL

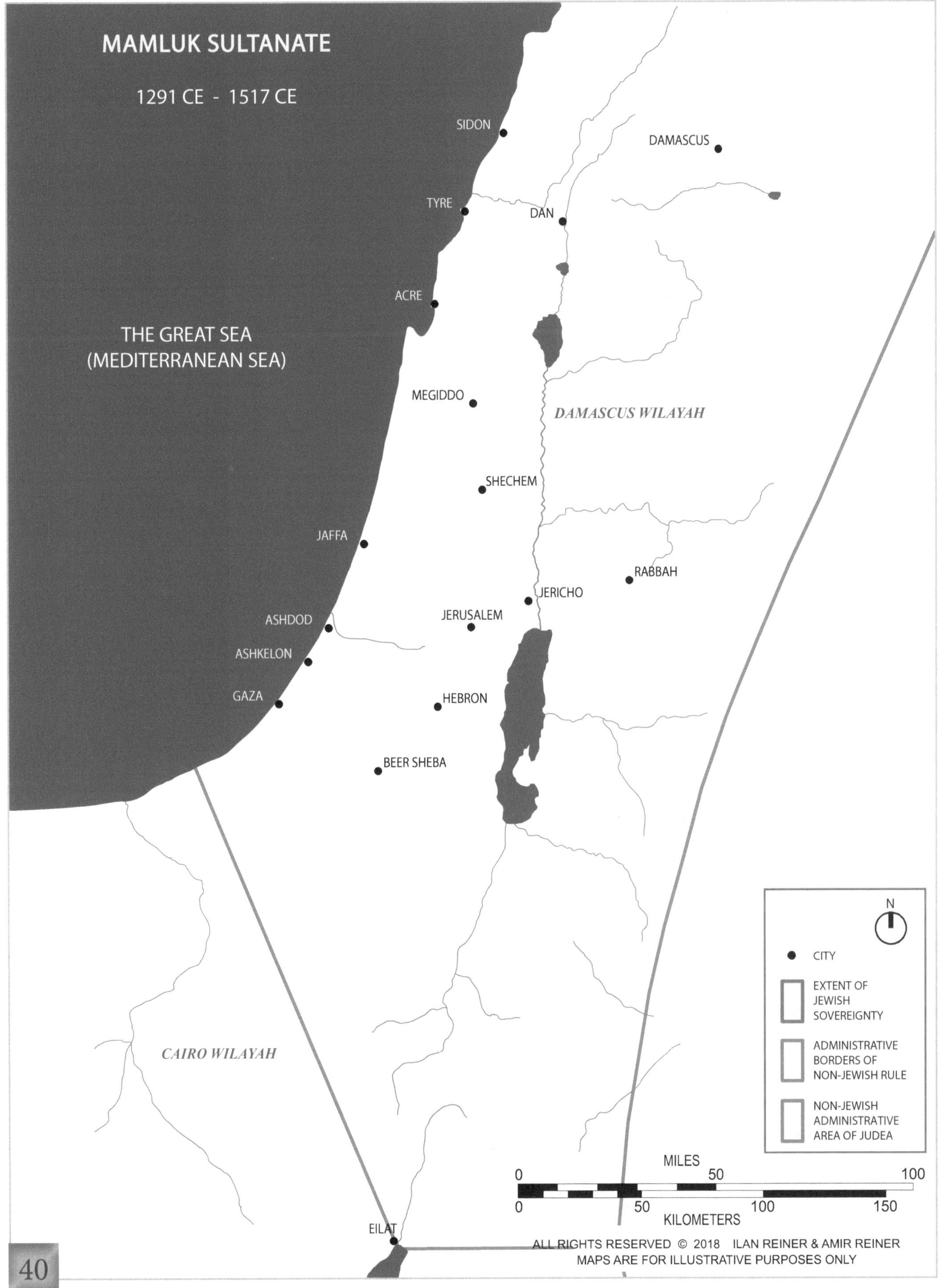
MAMLUK SULTANATE
1291 CE - 1517 CE
SIDON
DAMASCUS
TYRE
DAN
ACRE
THE GREAT SEA
(MEDITERRANEAN SEA)
MEGIDDO
DAMASCUS WILAYAH
SHECHEM
JAFFA
RABBAH
JERICHO
JERUSALEM
ASHDOD
ASHKELON
GAZA
HEBRON
BEER SHEBA
N
CITY
EXTENT OF JEWISH SOVEREIGNTY
ADMINISTRATIVE BORDERS OF NON-JEWISH RULE
NON-JEWISH ADMINISTRATIVE AREA OF JUDEA
CAIRO WILAYAH
MILES
0
50
100
0
50
100
150
KILOMETERS
EILAT
ALL RIGHTS RESERVED © 2018 ILAN REINER & AMIR REINER
MAPS ARE FOR ILLUSTRATIVE PURPOSES ONLY
40

Ottoman Rule
Syria (Damascus) Eyalet
about 1517 CE to 1872 CE

During the 15th and 16th centuries, the Ottoman Empire entered a long period of conquest and expanded her borders. The conquest of the land of Israel was vital in order to establish Ottoman rule in Egypt and naval presence in the Red Sea. Israel was included in Damascus Eyalet (Damascus Province) and was scarcely populated. During the reign of Suleiman the Magnificent in the 16th century, Jerusalem, named in Arabic, Al-Quds, enjoyed much development and flourished with new buildings and new city walls. In 1799 Napoleon briefly occupied the land and even planned a proclamation inviting Jews to create a national state for themselves. The proclamation was shelved following his defeat at Acre.

TIME LINE

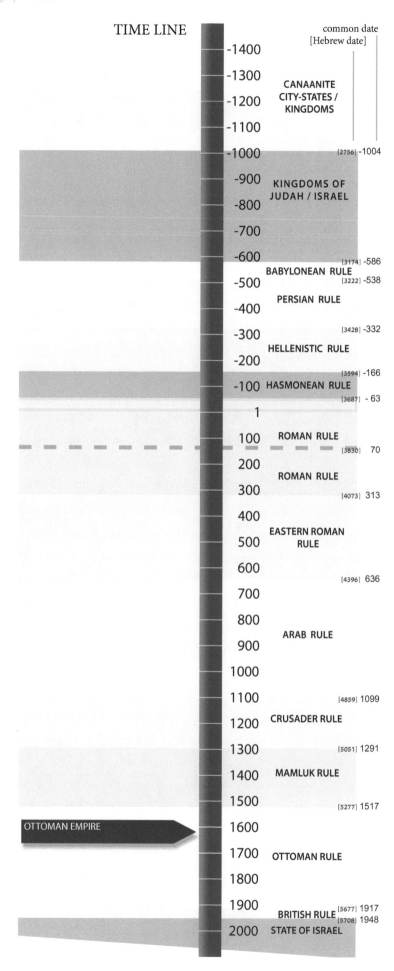

common date [Hebrew date]

Scale	Period	Dates
-1400, -1300, -1200, -1100	CANAANITE CITY-STATES / KINGDOMS	
-1000, -900, -800, -700, -600	KINGDOMS OF JUDAH / ISRAEL	[2756] -1004
	BABYLONEAN RULE	[3174] -586
-500, -400	PERSIAN RULE	[3222] -538
-300, -200	HELLENISTIC RULE	[3428] -332
-100	HASMONEAN RULE	[3594] -166
1, 100	ROMAN RULE	[3687] - 63
200, 300	ROMAN RULE	[3830] 70
400, 500, 600	EASTERN ROMAN RULE	[4073] 313
700, 800, 900, 1000	ARAB RULE	[4396] 636
1100, 1200	CRUSADER RULE	[4859] 1099
1300, 1400, 1500	MAMLUK RULE	[5051] 1291
1600, 1700, 1800	OTTOMAN RULE	[5277] 1517
1900	BRITISH RULE	[5677] 1917
2000	STATE OF ISRAEL	[5708] 1948

OTTOMAN EMPIRE

Jerusalem's City Walls as built by Sultan Suleiman the Magnificent

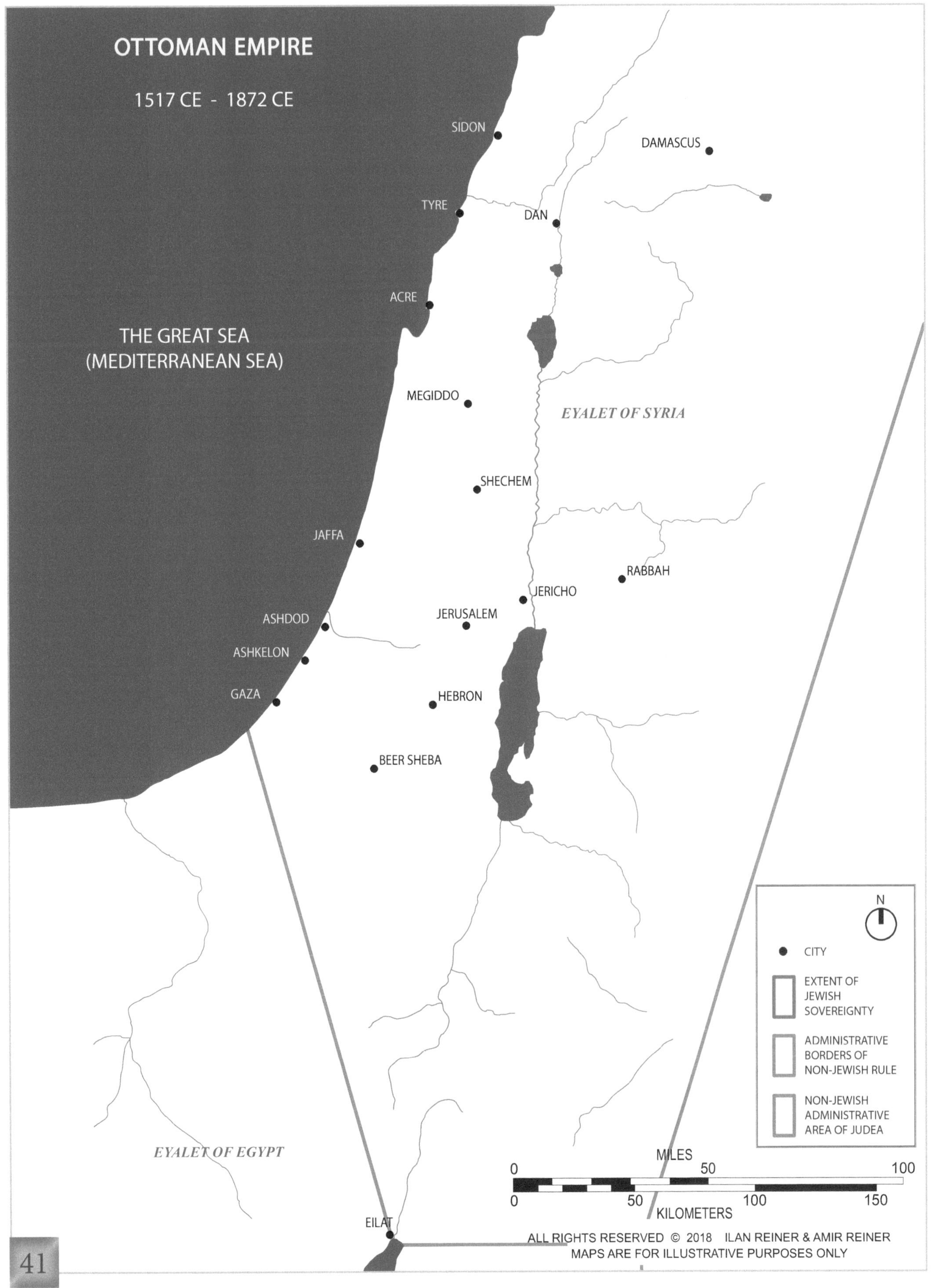
OTTOMAN EMPIRE
1517 CE - 1872 CE
SIDON
DAMASCUS
TYRE
DAN
ACRE
THE GREAT SEA
(MEDITERRANEAN SEA)
MEGIDDO
EYALET OF SYRIA
SHECHEM
JAFFA
RABBAH
JERICHO
JERUSALEM
ASHDOD
ASHKELON
GAZA
HEBRON
BEER SHEBA
N
CITY
EXTENT OF JEWISH SOVEREIGNTY
ADMINISTRATIVE BORDERS OF NON-JEWISH RULE
NON-JEWISH ADMINISTRATIVE AREA OF JUDEA
EYALET OF EGYPT
MILES
0
50
100
0
50
100
150
KILOMETERS
EILAT
41
ALL RIGHTS RESERVED © 2018 ILAN REINER & AMIR REINER
MAPS ARE FOR ILLUSTRATIVE PURPOSES ONLY

Ottoman Rule
Sanjak of Jerusalem
about 1874 CE to 1917 CE

One of the administrative changes made in Palestine during the mid-19th century, was subjecting Jerusalem directly to the administration in Istanbul. This reflected the rise in importance of Israel on an international level at the time. The arrival of many immigrants created the need to form a standard structure and administration for real-estate transactions (namely, the Tabo). The Tabo made it easier for Jews outside of Israel to purchase land in Israel.

The growing Zionist movement brought many Jewish immigrants from Europe and Russia. Those waves of immigration are called Aliyot (plural for Aliyah, literally, ascension). During the 1880's and 1890's Aliyah, about 30,000 Jews immigrated to Israel and established many agricultural settlements. During the Aliyah of the early 20th century (until World War I), about 35,000 Jews immigrated.

The Jewish population grew more than five times in size during this era, from about 22,000 in 1878 to about 84,000 in 1922. They became more significant and independent, creating their own local Jewish-Zionist lifestyle. Ottoman rule ended by the British conquest of Palestine at the end of World War I, which was greatly supported by the Jews.

Jews Immigrating to Israel
The Palmach Archives

TIME LINE

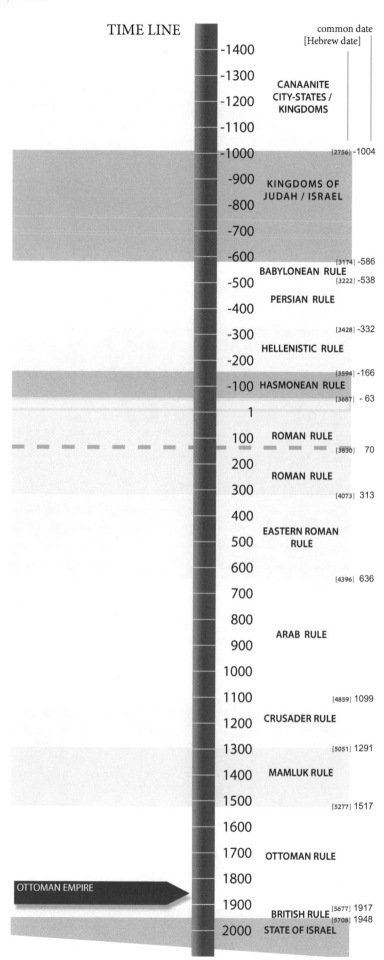

common date [Hebrew date]

Scale	Period	Date
-1400		
-1300	CANAANITE CITY-STATES / KINGDOMS	
-1200		
-1100		
-1000		[2756] -1004
-900	KINGDOMS OF JUDAH / ISRAEL	
-800		
-700		
-600		[3174] -586
-500	BABYLONEAN RULE	[3222] -538
-400	PERSIAN RULE	
-300		[3428] -332
-200	HELLENISTIC RULE	
-100		[3594] -166
	HASMONEAN RULE	[3687] - 63
1		
100	ROMAN RULE	[3830] 70
200	ROMAN RULE	
300		[4073] 313
400		
500	EASTERN ROMAN RULE	
600		[4396] 636
700		
800	ARAB RULE	
900		
1000		
1100		[4859] 1099
1200	CRUSADER RULE	
1300		[5051] 1291
1400	MAMLUK RULE	
1500		[5277] 1517
1600		
1700	OTTOMAN RULE	
1800	OTTOMAN EMPIRE	
1900	BRITISH RULE	[5677] 1917
2000	STATE OF ISRAEL	[5708] 1948

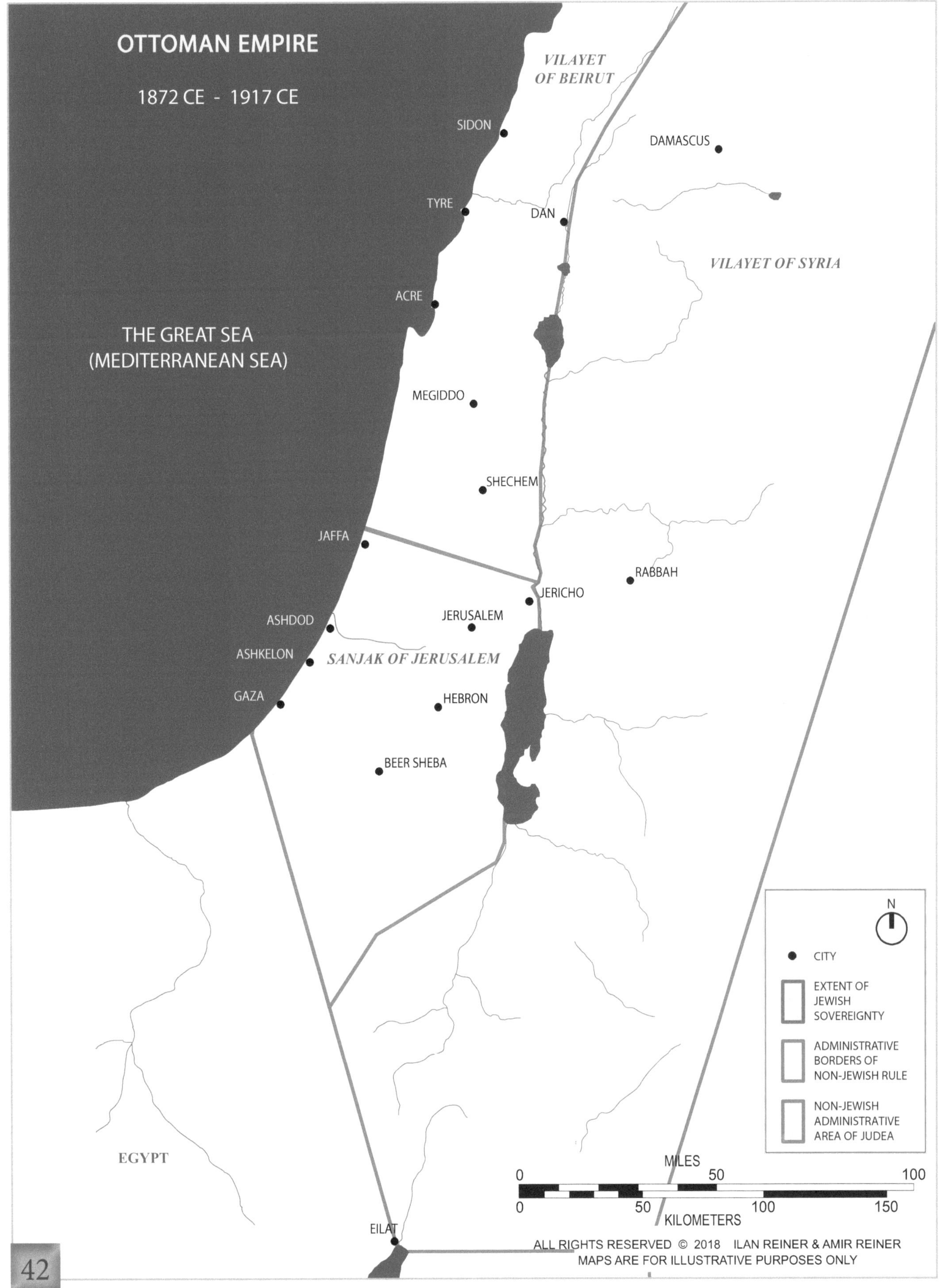
OTTOMAN EMPIRE
1872 CE - 1917 CE
VILAYET OF BEIRUT
SIDON
DAMASCUS
TYRE
DAN
VILAYET OF SYRIA
ACRE
THE GREAT SEA (MEDITERRANEAN SEA)
MEGIDDO
SHECHEM
JAFFA
RABBAH
JERICHO
JERUSALEM
ASHDOD
ASHKELON
SANJAK OF JERUSALEM
GAZA
HEBRON
BEER SHEBA
N
CITY
EXTENT OF JEWISH SOVEREIGNTY
ADMINISTRATIVE BORDERS OF NON-JEWISH RULE
NON-JEWISH ADMINISTRATIVE AREA OF JUDEA
EGYPT
MILES
0 50 100
0 50 100 150
KILOMETERS
EILAT
ALL RIGHTS RESERVED © 2018 ILAN REINER & AMIR REINER
MAPS ARE FOR ILLUSTRATIVE PURPOSES ONLY
42

British Rule
Occupied Enemy Territory Administration
1917 CE to 1923 CE

At the end of the First World War, Britain established an administration system to govern the territories captured in that war. The Occupied Enemy Territory Administration was created in Palestine and Trans-Jordan as a single administration. In November 1917, shortly after conquering Israel during World War I, British foreign minister Balfour issued "The Balfour Declaration". The declaration stated that the British would support the establishment of a Jewish home in Palestine. Jews considered this a very promising step towards establishing an independent Jewish state, and embraced the British mandate rule authorized by the League of Nations after World War I. However, Britain also made a promise to create an Emirate under the rule of the Hashemite family. This promise was the basis of the division of the administered territory as two separate mandates. In 1922 the League of Nations set out to create a Mandate system that would allow Britain to administer these territories "until such time as they are able to stand alone."

Arrival of Sir H. Samuel and other delegates
Available by G. Eric and Edith Matson Collection, Library of Congress

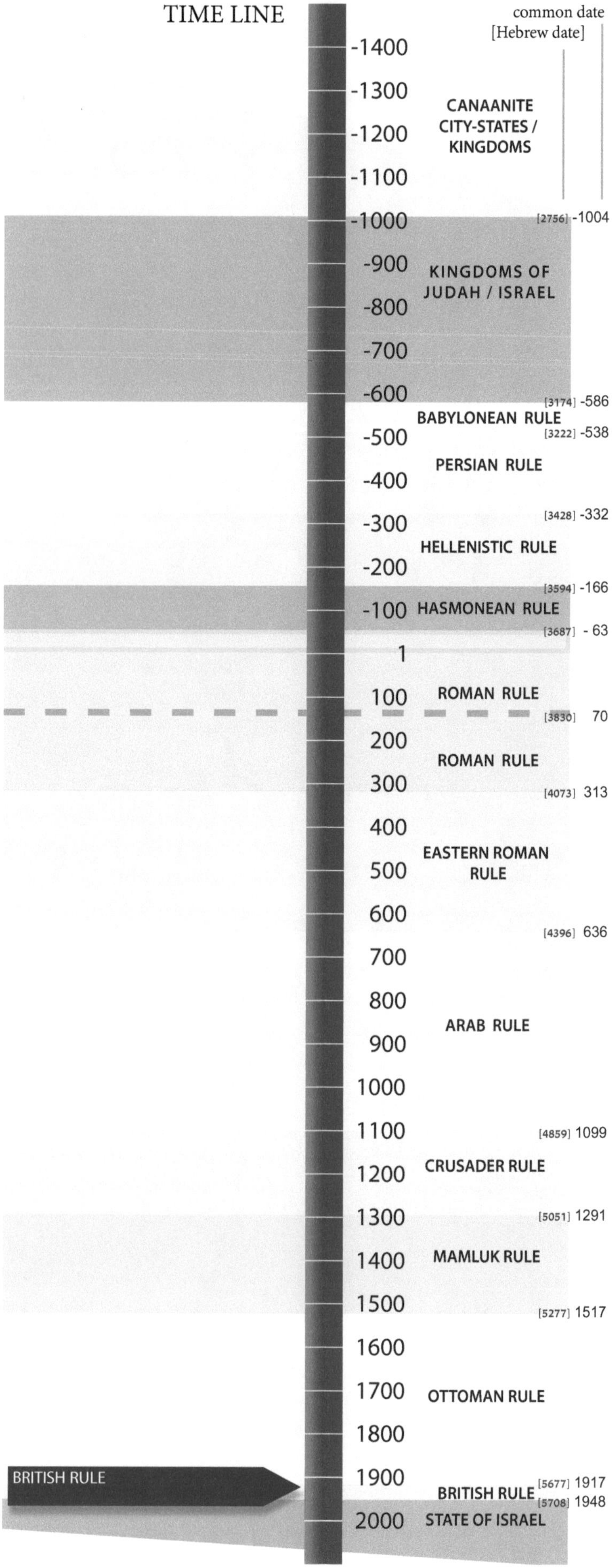

TIME LINE

common date
[Hebrew date]

-1400
-1300
CANAANITE CITY-STATES / KINGDOMS
-1200
-1100
[2756] -1004
-1000
-900
KINGDOMS OF JUDAH / ISRAEL
-800
-700
-600
[3174] -586
BABYLONEAN RULE
[3222] -538
-500
PERSIAN RULE
-400
[3428] -332
-300
HELLENISTIC RULE
-200
[3594] -166
-100 HASMONEAN RULE
[3687] - 63
1
100 ROMAN RULE
[3830] 70
200
ROMAN RULE
300
[4073] 313
400
EASTERN ROMAN RULE
500
600
[4396] 636
700
800
ARAB RULE
900
1000
1100
[4859] 1099
CRUSADER RULE
1200
1300
[5051] 1291
1400 MAMLUK RULE
1500
[5277] 1517
1600
1700 OTTOMAN RULE
1800
BRITISH RULE
1900
[5677] 1917
BRITISH RULE
[5708] 1948
2000 STATE OF ISRAEL

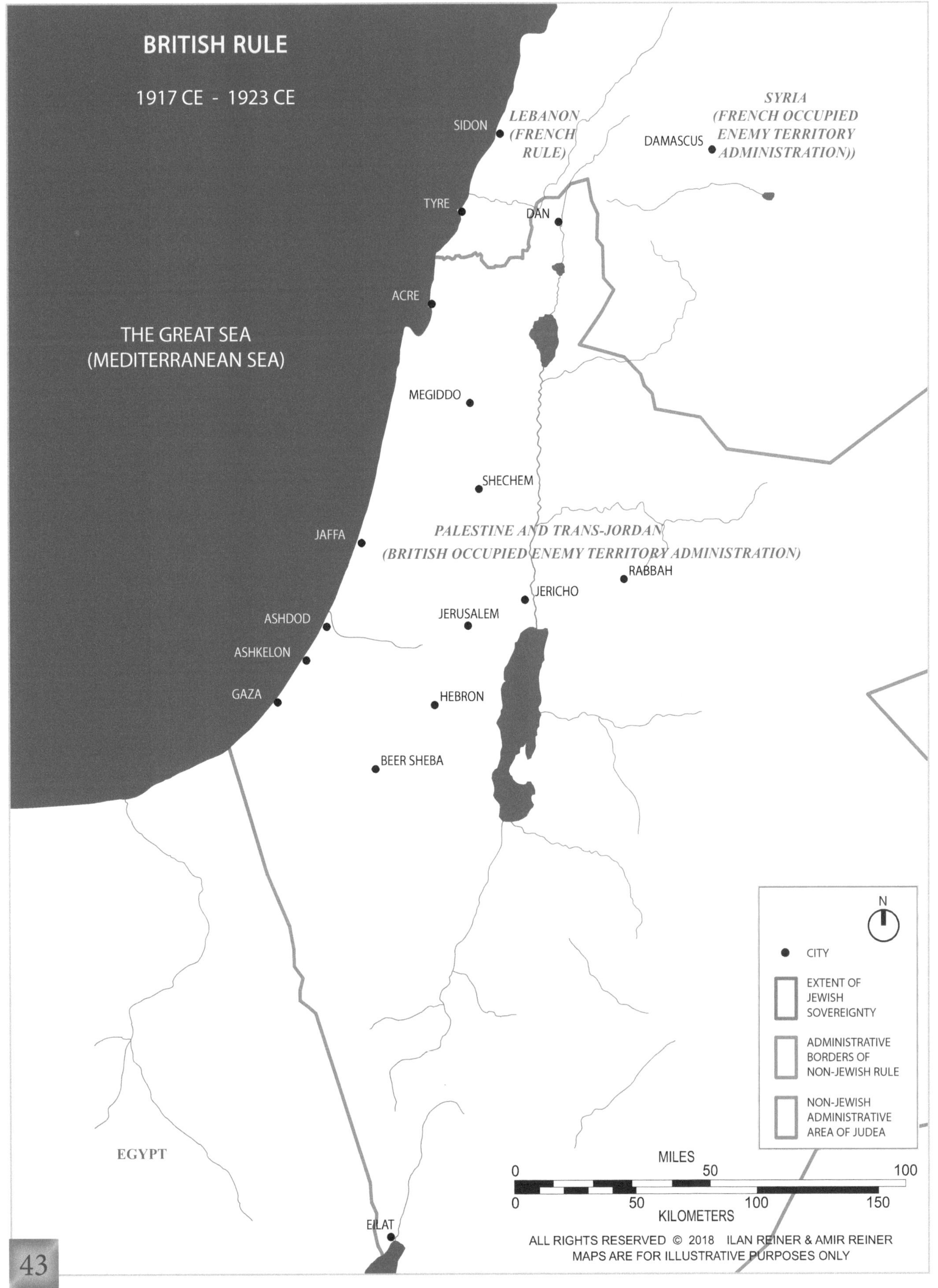

BRITISH RULE
1917 CE - 1923 CE
SIDON
LEBANON (FRENCH RULE)
DAMASCUS
SYRIA (FRENCH OCCUPIED ENEMY TERRITORY ADMINISTRATION))
TYRE
DAN
ACRE
THE GREAT SEA (MEDITERRANEAN SEA)
MEGIDDO
SHECHEM
JAFFA
PALESTINE AND TRANS-JORDAN (BRITISH OCCUPIED ENEMY TERRITORY ADMINISTRATION)
RABBAH
JERICHO
JERUSALEM
ASHDOD
ASHKELON
GAZA
HEBRON
BEER SHEBA
EGYPT
EILAT
N
CITY
EXTENT OF JEWISH SOVEREIGNTY
ADMINISTRATIVE BORDERS OF NON-JEWISH RULE
NON-JEWISH ADMINISTRATIVE AREA OF JUDEA
MILES
0 50 100
0 50 100 150
KILOMETERS
ALL RIGHTS RESERVED © 2018 ILAN REINER & AMIR REINER
MAPS ARE FOR ILLUSTRATIVE PURPOSES ONLY
43

British Rule
Mandatory Palestine
1923 CE to 1948 CE

In 1923 the Mandates for Palestine and Trans-Jordan were ratified by the League of Nations. Despite the initial intent to develop the mandates until they would become independent countries, Britain wasn't eager to give up the colony of Palestine so quickly, especially after making vast investments in infrastructure and industry, that became significantly important before and during World War II. Also the local Arab population didn't view favorably a creation of a Jewish state, and there were continuous violent clashes between the British, Arabs and Jews. Despite the many restrictions and efforts on behalf of the British to limit Jewish immigration, the Zionist Underground managed to smuggle thousands of Jewish immigrants into Israel, especially following the Holocaust in Europe. During the last years of the British Mandate, the Jews began preparing for an independent state by creating national authorities as well as armed forces (to defend against Arab resistance). Besides building many new towns, the Jews had significantly developed Israel during those years in all fields: public works, infrastructure, education, agriculture, science, architecture, the arts and more.

Anglo-Palestine Bank and Post Office Building
Was located on Jaffa Road, Jerusalem

TIME LINE

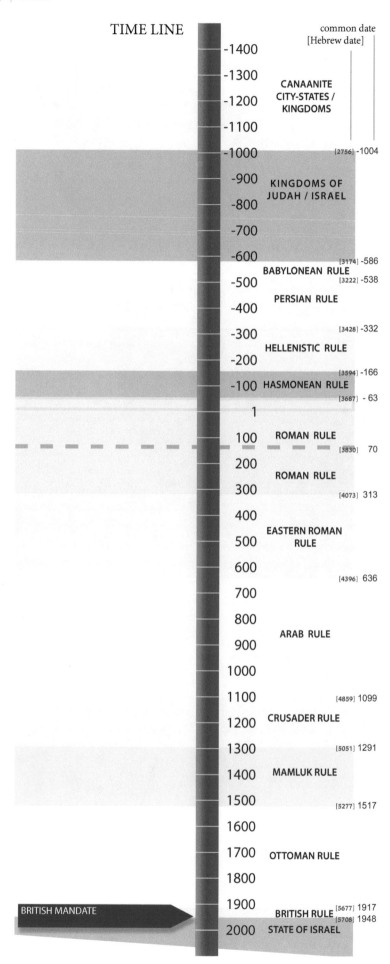

common date
[Hebrew date]

-1400
-1300
-1200
-1100
-1000
-900
-800
-700
-600
-500
-400
-300
-200
-100
1
100
200
300
400
500
600
700
800
900
1000
1100
1200
1300
1400
1500
1600
1700
1800
1900
2000

CANAANITE CITY-STATES / KINGDOMS
[2756] -1004
KINGDOMS OF JUDAH / ISRAEL
[3174] -586
BABYLONEAN RULE
[3222] -538
PERSIAN RULE
[3428] -332
HELLENISTIC RULE
[3594] -166
HASMONEAN RULE
[3687] - 63
ROMAN RULE
[3830] 70
ROMAN RULE
[4073] 313
EASTERN ROMAN RULE
[4396] 636
ARAB RULE
[4859] 1099
CRUSADER RULE
[5051] 1291
MAMLUK RULE
[5277] 1517
OTTOMAN RULE
[5677] 1917
BRITISH RULE
[5708] 1948
STATE OF ISRAEL

BRITISH MANDATE

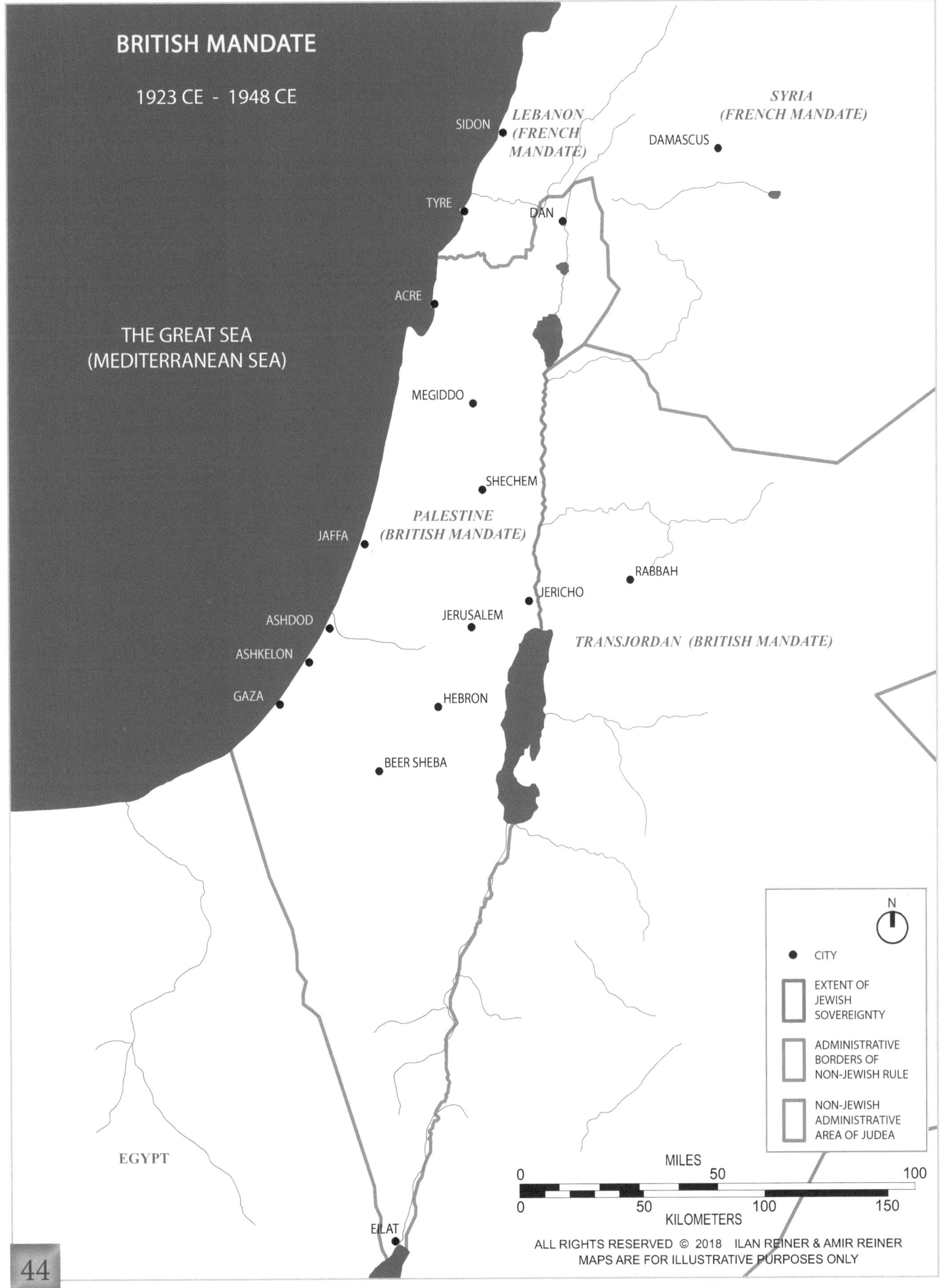
BRITISH MANDATE
1923 CE - 1948 CE
SIDON
LEBANON (FRENCH MANDATE)
SYRIA (FRENCH MANDATE)
DAMASCUS
TYRE
DAN
ACRE
THE GREAT SEA (MEDITERRANEAN SEA)
MEGIDDO
SHECHEM
PALESTINE (BRITISH MANDATE)
JAFFA
RABBAH
JERICHO
JERUSALEM
ASHDOD
ASHKELON
TRANSJORDAN (BRITISH MANDATE)
GAZA
HEBRON
BEER SHEBA
N
CITY
EXTENT OF JEWISH SOVEREIGNTY
ADMINISTRATIVE BORDERS OF NON-JEWISH RULE
NON-JEWISH ADMINISTRATIVE AREA OF JUDEA
EGYPT
MILES
0 50 100
0 50 100 150
KILOMETERS
EILAT
ALL RIGHTS RESERVED © 2018 ILAN REINER & AMIR REINER
MAPS ARE FOR ILLUSTRATIVE PURPOSES ONLY
44

Pre "State of Israel"
United Nations Partition Plan
1947 CE

Several commissions were suggesting how to divide Mandatory Palestine between a Jewish state and an Arab state. These were presented to the United Kingdom, then controlling the mandate over Israel, and to the United Nations, which was committed to resolving the constant conflict between Jews, Arabs and the British. On November 29, 1947, the United Nations adopted the Partition Plan as it was suggested by the United Nations Special Committee on Palestine. This plan designated about 55% to a Jewish state, about 45% to an Arab state and less than 1%, the area of Jerusalem and Bethlehem, for international government. But as the Jewish leadership accepted the plan and the Jews rejoiced the coming independence, the Arab leadership and people rejected the plan and said that the only partition would be that of "fire and blood" (expressed by Arab League Chairman Azzam Pasha).

Rejoicing on November 29 in the streets of Tel Aviv
Photo by Hans Pins/GPO

TIME LINE

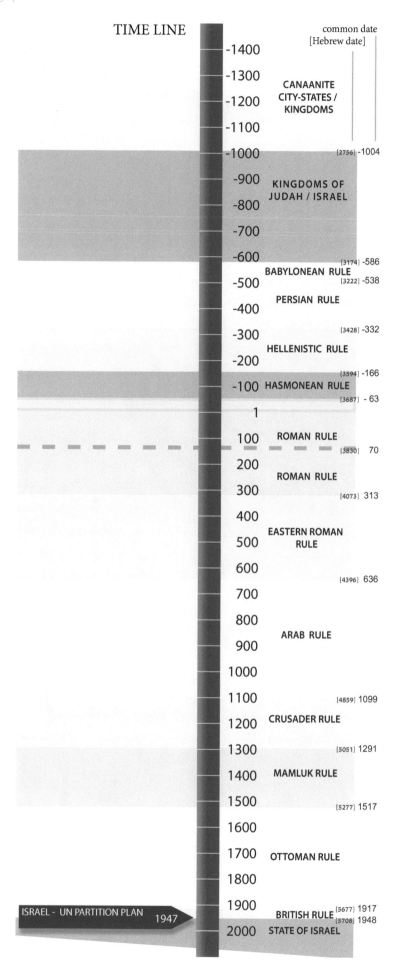

common date
[Hebrew date]

-1400
-1300
-1200
-1100
CANAANITE CITY-STATES / KINGDOMS
-1000
[2756] -1004
-900
-800
-700
KINGDOMS OF JUDAH / ISRAEL
-600
[3174] -586
BABYLONEAN RULE
-500
[3222] -538
PERSIAN RULE
-400
-300
[3428] -332
HELLENISTIC RULE
-200
[3594] -166
-100
HASMONEAN RULE
[3687] - 63
1
100
ROMAN RULE
[3830] 70
200
ROMAN RULE
300
[4073] 313
400
500
EASTERN ROMAN RULE
600
[4396] 636
700
800
900
ARAB RULE
1000
1100
[4859] 1099
1200
CRUSADER RULE
1300
[5051] 1291
1400
MAMLUK RULE
1500
[5277] 1517
1600
1700
OTTOMAN RULE
1800
1900
ISRAEL - UN PARTITION PLAN 1947
[5677] 1917
BRITISH RULE
[5708] 1948
2000
STATE OF ISRAEL

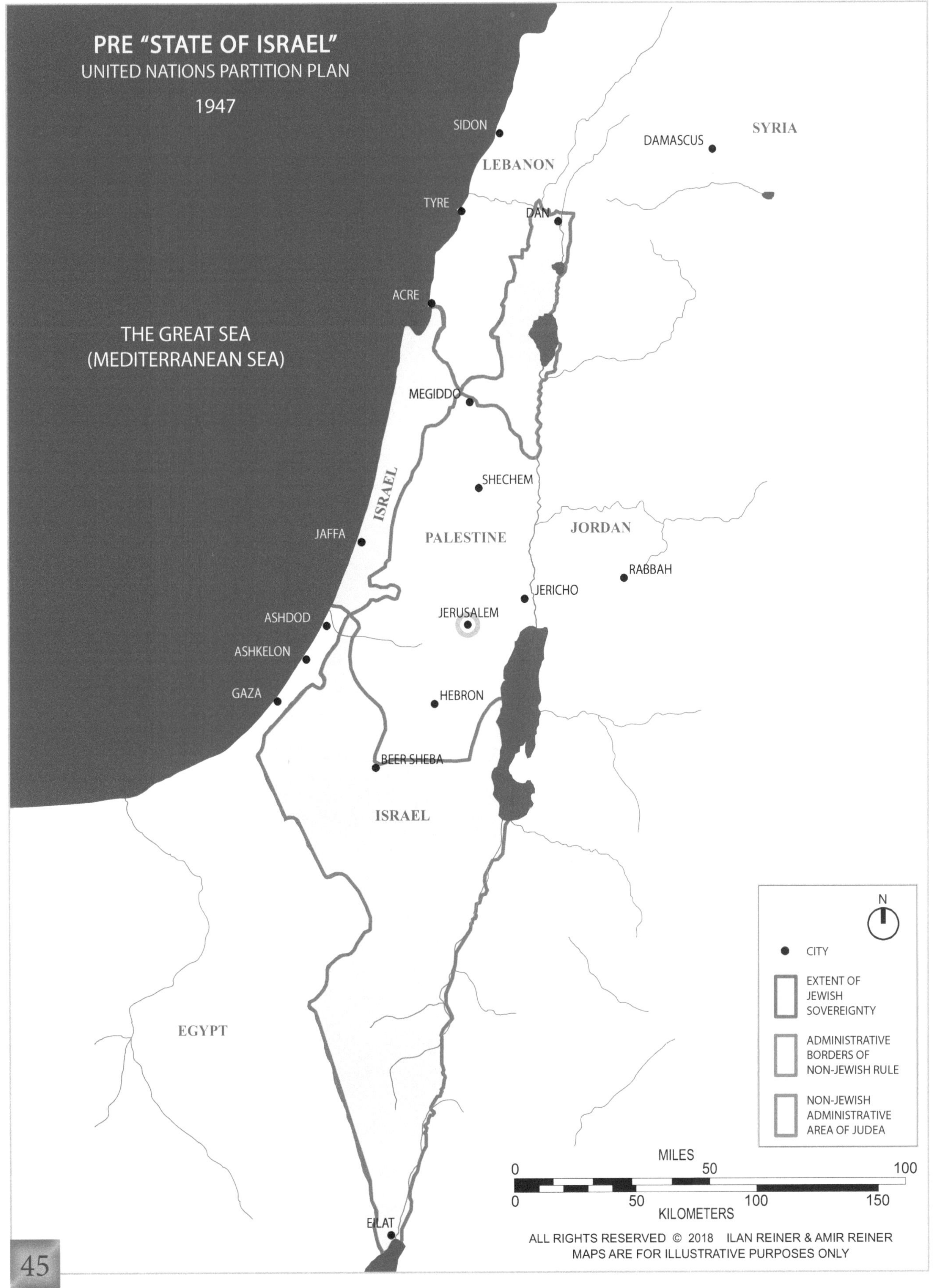
PRE "STATE OF ISRAEL"
UNITED NATIONS PARTITION PLAN
1947
SIDON
DAMASCUS
SYRIA
LEBANON
TYRE
DAN
ACRE
THE GREAT SEA
(MEDITERRANEAN SEA)
MEGIDDO
ISRAEL
SHECHEM
JORDAN
JAFFA
PALESTINE
RABBAH
JERICHO
ASHDOD
JERUSALEM
ASHKELON
GAZA
HEBRON
BEER SHEBA
ISRAEL
EGYPT
N
CITY
EXTENT OF JEWISH SOVEREIGNTY
ADMINISTRATIVE BORDERS OF NON-JEWISH RULE
NON-JEWISH ADMINISTRATIVE AREA OF JUDEA
MILES
0
50
100
0
50
100
150
KILOMETERS
EILAT
ALL RIGHTS RESERVED © 2018 ILAN REINER & AMIR REINER
MAPS ARE FOR ILLUSTRATIVE PURPOSES ONLY
45

Beginning of the Third Era of Jewish Rule in the Land of Israel

1948 CE to Present

The Third Era begins with the establishment of the Sovereign State of Israel in May 1948. It continues through the various conflicts that the State of Israel was involved in and the peace accords that Israel signed with her neighbors, until the present day. In this era it is demonstrated how the borders of the new country, created under mandate of the United Nations, shifted significantly in less than seven decades. The borders of the newly established state were theoretical since Israel was born into war. The cease-fire borders were significantly different. Israel expanded her borders considerably after the Six Day War, and returned most of that new territory after signing the peace treaty with Egypt and later on with Jordan. Several other territories were given to the Arab Palestinians for self governing initiative following various agreements with the Palestinian Authority.

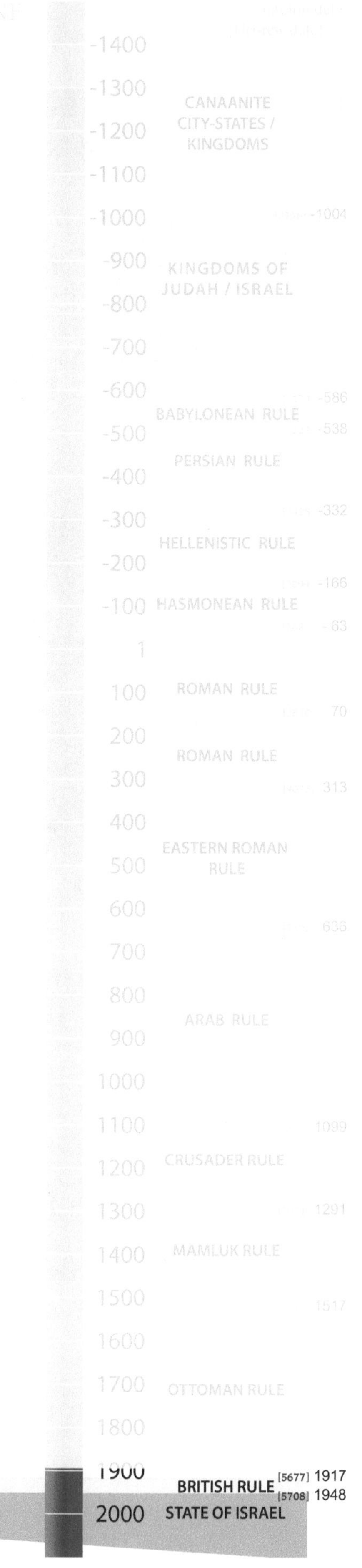

BEGINNING OF THE THIRD ERA OF JEWISH RULE IN THE LAND OF ISRAEL

STATE OF ISRAEL ESTABLISHED

1948

Ben Gurion reads Israel's Declaration of Independence
State of Israel's national photo collection

State of Israel
After War of Independence
1949 CE to 1956 CE

The young state was born into war with her Arab neighbors. Following the armistice agreements after the War of Independence, Israeli leadership swiftly moved towards unifying the various organizations and groups into a single army and government. Israel knew extreme growth as her population doubled after just a few years due to increasing immigration from Europe after World War II and from surrounding Arab countries. Economic recession soon followed and the government tried various courses of action in order to keep the economy solvent. During this time, clashes between Arabs and Jews continued, as terrorists penetrated the borders and attacked Israeli towns. The Israeli army retaliated with counter attacks on the terrorists, in an effort to keep the towns along the borders safe and secured.

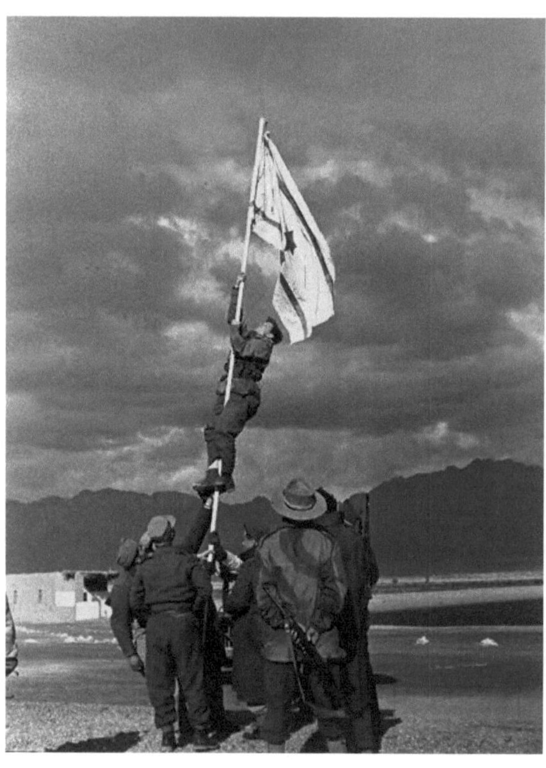

Ink-drawn flag of Israel flies at Um Rashrash (Eilat)
Photo by: Micha Perry, March 1949

TIME LINE

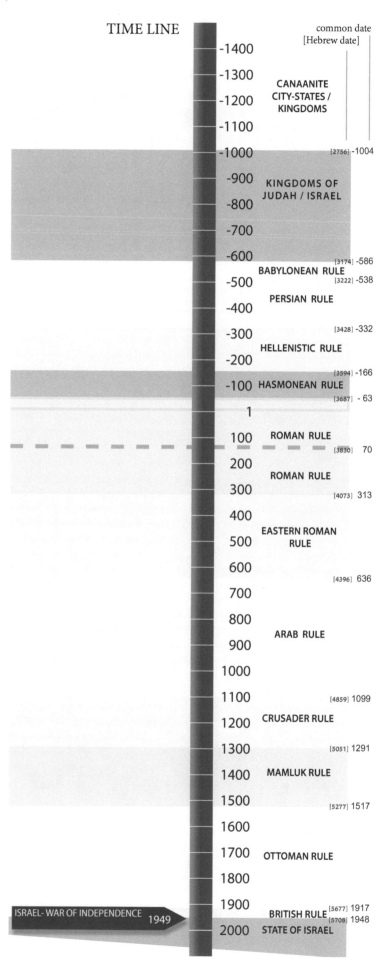

common date
[Hebrew date]

-1400
-1300
-1200
-1100
-1000
-900
-800
-700
-600
-500
-400
-300
-200
-100
1
100
200
300
400
500
600
700
800
900
1000
1100
1200
1300
1400
1500
1600
1700
1800
1900
2000

CANAANITE CITY-STATES / KINGDOMS
[2756] -1004
KINGDOMS OF JUDAH / ISRAEL
[3174] -586
BABYLONEAN RULE
[3222] -538
PERSIAN RULE
[3428] -332
HELLENISTIC RULE
[3594] -166
HASMONEAN RULE
[3687] - 63
ROMAN RULE
[3830] 70
ROMAN RULE
[4073] 313
EASTERN ROMAN RULE
[4396] 636
ARAB RULE
[4859] 1099
CRUSADER RULE
[5051] 1291
MAMLUK RULE
[5277] 1517
OTTOMAN RULE
[5677] 1917
BRITISH RULE
[5708] 1948
STATE OF ISRAEL

ISRAEL- WAR OF INDEPENDENCE 1949

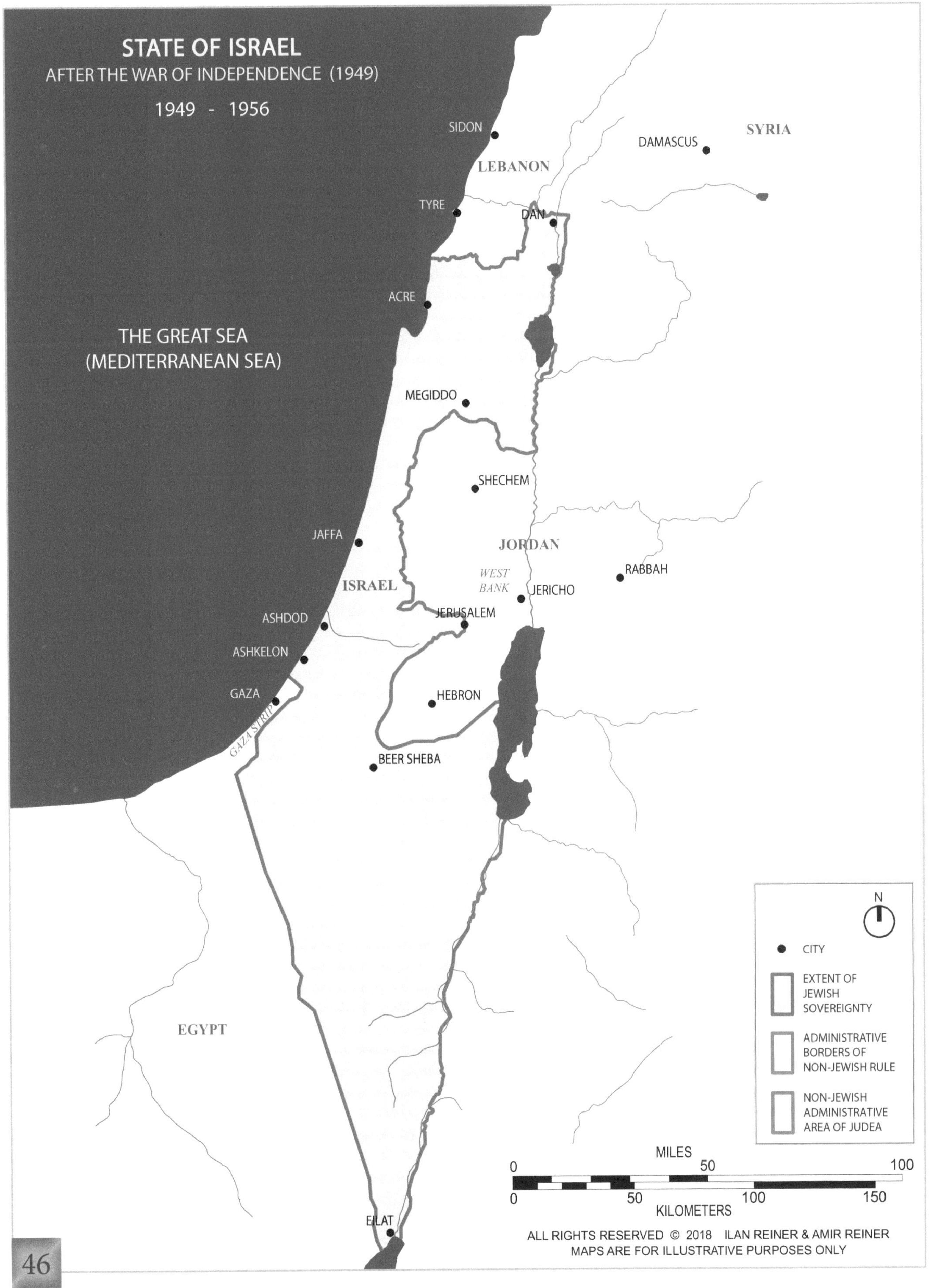

STATE OF ISRAEL
AFTER THE WAR OF INDEPENDENCE (1949)
1949 - 1956
SIDON
DAMASCUS
SYRIA
LEBANON
TYRE
DAN
ACRE
THE GREAT SEA
(MEDITERRANEAN SEA)
MEGIDDO
SHECHEM
JAFFA
JORDAN
WEST
BANK
RABBAH
JERICHO
ISRAEL
ASHDOD
JERUSALEM
ASHKELON
GAZA
HEBRON
GAZA STRIP
BEER SHEBA
EGYPT
N
CITY
EXTENT OF JEWISH SOVEREIGNTY
ADMINISTRATIVE BORDERS OF NON-JEWISH RULE
NON-JEWISH ADMINISTRATIVE AREA OF JUDEA
MILES
0
50
100
0
50
100
150
KILOMETERS
EILAT
ALL RIGHTS RESERVED © 2018 ILAN REINER & AMIR REINER
MAPS ARE FOR ILLUSTRATIVE PURPOSES ONLY
46

State of Israel
After the Kadesh Campaign (Sinai War)
1956 CE to 1957 CE

In 1956 Egypt took control over the Suez Canal and closed the passage to all Israeli ships, in what will be called the "Suez Crisis". Both Britain and France secretly encouraged Israel to go into a military operation and seize the Sinai peninsula and the Suez Canal. From a military standpoint the Kadesh Campaign was successful. The Israeli troops gained control over the Gaza Strip and the Sinai peninsula, stopping about 10 miles east of the canal (as ordered by Britain and France). The IDF seized much military equipment and destroyed the Egyptian military infrastructure. From a political standpoint the operation was a disaster, and soon after it the United States and USSR forced Israel to withdraw completely from the seized territories.

Israeli soldier stands next to an Egyptian cannon that had blocked the Tiran Straits.

TIME LINE

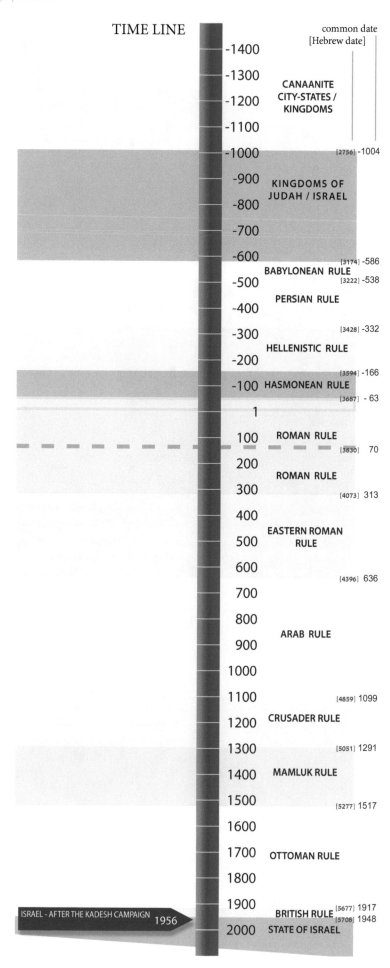

common date
[Hebrew date]

-1400
-1300
-1200
-1100
CANAANITE CITY-STATES / KINGDOMS
-1000 [2756] -1004
-900
-800
-700
KINGDOMS OF JUDAH / ISRAEL
-600 [3174] -586
BABYLONEAN RULE
-500 [3222] -538
PERSIAN RULE
-400
-300 [3428] -332
HELLENISTIC RULE
-200
[3594] -166
-100 HASMONEAN RULE
[3687] - 63
1
100 ROMAN RULE
[3830] 70
200
ROMAN RULE
300 [4073] 313
400
EASTERN ROMAN RULE
500
600
[4396] 636
700
800
ARAB RULE
900
1000
1100 [4859] 1099
CRUSADER RULE
1200
1300 [5051] 1291
1400 MAMLUK RULE
1500 [5277] 1517
1600
1700 OTTOMAN RULE
1800
1900
BRITISH RULE [5677] 1917
[5708] 1948
2000 STATE OF ISRAEL

ISRAEL - AFTER THE KADESH CAMPAIGN 1956

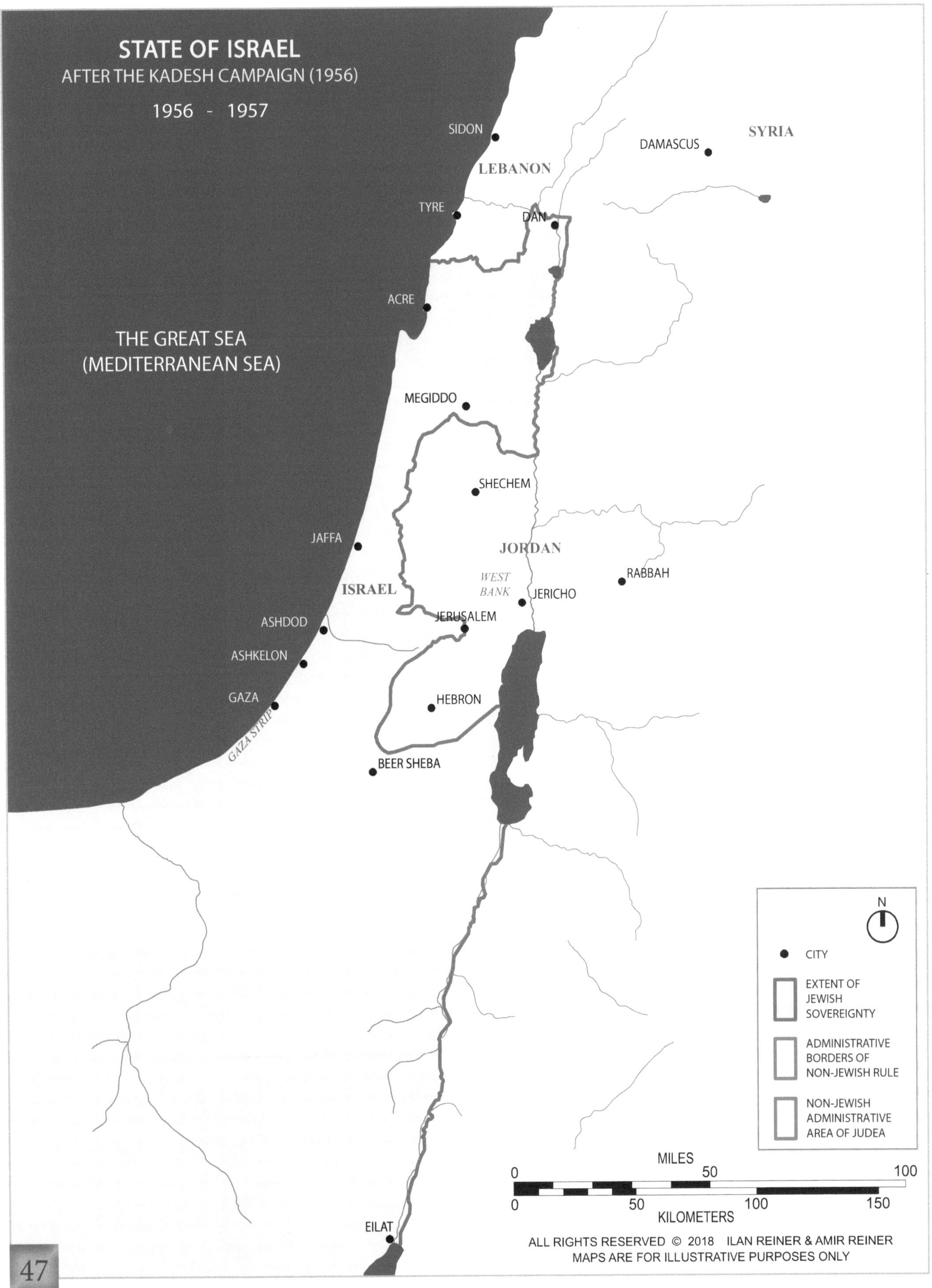
STATE OF ISRAEL
AFTER THE KADESH CAMPAIGN (1956)
1956 - 1957
SIDON
DAMASCUS
SYRIA
LEBANON
TYRE
DAN
ACRE
THE GREAT SEA
(MEDITERRANEAN SEA)
MEGIDDO
SHECHEM
JAFFA
JORDAN
RABBAH
WEST
BANK
ISRAEL
JERICHO
ASHDOD
JERUSALEM
ASHKELON
GAZA
HEBRON
GAZA STRIP
BEER SHEBA
N
CITY
EXTENT OF
JEWISH
SOVEREIGNTY
ADMINISTRATIVE
BORDERS OF
NON-JEWISH RULE
NON-JEWISH
ADMINISTRATIVE
AREA OF JUDEA
MILES
0
50
100
0
50
100
150
KILOMETERS
EILAT
ALL RIGHTS RESERVED © 2018 ILAN REINER & AMIR REINER
MAPS ARE FOR ILLUSTRATIVE PURPOSES ONLY
47

State of Israel
After the Withdrawal from Sinai
1957 CE to 1967 CE

During this time the young country needed to deal with several issues while it continued to grow and undergo rapid development. There were several cases of civil unrest accompanied by political scandals. Still, some great infrastructure projects were completed, such as the Port of Ashdod and the National Aqueduct. From a national defense perspective, there were several major developments. One such development was the construction of the nuclear facility in Dimona and another in 1961 was the successful launch of the Shavit II rocket. These national accomplishments created a message of deterrence to Israel's enemies. Yet, these developments also intensified the arms race in the region. This, along with rising Arab nationalism (and other factors) might have led to the rise in hostilities that escalated to the Six Day War.

Shavit Rocked Launched
Israel Aerospace Industries

TIME LINE

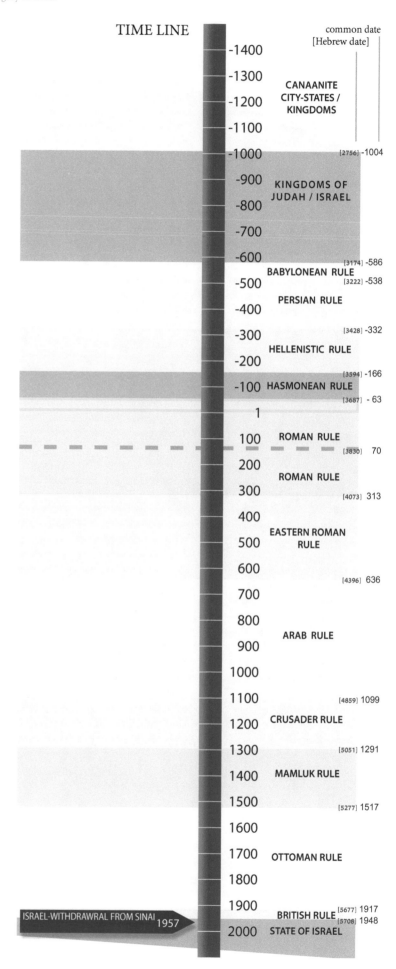

common date
[Hebrew date]

-1400
-1300
-1200
-1100
-1000
-900
-800
-700
-600
-500
-400
-300
-200
-100
1
100
200
300
400
500
600
700
800
900
1000
1100
1200
1300
1400
1500
1600
1700
1800
1900
2000

CANAANITE CITY-STATES / KINGDOMS
[2756] -1004
KINGDOMS OF JUDAH / ISRAEL
[3174] -586
BABYLONEAN RULE
[3222] -538
PERSIAN RULE
[3428] -332
HELLENISTIC RULE
[3594] -166
HASMONEAN RULE
[3687] - 63
ROMAN RULE
[3830] 70
ROMAN RULE
[4073] 313
EASTERN ROMAN RULE
[4396] 636
ARAB RULE
[4859] 1099
CRUSADER RULE
[5051] 1291
MAMLUK RULE
[5277] 1517
OTTOMAN RULE
[5677] 1917
BRITISH RULE
[5708] 1948
STATE OF ISRAEL

ISRAEL-WITHDRAWRAL FROM SINAI 1957

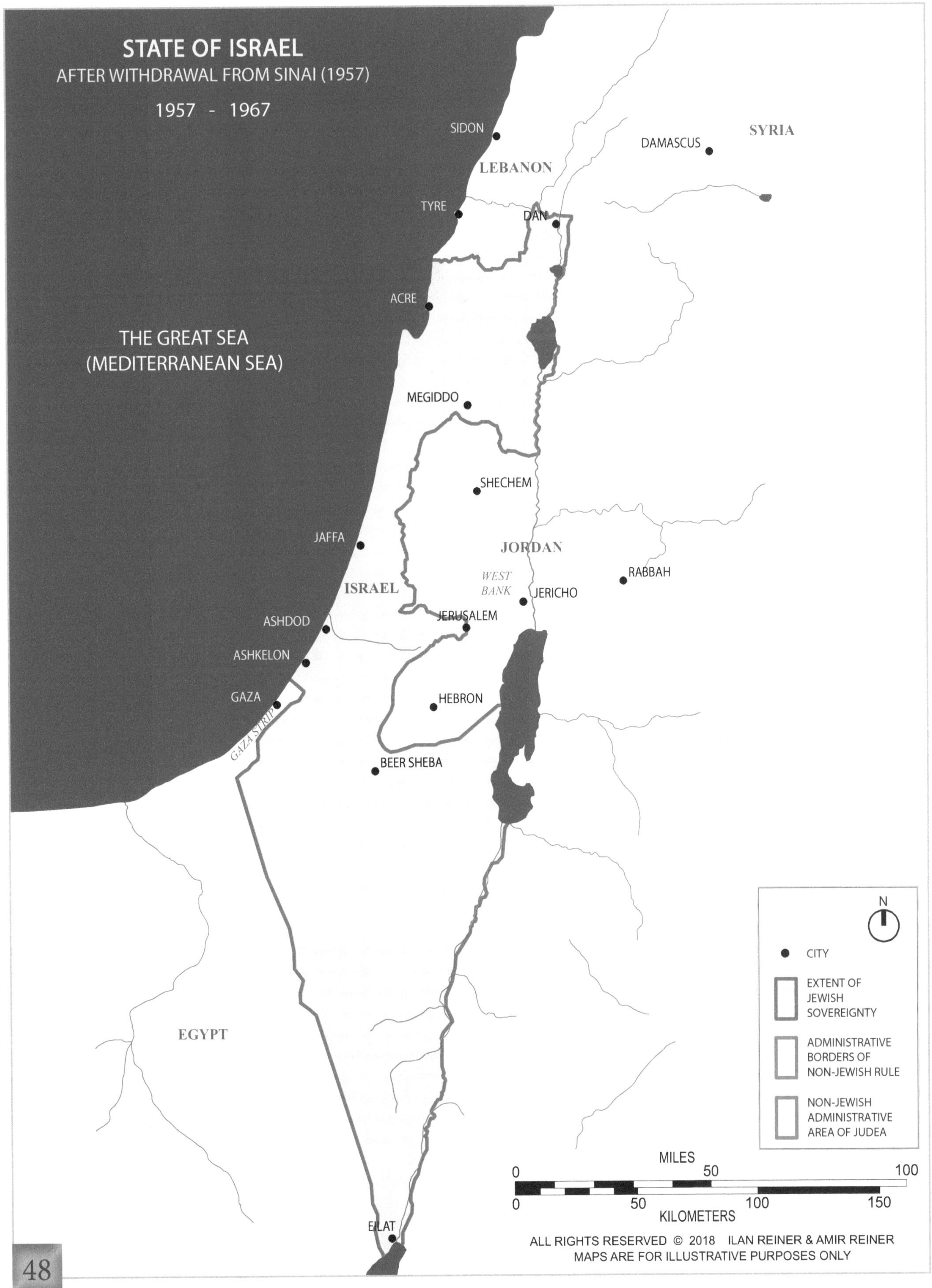

STATE OF ISRAEL
AFTER WITHDRAWAL FROM SINAI (1957)
1957 - 1967
THE GREAT SEA
(MEDITERRANEAN SEA)
SIDON
LEBANON
DAMASCUS
SYRIA
TYRE
DAN
ACRE
MEGIDDO
SHECHEM
JAFFA
JORDAN
WEST BANK
RABBAH
JERICHO
ISRAEL
ASHDOD
JERUSALEM
ASHKELON
GAZA
GAZA STRIP
HEBRON
BEER SHEBA
EGYPT
EILAT
N
CITY
EXTENT OF JEWISH SOVEREIGNTY
ADMINISTRATIVE BORDERS OF NON-JEWISH RULE
NON-JEWISH ADMINISTRATIVE AREA OF JUDEA
MILES
0 50 100
0 50 100 150
KILOMETERS
ALL RIGHTS RESERVED © 2018 ILAN REINER & AMIR REINER
MAPS ARE FOR ILLUSTRATIVE PURPOSES ONLY
48

State of Israel
After the Six Day War And Yom Kippur War
1967 CE to 1980 CE

The Middle East changed significantly after the Six Day War of June 1967. Following ongoing hostilities and preparations for war from the surrounding Arab countries, specifically Egypt, Israel launched a preemptive strike on Egypt and Syria. Within hours the Israeli Air Force crippled the Egyptian and Syrian Air Forces. In a rapid advance, Israeli armies swept south into the Sinai, east towards the Jordan River and north into the Golan Heights and Syria. After nearly 2000 years, Jerusalem and the Temple Mount were once again under complete and full Jewish sovereignty. Israel won a huge victory and almost tripled her land area, including the Golan Heights, West Bank, Gaza Strip and the Sinai Peninsula. Egypt and Syria could not accept their defeat and attacked Israel again six years later on the most sacred Jewish holiday of Yom Kippur, but were defeated. These expanded borders and occupied territories, that were held also after the Yom Kippur War of 1973, have raised many political and moral debates that continue to be at the heart of Israeli and international politics to this present day.

Rabbi Shlomo Goren blows the Shofar after capturing the Western Wall *Photo by: David Rubinger / GPO*

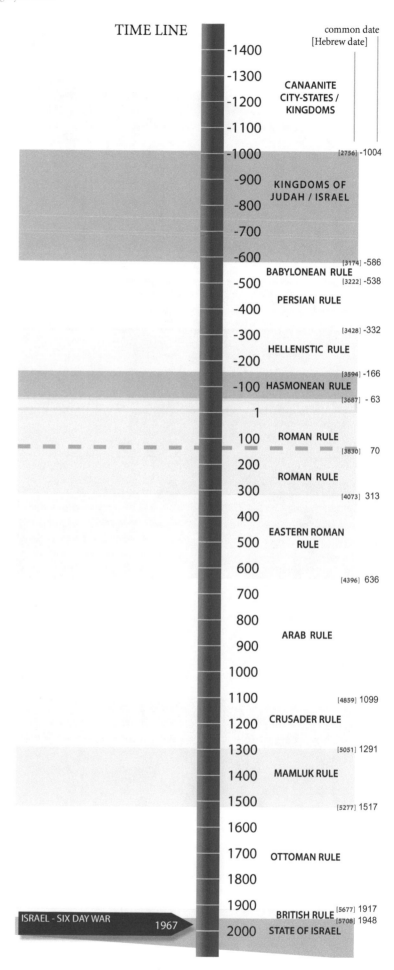

TIME LINE

common date [Hebrew date]

-1400 -1300 -1200 -1100 -1000 -900 -800 -700 -600 -500 -400 -300 -200 -100 1 100 200 300 400 500 600 700 800 900 1000 1100 1200 1300 1400 1500 1600 1700 1800 1900 2000

Period	Ends (common date [Hebrew date])
CANAANITE CITY-STATES / KINGDOMS	[2756] -1004
KINGDOMS OF JUDAH / ISRAEL	[3174] -586
BABYLONEAN RULE	[3222] -538
PERSIAN RULE	[3428] -332
HELLENISTIC RULE	[3594] -166
HASMONEAN RULE	[3687] - 63
ROMAN RULE	[3830] 70
ROMAN RULE	[4073] 313
EASTERN ROMAN RULE	[4396] 636
ARAB RULE	[4859] 1099
CRUSADER RULE	[5051] 1291
MAMLUK RULE	[5277] 1517
OTTOMAN RULE	[5677] 1917
BRITISH RULE	[5708] 1948
STATE OF ISRAEL	

ISRAEL - SIX DAY WAR 1967

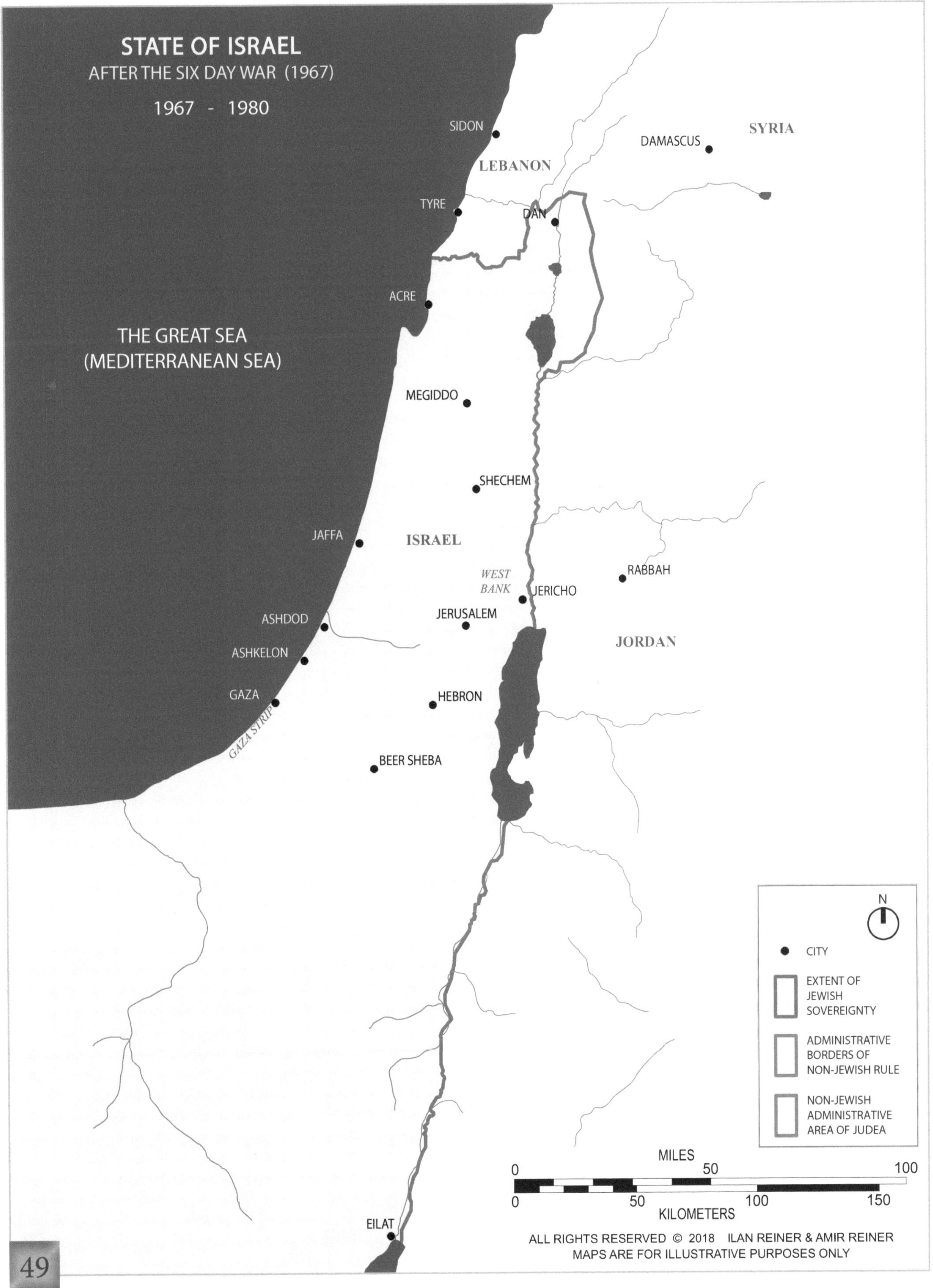
STATE OF ISRAEL
AFTER THE SIX DAY WAR (1967)
1967 - 1980
SIDON
DAMASCUS
SYRIA
LEBANON
TYRE
DAN
ACRE
THE GREAT SEA
(MEDITERRANEAN SEA)
MEGIDDO
SHECHEM
JAFFA
ISRAEL
WEST
BANK
RABBAH
JERICHO
JERUSALEM
ASHDOD
JORDAN
ASHKELON
GAZA
GAZA STRIP
HEBRON
BEER SHEBA
N
CITY
EXTENT OF
JEWISH
SOVEREIGNTY
ADMINISTRATIVE
BORDERS OF
NON-JEWISH RULE
NON-JEWISH
ADMINISTRATIVE
AREA OF JUDEA
MILES
0
50
100
0
50
100
150
KILOMETERS
EILAT
49

State of Israel
After Signing Peace Treaty with Egypt in 1979

1980 CE to 1982 CE

In 1979 Israel and Egypt signed an historic peace accord. Following the signing, Israel gradually retreated from the Sinai peninsula it occupied since the Six Day War, evacuating dozens of Israeli towns and causing much civil unrest and controversy. Relations between the countries slowly normalized but it was never a warm friendship. The Gaza strip remained under Israeli rule with the agreement that it would eventually become part of a Palestinian state. Securing its southern border, Israel turned to address potential enemies farther away from home. In 1981 the Israeli Air Force struck and destroyed the Iraqi nuclear facility to prevent Iraq from developing nuclear weapons.

Israeli PM Begin and Egyptian President Sadat with U.S. President Carter at Camp David in 1978

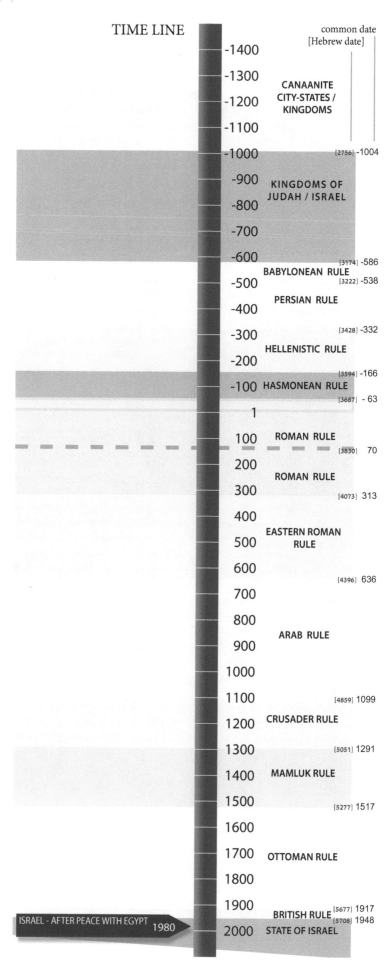

TIME LINE

common date [Hebrew date]

Period	Ends (common date [Hebrew date])
CANAANITE CITY-STATES / KINGDOMS	[2756] -1004
KINGDOMS OF JUDAH / ISRAEL	[3174] -586
BABYLONEAN RULE	[3222] -538
PERSIAN RULE	[3428] -332
HELLENISTIC RULE	[3594] -166
HASMONEAN RULE	[3687] - 63
ROMAN RULE	[3830] 70
ROMAN RULE	[4073] 313
EASTERN ROMAN RULE	[4396] 636
ARAB RULE	[4859] 1099
CRUSADER RULE	[5051] 1291
MAMLUK RULE	[5277] 1517
OTTOMAN RULE	[5677] 1917
BRITISH RULE	[5708] 1948
STATE OF ISRAEL	

Scale: -1400, -1300, -1200, -1100, -1000, -900, -800, -700, -600, -500, -400, -300, -200, -100, 1, 100, 200, 300, 400, 500, 600, 700, 800, 900, 1000, 1100, 1200, 1300, 1400, 1500, 1600, 1700, 1800, 1900, 2000

ISRAEL - AFTER PEACE WITH EGYPT 1980

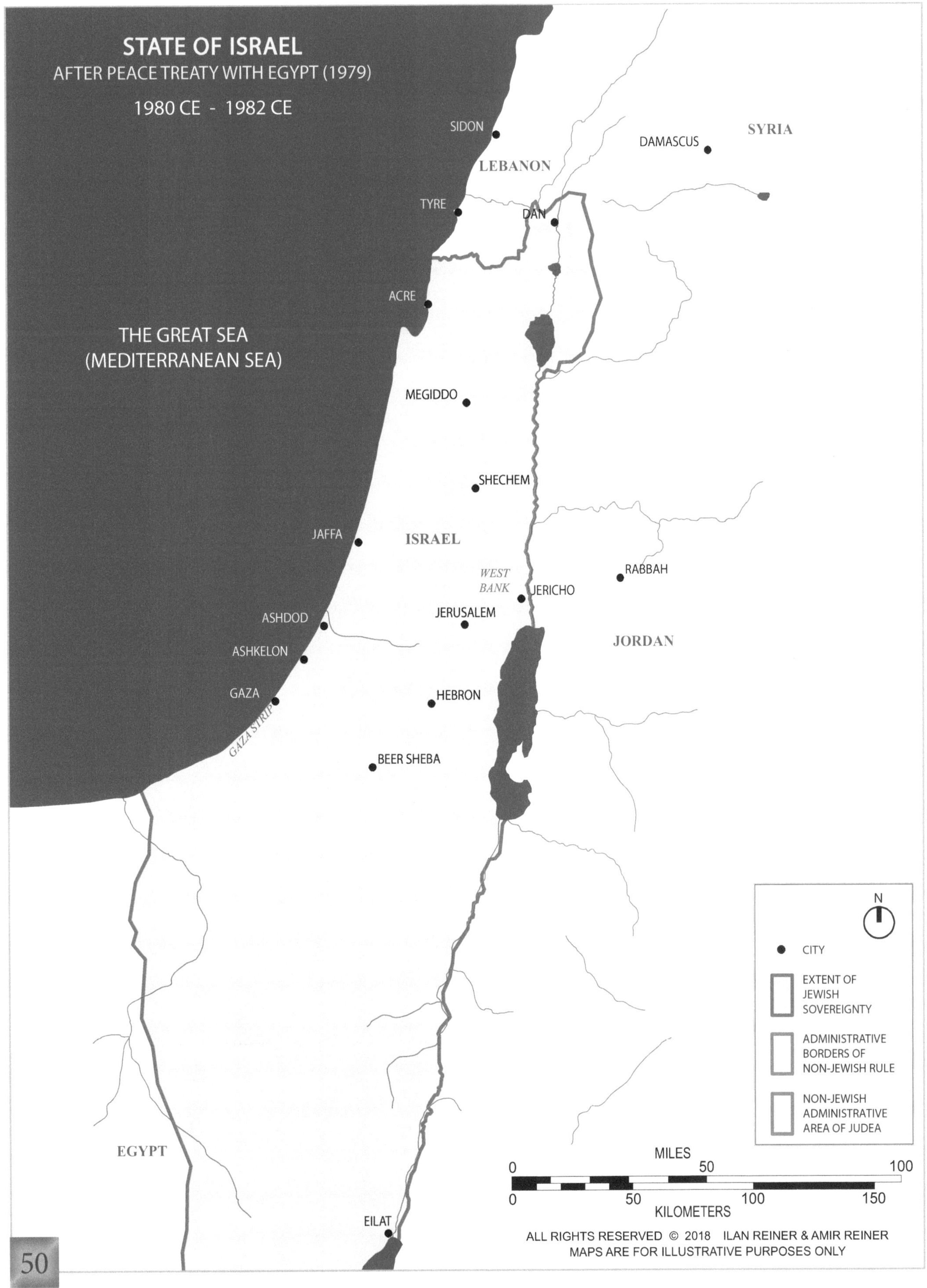

STATE OF ISRAEL
AFTER PEACE TREATY WITH EGYPT (1979)
1980 CE - 1982 CE
SIDON
DAMASCUS
SYRIA
LEBANON
TYRE
DAN
ACRE
THE GREAT SEA
(MEDITERRANEAN SEA)
MEGIDDO
SHECHEM
JAFFA
ISRAEL
WEST
BANK
RABBAH
JERICHO
JERUSALEM
ASHDOD
ASHKELON
JORDAN
GAZA
HEBRON
GAZA STRIP
BEER SHEBA
N
CITY
EXTENT OF JEWISH SOVEREIGNTY
ADMINISTRATIVE BORDERS OF NON-JEWISH RULE
NON-JEWISH ADMINISTRATIVE AREA OF JUDEA
EGYPT
MILES
0
50
100
0
50
100
150
KILOMETERS
EILAT
50

State of Israel
After Withdrawal from Sinai (1982)

1982 CE to 1993 CE

As Israel secured the borders in the south with the full retreat from Sinai, problems started to arise in the north, where masses of Palestinian terrorists, escaping from Jordan, settled in southern Lebanon and began terrorizing Northern Israel. As a response, Israel invaded Lebanon (the First Lebanon War) and forced out many of the terrorists. Israeli army remained in southern Lebanon 'Security Zone' for almost two decades.

The Israeli economy flourished with new industries and opportunities during the 1980's. In 1987, the First Intifada (uprising) broke out in the West Bank, starting off as a Palestinian civilian uprising and escalating to a full campaign of terrorism against Israel. Suicide bombers exploded in buses, shopping malls and other civilian centers. Only after great efforts, were the Israeli security forces able to put down the Intifada.

Following the dissolution of the Soviet Union (1991), approximately one million Jews immigrated to Israel from the former Soviet states. The Rabin administration, in the early 1990's, advanced the peace process with Israel's neighbors. The Oslo accords with the Palestinians was signed in 1993. Following that, in 1994, Jordan signed a treaty of peace with Israel.

US President Bill Clinton, Israel PM Yitzhak Rabin, PLO Chairman Yasser Arafat, at the White House

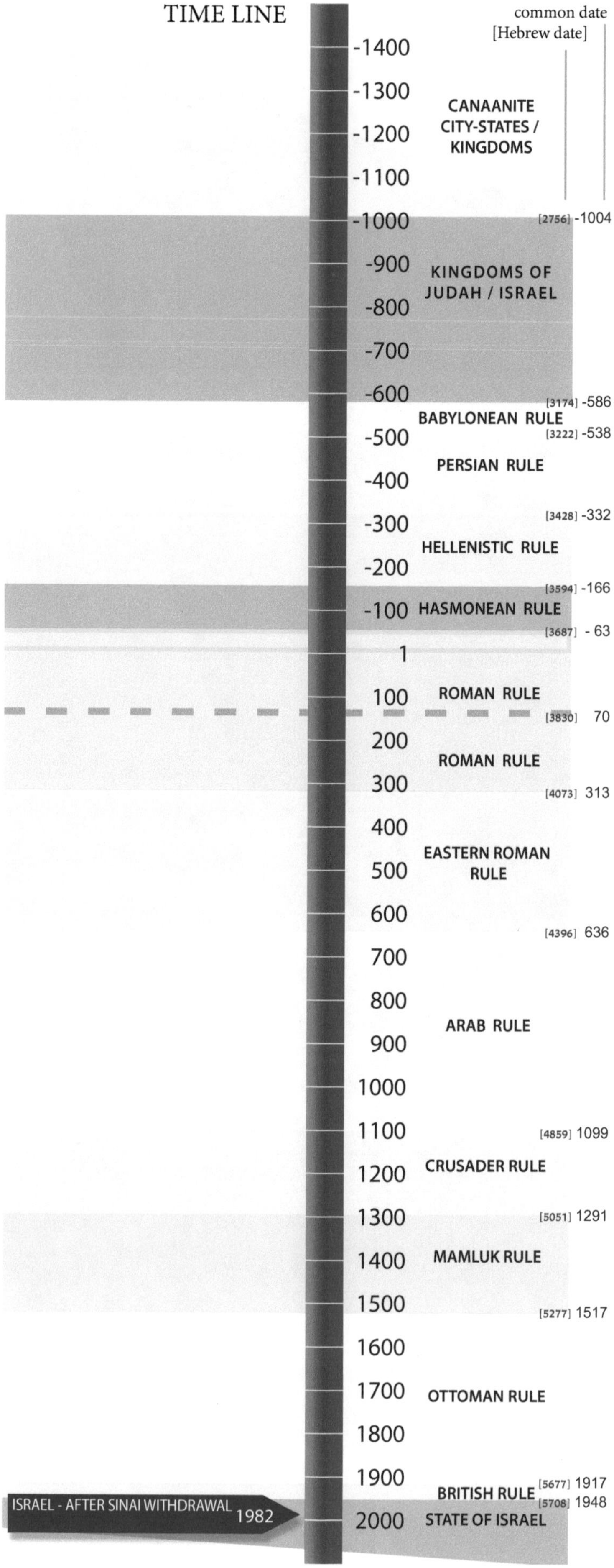

TIME LINE

Period	common date [Hebrew date]
CANAANITE CITY-STATES / KINGDOMS	[2756] -1004
KINGDOMS OF JUDAH / ISRAEL	[3174] -586
BABYLONEAN RULE	[3222] -538
PERSIAN RULE	[3428] -332
HELLENISTIC RULE	[3594] -166
HASMONEAN RULE	[3687] - 63
ROMAN RULE	[3830] 70
ROMAN RULE	[4073] 313
EASTERN ROMAN RULE	[4396] 636
ARAB RULE	[4859] 1099
CRUSADER RULE	[5051] 1291
MAMLUK RULE	[5277] 1517
OTTOMAN RULE	[5677] 1917
BRITISH RULE	[5708] 1948
STATE OF ISRAEL	

Scale: -1400, -1300, -1200, -1100, -1000, -900, -800, -700, -600, -500, -400, -300, -200, -100, 1, 100, 200, 300, 400, 500, 600, 700, 800, 900, 1000, 1100, 1200, 1300, 1400, 1500, 1600, 1700, 1800, 1900, 2000

ISRAEL - AFTER SINAI WITHDRAWAL 1982

STATE OF ISRAEL
AFTER WITHDRAWAL FROM SINAI (1982)
1982 - 1993
SIDON
DAMASCUS
SYRIA
LEBANON
TYRE
DAN
ACRE
THE GREAT SEA
(MEDITERRANEAN SEA)
MEGIDDO
SHECHEM
JAFFA
ISRAEL
WEST
BANK
JERICHO
RABBAH
JERUSALEM
ASHDOD
ASHKELON
JORDAN
GAZA
HEBRON
GAZA STRIP
BEER SHEBA
N
CITY
EXTENT OF
JEWISH
SOVEREIGNTY
ADMINISTRATIVE
BORDERS OF
NON-JEWISH RULE
NON-JEWISH
ADMINISTRATIVE
AREA OF JUDEA
EGYPT
MILES
0
50
100
0
50
100
150
KILOMETERS
EILAT
51

State of Israel
Following the Oslo Accords (1993)
1993 CE to 2005 CE

Following the signing of the Oslo Accords, Israel gradually gave partial autonomous rule to the Palestinian Authority throughout the West Bank and the Gaza Strip. A new wave of Palestinian terrorism made any further negotiations with the Palestinian Authority impossible. In 1994, the Israel–Jordan Peace Treaty was signed, making Jordan the second Arab country to normalize relations with Israel. In 2000, the Israeli Defence Force (IDF) retreated from the entire 'security zone' in south Lebanon, a very controversial move, since Hezbollah (the Lebanese terrorist organization) took over the area and sporadically fired rockets at Israeli towns.

The Second Intifada (uprising) broke out that year. Palestinians fired rockets on Israeli towns and sent suicide bombers to buses and shopping malls. The Palestinian Authority was unwilling to fight this terrorism, so the Israeli security forces went into Palestinian areas and temporarily seized entire cities, in order to eradicate terrorism.

One of the outcomes of this Intifada was the construction of the Separation Barrier (Security fence / wall) along the West Bank, to prevent terrorists from crossing into Israel. (See heavy dashed line in the next map).

The Separation Fence (Barrier) between Israel and the Palestinian Authority in the West Bank

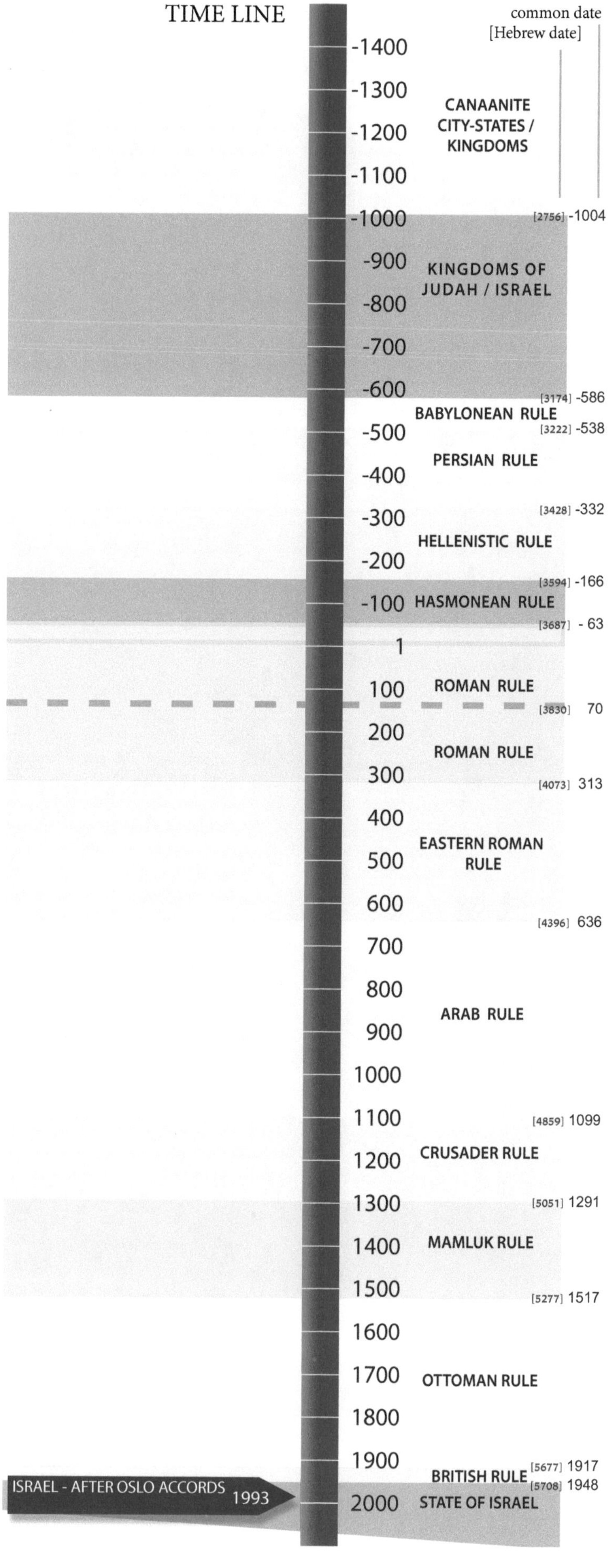

TIME LINE

common date
[Hebrew date]

-1400
-1300
CANAANITE CITY-STATES / KINGDOMS
-1200
-1100
[2756] -1004
-1000
-900
KINGDOMS OF JUDAH / ISRAEL
-800
-700
-600
[3174] -586
BABYLONEAN RULE
-500
[3222] -538
PERSIAN RULE
-400
[3428] -332
-300
HELLENISTIC RULE
-200
[3594] -166
-100
HASMONEAN RULE
[3687] - 63
1
100
ROMAN RULE
[3830] 70
200
ROMAN RULE
300
[4073] 313
400
EASTERN ROMAN RULE
500
600
[4396] 636
700
800
ARAB RULE
900
1000
1100
[4859] 1099
CRUSADER RULE
1200
1300
[5051] 1291
1400
MAMLUK RULE
1500
[5277] 1517
1600
1700
OTTOMAN RULE
1800
1900
[5677] 1917
BRITISH RULE
[5708] 1948
ISRAEL - AFTER OSLO ACCORDS 1993
2000
STATE OF ISRAEL

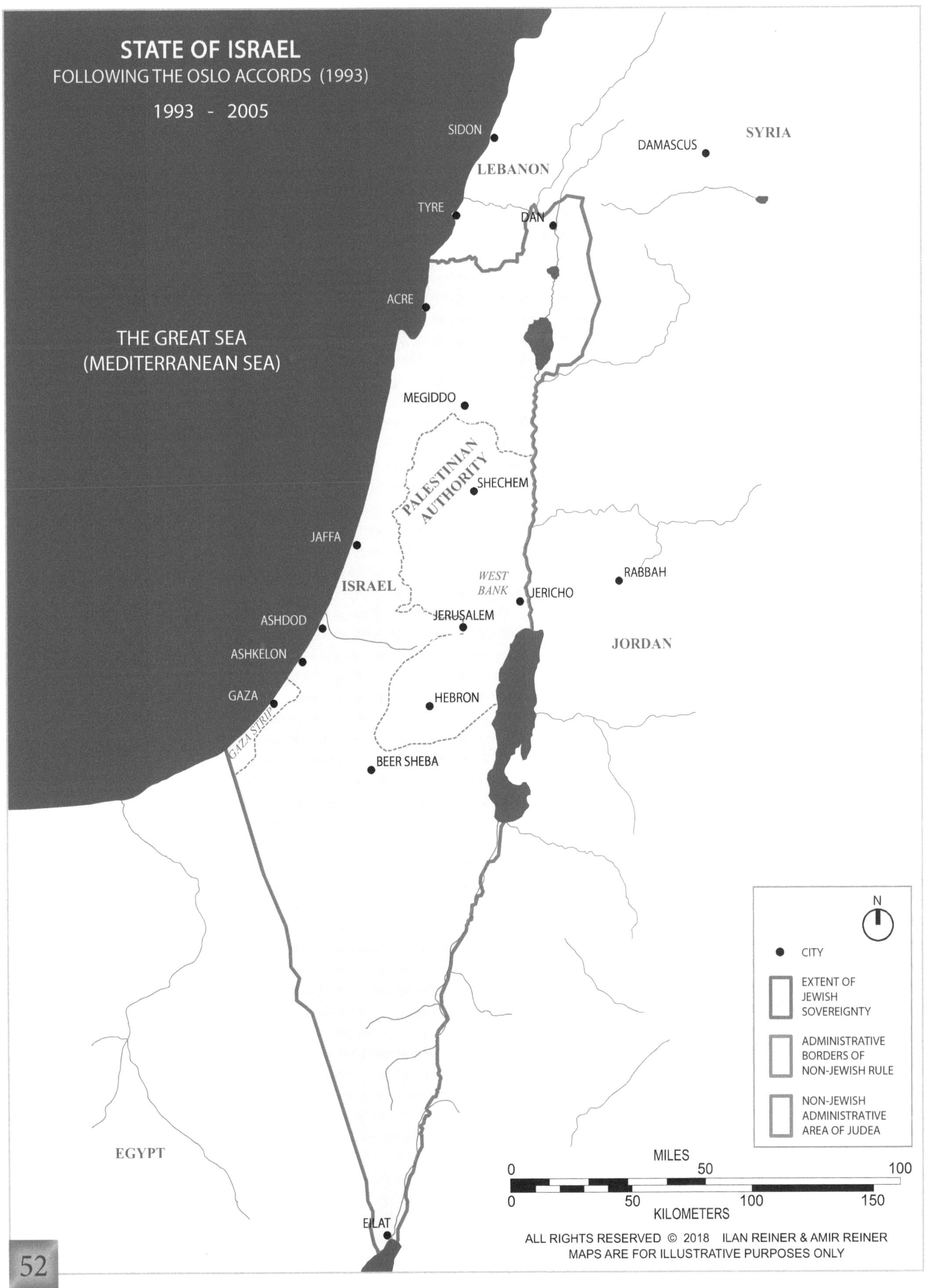
STATE OF ISRAEL
FOLLOWING THE OSLO ACCORDS (1993)
1993 - 2005
SIDON
DAMASCUS
SYRIA
LEBANON
TYRE
DAN
ACRE
THE GREAT SEA
(MEDITERRANEAN SEA)
MEGIDDO
PALESTINIAN AUTHORITY
SHECHEM
JAFFA
RABBAH
WEST BANK
ISRAEL
JERICHO
ASHDOD
JERUSALEM
JORDAN
ASHKELON
GAZA
HEBRON
GAZA STRIP
BEER SHEBA
N
CITY
EXTENT OF JEWISH SOVEREIGNTY
ADMINISTRATIVE BORDERS OF NON-JEWISH RULE
NON-JEWISH ADMINISTRATIVE AREA OF JUDEA
EGYPT
MILES
0
50
100
0
50
100
150
KILOMETERS
EILAT
ALL RIGHTS RESERVED © 2018 ILAN REINER & AMIR REINER
MAPS ARE FOR ILLUSTRATIVE PURPOSES ONLY

52

State of Israel
Following the Disengagement (2005)
2005 CE to 2011 CE

The Separation Fence / Barrier was continued to be built (shown in heavy dashed line), making it more difficult for terrorist to cross over from the Palestinian Authority into Israel. In the summer of 2005, Israel retreated unilaterally from the Gaza Strip and parts of the West Bank, demolishing the Israeli settlements there. This "Disengagement" was highly controversial and its merits are still subject to public debate. Soon after Israel unilaterally withdrew, the Gaza Strip fell under control of the extremist Muslim Hamas terrorist organization.
In 2006, both Hamas and Hezbollah attacked, killed and kidnapped Israeli soldiers, as well as launching hundreds of rockets at Israeli northern towns and cities, leading to the Second Lebanon War. In 2008, after suffering thousands of rocket attacks by Hamas, Israel invaded Gaza, seriously damaging Hamas facilities and military infrastructure. During all this time, Israel's economy grew (surviving

Evacuation of Kfar Darom During the Disengagement
Photo by: Israel Defence Force

TIME LINE

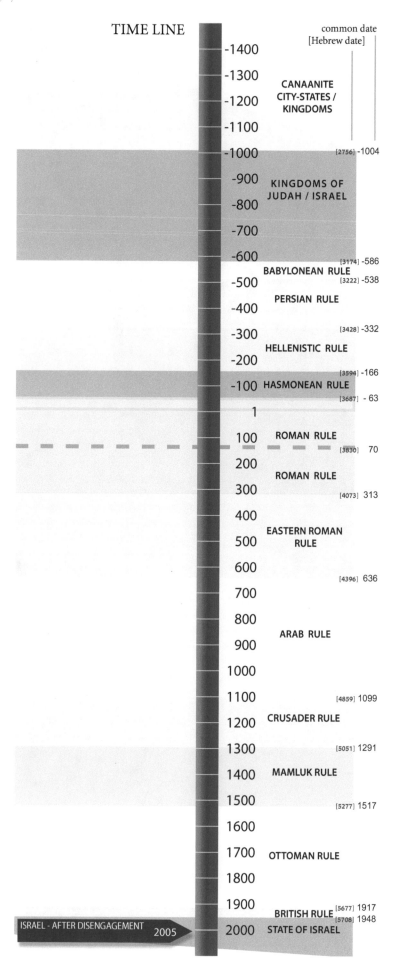

common date
[Hebrew date]

-1400
-1300
CANAANITE CITY-STATES / KINGDOMS
-1200
-1100
[2756] -1004
-1000
-900
KINGDOMS OF JUDAH / ISRAEL
-800
-700
-600
[3174] -586
BABYLONEAN RULE
-500
[3222] -538
PERSIAN RULE
-400
-300
[3428] -332
HELLENISTIC RULE
-200
[3594] -166
-100 HASMONEAN RULE
[3687] - 63
1
100
ROMAN RULE
[3830] 70
200
ROMAN RULE
300
[4073] 313
400
EASTERN ROMAN RULE
500
600
[4396] 636
700
800
ARAB RULE
900
1000
1100
[4859] 1099
CRUSADER RULE
1200
1300
[5051] 1291
1400
MAMLUK RULE
1500
[5277] 1517
1600
1700
OTTOMAN RULE
1800
1900
[5677] 1917
BRITISH RULE
[5708] 1948
ISRAEL - AFTER DISENGAGEMENT 2005
2000
STATE OF ISRAEL

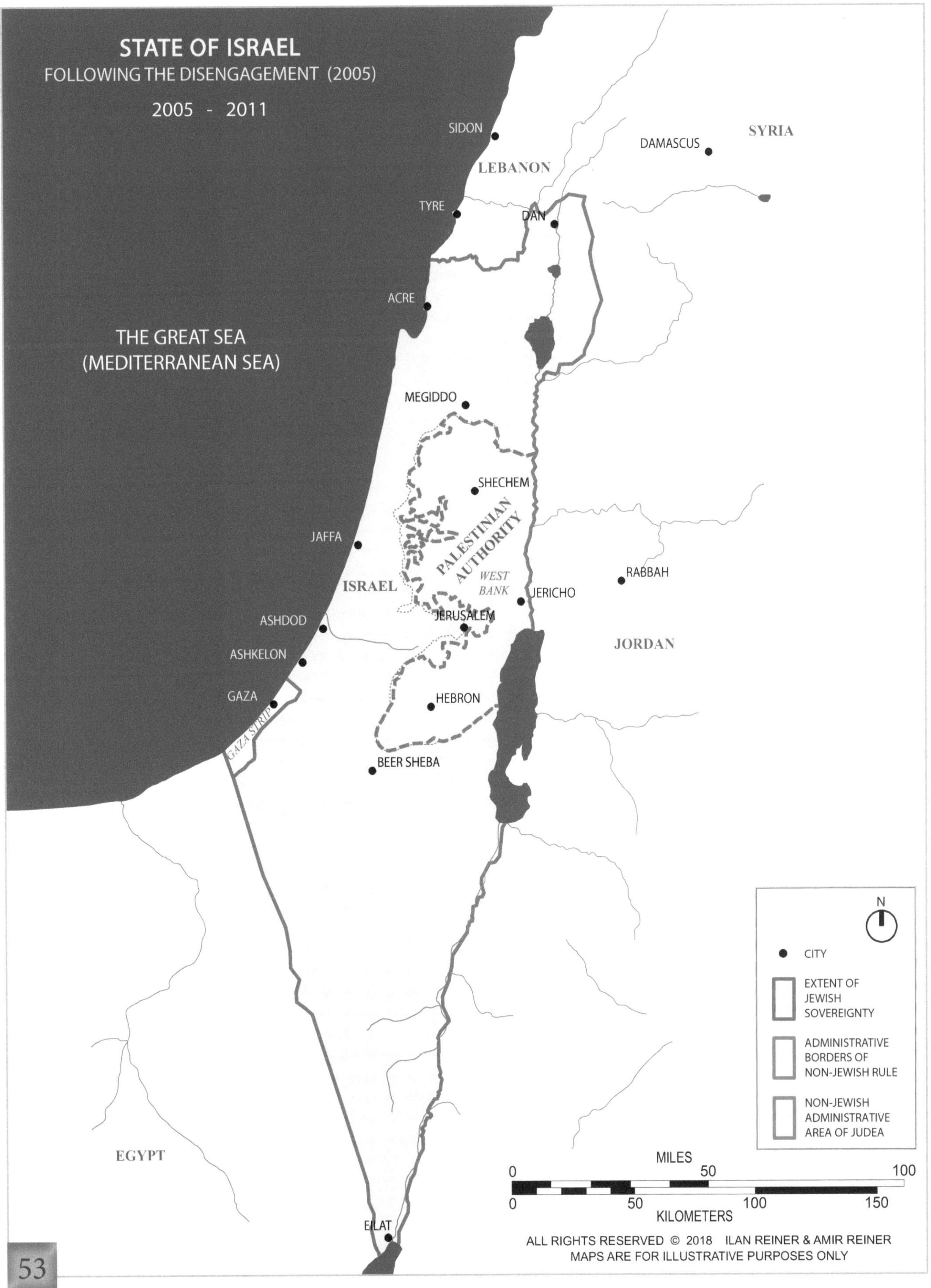
STATE OF ISRAEL
FOLLOWING THE DISENGAGEMENT (2005)
2005 - 2011
SIDON
DAMASCUS
SYRIA
LEBANON
TYRE
DAN
ACRE
THE GREAT SEA
(MEDITERRANEAN SEA)
MEGIDDO
SHECHEM
PALESTINIAN AUTHORITY
JAFFA
WEST BANK
RABBAH
ISRAEL
JERICHO
ASHDOD
JERUSALEM
ASHKELON
JORDAN
GAZA
HEBRON
GAZA STRIP
BEER SHEBA
N
CITY
EXTENT OF JEWISH SOVEREIGNTY
ADMINISTRATIVE BORDERS OF NON-JEWISH RULE
NON-JEWISH ADMINISTRATIVE AREA OF JUDEA
EGYPT
MILES
0
50
100
0
50
100
150
KILOMETERS
EILAT
53

State of Israel
Towards 70th Independence Day
2011 CE to 2018 CE (Present)

At her 70th birthday, Israel builds on successes and write greater chapters for her future.
The past decade appeared to be a repetition of threats, escalation of violence, retaliation and campaigns between wars. Syria built a nuclear reactor and Israel destroyed it. Hamas in the Gaza Strip escalated violence and Israel invaded. Twice (2012 and 2014). Rockets were fired at Israeli towns and Israel developed the famed Iron Dome for protection. Attack tunnels were dug and Israel destroyed them. Israel and the Palestinians continuously refused to negotiate peace. Will the next decade be any different?
Israel boasts the enormous accomplishments it achieved since it was established, particularly in the past decade - in medicine, technology, agriculture and in international relationships. One political milestone was marked in 2017, when US President Trump officially recognized Jerusalem as the capital of Israel. In March 2019, President Trump formally recognized Israeli sovereignty over the Golan Heights.
Internally, media coverage conveyed rifts between Israel's many factions (or "tribes", as referred by the media). However, upon a closer look, these rifts actually seem like healthy democratic disagreements. When in need, most Israelis unite behind a cause, whether it be in support of the IDF, helping the needy, calling for social justice or supporting African refugees.
For Israelis - Jewish, Muslim, Druze, Christian, et al, who love their country, it is not a question of what will be written in the future chapters, but rather *how can they write these chapters together* — in order to continue flourishing.

Israeli Jews, Arabs and others protesting together for a same cause
Photo by: Shatil PR

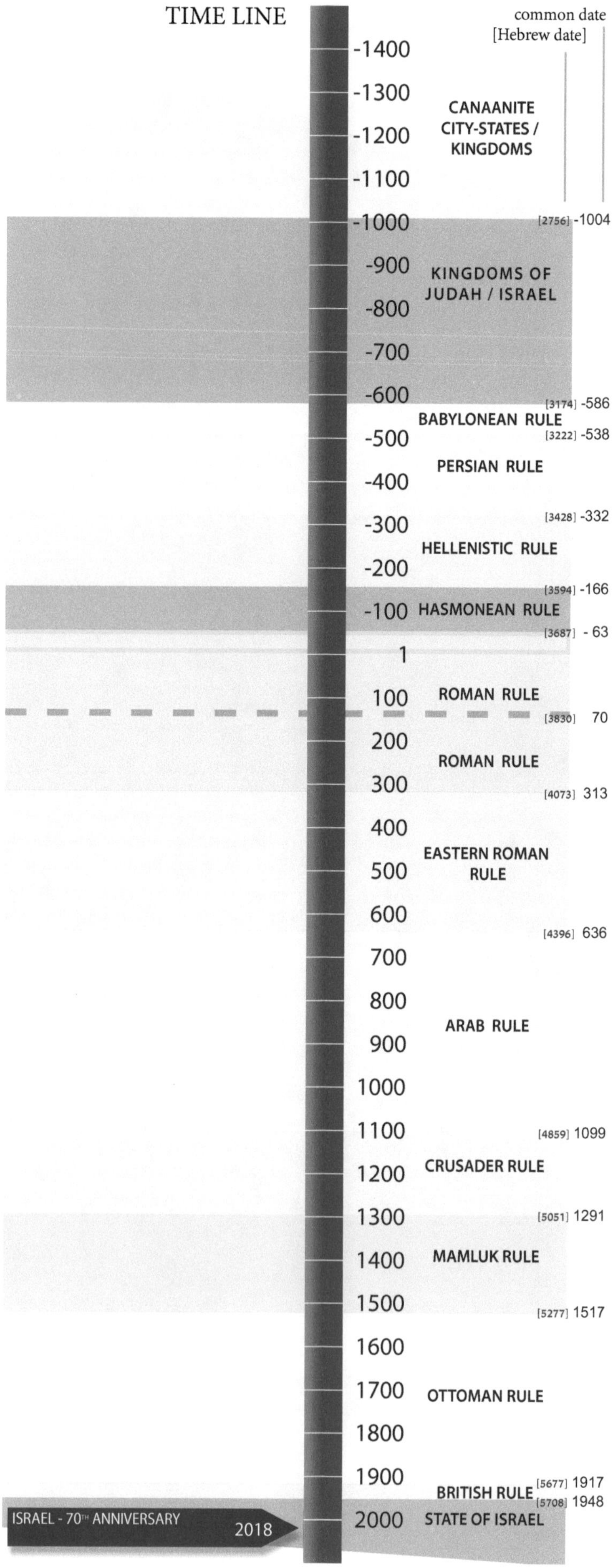

TIME LINE

	common date [Hebrew date]
CANAANITE CITY-STATES / KINGDOMS	[2756] -1004
KINGDOMS OF JUDAH / ISRAEL	[3174] -586
BABYLONEAN RULE	[3222] -538
PERSIAN RULE	[3428] -332
HELLENISTIC RULE	[3594] -166
HASMONEAN RULE	[3687] - 63
ROMAN RULE	[3830] 70
ROMAN RULE	[4073] 313
EASTERN ROMAN RULE	[4396] 636
ARAB RULE	[4859] 1099
CRUSADER RULE	[5051] 1291
MAMLUK RULE	[5277] 1517
OTTOMAN RULE	[5677] 1917
BRITISH RULE	[5708] 1948
STATE OF ISRAEL	

Scale: -1400, -1300, -1200, -1100, -1000, -900, -800, -700, -600, -500, -400, -300, -200, -100, 1, 100, 200, 300, 400, 500, 600, 700, 800, 900, 1000, 1100, 1200, 1300, 1400, 1500, 1600, 1700, 1800, 1900, 2000

ISRAEL - 70TH ANNIVERSARY 2018

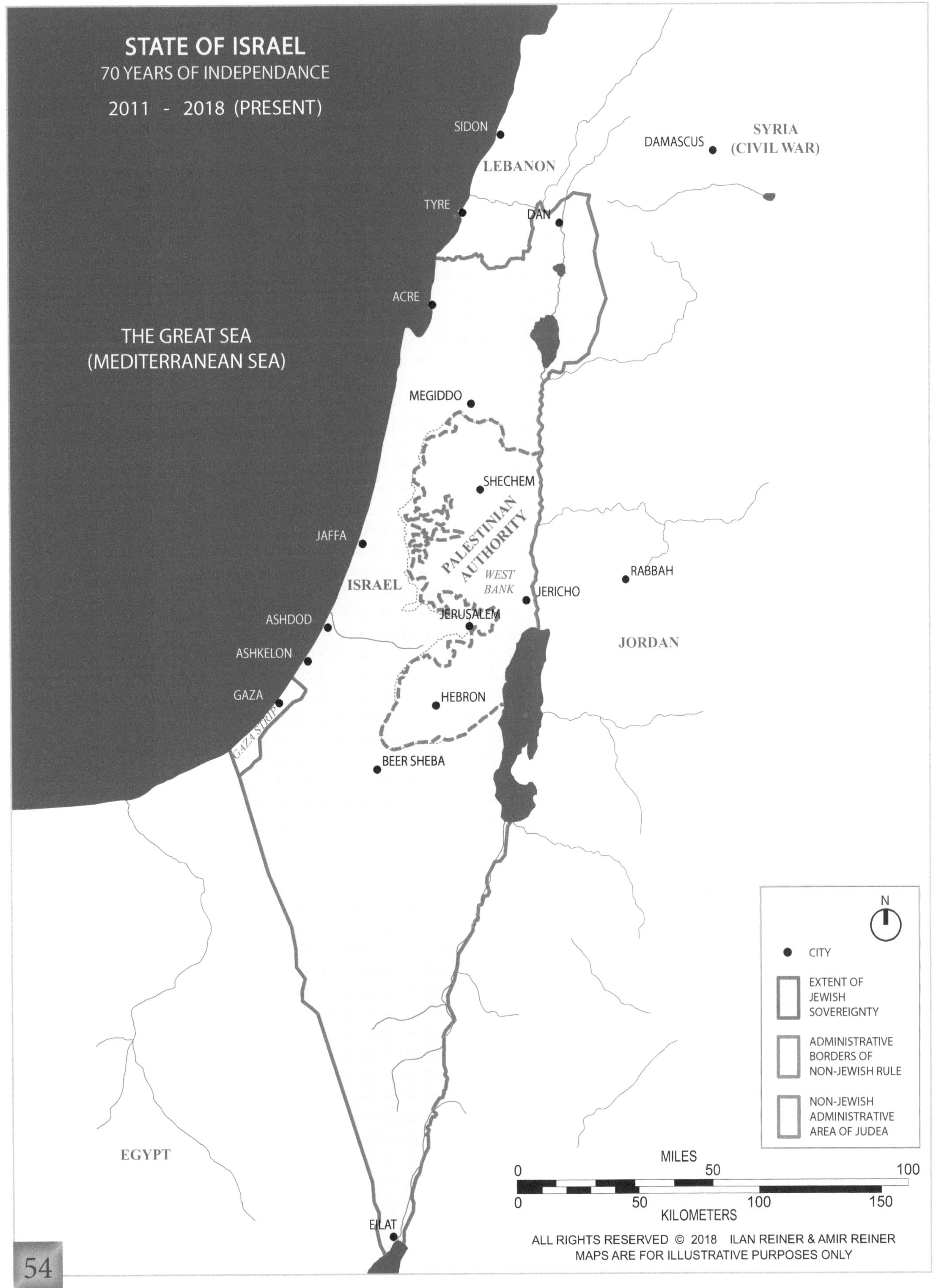
STATE OF ISRAEL
70 YEARS OF INDEPENDANCE
2011 - 2018 (PRESENT)
SIDON
DAMASCUS
SYRIA
(CIVIL WAR)
LEBANON
TYRE
DAN
ACRE
THE GREAT SEA
(MEDITERRANEAN SEA)
MEGIDDO
SHECHEM
PALESTINIAN
AUTHORITY
WEST
BANK
JAFFA
RABBAH
ISRAEL
JERICHO
ASHDOD
JERUSALEM
ASHKELON
JORDAN
GAZA
HEBRON
GAZA STRIP
BEER SHEBA
N
CITY
EXTENT OF
JEWISH
SOVEREIGNTY
ADMINISTRATIVE
BORDERS OF
NON-JEWISH RULE
NON-JEWISH
ADMINISTRATIVE
AREA OF JUDEA
EGYPT
MILES
0
50
100
0
50
100
150
KILOMETERS
EILAT
ALL RIGHTS RESERVED © 2018 ILAN REINER & AMIR REINER
MAPS ARE FOR ILLUSTRATIVE PURPOSES ONLY
54

Prayer for Peace
Universal (Non-Denominational)

May it be Your will, Our Lord our God and God of our ancestors,
that You abolish all wars and bloodshed from this world
and extend great and wonderful peace in the world.
Nations shall not lift up the sword against one another,
neither shall they learn to make war any more.

May all the inhabitants of this universe acknowledge the one great truth;
that we have not come into this world for friction and dissension,
nor enmity and jealousy and vexation and bloodshed.
We have come into the world solely that we might know You, eternally blessed One.

And therefore have mercy upon us
that through us the written word will become a reality.
"And I will grant peace in the land, and you shall lie down untroubled by anyone;
I will give the land respite from vicious beasts and no sword shall cross your land." (Lev. 26:6)
"But let justice well up like water, righteousness like an unfailing stream." (Amos 5:24)
"For the land shall be filled with devotion to God as water covers the sea." (Is. 11:9)

Based on the prayer of Rabbi Nachman of Bratslav,
from Siddur Ha'avodah She'ba'lev, Service of the Heart.

SIDON
DAMASCUS
TYRE
DAN
ACRE
MEGIDDO
SHECHEM
JAFFA
RABBAH
JERICHO
ASHDOD
JERUSALEM
ASHKELON
GAZA
HEBRON
BEER SHEBA
MILES
0
50
100
0
50
100
150
KILOMETERS
EILAT
ALL RIGHTS RESERVED © 2016 ILAN REINER & AMIR REINER
MAPS ARE FOR ILLUSTRATIVE PURPOSES ONLY

Bibliography

Aharoni, Yochanan (Ed.), *Carta's Atlas of the Bible*, Jerusalem: Carta Jerusalem Press, 1974 (Heb.).

Aharoni, Yohanan, Michael Avi-Yonah, Anson F. Rainey, & Ze'ev Safrai, *The Carta Bible Atlas* (5th edn.), Jerusalem: Carta Jerusalem Press, 2011.

Avi-Yonah, Michael (Ed.), *The Holy Land – A Historical Geography from the Persian to the Arab Conquest*, Jerusalem: Carta Jerusalem Press, 2002.

Avi-Yonah, Michael (Ed.), *Carta's Atlas of the Period of the Second Temple, the Mishna and Talmud*, Jerusalem: Carta Jerusalem Press, 1974 (Heb.).

Barnavi, Eli, *A Historical Atlas of the Jewish People: From the Time of the Patriarchs to the Present*, New York: Schocken Books Inc., 1992.

Barnes, Ian and Joshephine Bacon, *The Historical Atlas of Judaism*, Edison, NJ: Chartwell Books, 2009.

Bright, John, *A History of Israel*, London: SCM Press, 1972.

Bruce, Federick F., *The Illustrated Bible Atlas*, Jerusalem: Carta Jerusalem Press, 1994.

Broudi, Yehudit and Fisher, Shlomo (Ed.), *Jewish Society During the Second Temple: Developments and Struggles in the Period Between the Return to Zion and the Bar Kochva Revolt*, Jerusalem: Israel Department of Education, 1991 (Heb.).

Elitzur, Yehuda and Yehuda Keel (Eds.), *The Daat Mikra Bible Atlas: A Comprehensive Guide to Biblical Geography and History*, Jerusalem: Mosad HaRav Kuk, 2011 (Heb.).

Elitzur, Yehudah and Yoel Elitzur (Eds.), *Israel and the Bible: Studies in Geography, History and Biblical Thought*, Ramat-Gan: Bar-Ilan University Press, 1999 (Heb.).

Gelb, Norman, *Kings of the Jews: Exploring the Origins of the Jewish Nation*, Philadelphia, PA: The Jewish Publication Society, 2008.

Gichon, Mordechai (Ed.), *Atlas Carta for the History of the Land of Israel from Beitar until Tel Chai*, Jerusalem: Carta Jerusalem Press, 1974 (Heb.).

Gil, Moshe, A History of Palestine, 634-1099, Cambridge, UK: Cambridge University Press, 1992.

Goodnick-Wetenholz, Joan, *Royal Cities of the Biblical World*, Jerusalem: Bible Lands Museum, 1996.

Hertzog College Jewish and Spiritual Studies database: http://www.daat.co.il/

Isbouts, Jean-Pierre, *The Biblical World: An Illustrated Atlas*, Washington, D.C.: National Geographic Society, 2007.

Jones, A.H.M., *The Herods of Judea*, Oxford: Clarendon, 1938.

The Koren Tanakh (Hebrew Bible), Jerusalem: Koren Publishers, 2013.

Sachar, Howard M., *A History of Israel: From the Rise of Zionism to Our Time* (3rd ed.), New York: Random House Inc., 2007.

Safrai, Ze'ev and Eyal Regev, *The Land of Israel During the Second Temple, Mishnah and Talmud Periods: From the Hellenistic Conquest to the Days of Islam*, Jerusalem: Carta Jerusalem Press, 2011 (Heb.).

Safrai, Shmuel and Menahem Stern (Eds.), T*he Jewish People in the First Century: Historical Geography, Political History, Social, Cultural and Religious Life and Institutions*, Uitgeverij Van Gorcum, 1987

Sarel, Baruch, *Understanding the Old Testament – An Introductory Atlas to the Hebrew Bible*, Jerusalem: Carta Jerusalem Press, 1997.

Schur, Natan, *History of the Holy Land*, Tel Aviv: Dvir Publishing House, 1998.

Shulman, Eliezer, *The Sequence of Events in the Old Testament*, Jerusalem: Gefen Books, 1995

Smallwood, E. Mary, *The Jews under Roman Rule,* Leiden: Brill Academic Pub, 1997.

State of Israel Ministry of Foreign Affairs: http://www.mfa.gov.il/MFA/History

Wallach, Yehuda, *Atlas Carta of the History of the State of Israel – Vol. 1*, Jerusalem: Carta Jerusalem Press, 1978.

Wallach, Yehuda, *Atlas Carta of the History of the State of Israel – Vol. 2*, Jerusalem: Carta Jerusalem Press, 1980.

Wallach, Yehuda, *Atlas Carta of the History of the State of Israel – Vol. 3*, Jerusalem: Carta Jerusalem Press, 1983.

Printed in the USA
CPSIA information can be obtained
at www.ICGtesting.com
LVHW060224151223
766577LV00003B/20

* 9 7 8 0 6 9 2 4 5 9 3 2 4 *